My Old Acquaintance

YESTERDAY IN CYPRUS

Barbara Cornwall Lyssarides

My Old Acquaintance

First published in 1999
by Barbara Cornwall Lyssarides
Nicosia - Cyprus

ISBN 9963-8428-0-1

Designed by EN TIPIS Voula Kokkinou
9A Avlonos str., 1075 Nicosia Cyprus
Tel.: 357-2-767291, Fax: 357-2-765438

Printed and bound in Cyprus, April, 1999
by Kailas Printers & Lithographers Ltd.

Cover black & white image of the harbour at Paphos by Lakis Demetriades; colour image of the arch detail from Axiothea building in old Nicosia. Back cover painting by Christos Lyssiotes.Inside front & back cover, black & white image by Haigaz Mangoian.

For my mother
With love and admiration

ABOUT THE AUTHOR

Barbara Cornwall Lyssarides has lived most of her adult life in the Middle East, mainly in Cyprus, and much of it as a journalist writing for local and foreign newspapers.

She was born in Detroit, Michigan and holds a degree in History from Wayne State University, where she also studied Journalism. Her previous publications include a first-hand account of guerrilla warfare in the former Portuguese colonies of Africa, published in New York and London.

During the EOKA rebellion against colonial Britain in the 1950's which led to the island's independence, she was a staff reporter and feature writer on the daily "Times of Cyprus." Later, she edited the lifestyle section of a local, Greek-language daily.

Her other interests include archaeology, history, the Middle East and Central Asia.

For the past three years she has been a contributor to the "Cyprus Weekly" newspaper. She is married to Dr. Vassos Lyssarides, a well-known Greek Cypriot politician and member of Parliament.

How does my old acquaintance of this isle?
Honey, you shall be well desired in Cyprus;
I have found great love amongst them.

Othello, Act II, Scene 1

INTRODUCTION

"My Old Acquaintance" is not a history of Cyprus, although certainly history fills its pages. Rather it was written for the general reader curious to know what yesterday looked like in a small island in the Eastern Mediterranean.

It offers, I hope, a picture of those times, not only through my own research, but through the eyes of a number of men and women from many nations who came to the island over the past centuries, and on whose accounts I have relied.

They included colonisers, pilgrims, churchmen, adventurers, military men, travellers and scholars who left their impressions or experiences behind them in books or diaries. I also drew on original papers and reports kept in the library of the Cyprus Parliament, and on other sources, such as historical or archaeological reports.

The stories and articles in this book first appeared as part of a series in the "Cyprus Weekly" newspaper, and I am indebted to the editors for their permission to re-publish them here.

Sometimes, sojourners to the island were as intriguing as the people and places they described, telling of hair-raising sea voyages enroute, and their sometimes bizarre encounters once ashore. They also tell of overland sojourns by carriage or mule, how people lived in forgotten villages, what they ate, and of the beauties of mountains and sea.

Personally, I don't think that it is ever possible to really know a country such as Cyprus. Although I have lived here for so many years, for me it is still an old and much-treasured acquaintance. Hence the title of the book. Its people continually surprise me, as I think they often do each other.

Cyprus has had a long, sometimes brilliant, but often very turbulent and tragic history that reaches back thousands of years, as evidenced by archaeological finds.

Its vulnerable position as a very small island between Europe and the East has brought it face to face with many conquering empires and armies, often going in opposite directions.

Sometimes the intention had been outright invasion and occupation, sometimes it was an afterthought, as in the case of Richard the Lionheart and the crusaders. Almost all ruling powers left behind them in varying degrees another set of beliefs or ideas to add to previous layers. Sometimes even other gods. All left memories of themselves.

Over the millennia, Cyprus has been sold, colonised, inherited, borrowed, lent, defeated, delivered, neglected, isolated, annexed, mis-ruled, sometimes well-governed, often betrayed. It has been independent since 1960.

To me, it is astonishing that its people have survived at all, not only physically but with religion intact for almost 2,000 years, language even longer, and with customs and beliefs little changed even after centuries of foreign impact.

This is possibly a testimony to the tenacity of the island's Homeric roots, and as historian Sir David Hunt remarked, to the legacy of Athens and Constantinople.

It is also a testimony, I think, to a nation's ability to withdraw into itself, an instinctive form of passive resistance, perhaps, to protect its identity through its social and religious armour. How many times, after all, must a nation be asked to re-define itself?

It is the archaeologists and historians of course, who have provided the striking insights and theories into how the ancients lived.

I have not touched on current affairs, as this was not the scope of the series. I have, however, included a story about Cypriot emigrants to England over the past decades, and their experiences in another, very different island. Meanwhile, I hope that I have succeeded in sharing with the reader a sincere attachment to a very beloved island and its people. Survivors all.

Barbara Cornwall Lyssarides

CONTENTS

LEGENDS ON MULEBACK

It took them longer to get here, but 19th century western women must have been more intrepid than many of us thought, popping up round Cyprus and the Middle East on camel and muleback and then loping back to write a book about it.

They talked about people's faces, politics, scenery, bazaars, body lice and the weather, and if there was any kissing along the way there was rarely any telling.

They opened sun parasols on muleback and rode side-saddle, often spoke a second language fairly well, and visited monasteries and archaeological sites where they recalled ancient verse while surreptitiously poking about for pre-Christian artifacts. They lapped up legends about goddesses and sorcerers, and praised the picturesque local folk for their kind and hospitable ways.

If the authors were British, they believed that the local populations could only gain from the new colonial administration, with its sound moral and civilising influences. They also noted the self-effacement of women in the East.

Readers may recall accounts about the visit to Cyprus in the 1880's of writer Agnes Smith and her travelling companion, Violet, who could harness a mule with the best of 'em. Agnes' book, "Through Cyprus", was published in London in 1887, just nine years after the British takeover of the island from Ottoman Turkey.

Perhaps the most hair-raising incidents of their trip to the island occurred before their arrival, during a train journey from London to Marseilles via Paris, where there were unseemly scuffles between the two ladies and disagreeable fellow passengers in the first class carriage.

Space was cramped on the overhead rack and at one point a stout Frenchman, in a failed attempt to hurl Agnes' rug-case from the window, struck her head with his arm and knocked her hat off. Other male passengers smoked heavily but refused to open the windows, while one young couple flirted outrageously. Agnes suspected that they were married to two other people.

She later regretted her decision not to write to the "Times" about their treatment, especially after hearing soon after of a murder on the Paris-Cherbourg line.

The island's backwoods and bays, with its tales of brigandage and pirates, must have seemed tame in comparison. Throughout their tour round the towns and countryside, the ladies were protected by trusted, robed dragomen, muleteers and servants, who led them through mountain and bush and pitched their snow-white tents at sundown. At least three were called George or Georgie, after the dragon-slaying saint.

We hear of mishaps as well, including the time that Violet's bed caught fire, and of near accidents with gangly horses or mules scrabbling for footholds on stony ridges and "giddy paths." She also writes about the picturesque villages and the softness of the light and how, during a journey from Lefka to Kykko, they "passed into even deeper solitude, seeing no trace of man save our path... and heard the cuckoo's cry."

Then there was the time that Agnes and Violet had wide-ranging discussions with the Bishop of Kyrenia which included the prospects of a union between the Greek and Anglican churches (Agnes was a Presbyterian). The bishop pointed out that there were two very practical difficulties in the way of such a merger - the Church of England did not accept images, nor did it insist on fasting as did the Orthodox.

Further, "With you, I suppose, anyone can be a pastor," he told them. Agnes thought that he had confounded them with some other body of Protestants. The bishop also thought it a "great abuse" that the Prime Minister appointed the Archbishop. The ladies and the bishop had a long talk about homeopathy before their departure next day -- their tents had been pitched beneath branching pines outside the monastery -- and he gave them presents of wine, cheese and honey for their journey.

Reaching Kyrenia, acquaintances urged them to stay longer in that town. It was the finest part of Cyprus, they were told, with the best prison in the island containing 150 criminals, mostly murderers.

"What more could we want?" remarks Agnes.

Kyrenia streets boasted English names, she pointed out, and there was a quiet bathing place for ladies close to the castle. And no earwigs, as in Nicosia. Only a decade before the arrival of the British, the amateur archaeologist, Cesnola, had reported the town as being dirty, small and dangerous, where as a visitor he needed a strong guard of soldiers and police, including a general. Perhaps the majority Moslem population had been aware of how many ancient artifacts he had excavated from other parts of Cyprus and shipped abroad for sale.

Now the ladies were sleeping on the same ground and guarded by servants whose only weapons of defence were their staves, Agnes wrote. "Nor did we hear a whisper of danger. Yet it is said that the English have done nothing for Cyprus."

She compared the scenery round Kyrenia to that of the Riviera, but finer and fresher and with no snarling dogs or sullen peasants.

The village of Lefka was their next destination, a perfect oasis of verdure, she later called it, on a spur of the mountains overlooking Morphou bay in the northwest.

They rode across a range of thyme-scented hills and through the Messaoria plain to Morphou, where their tents were pitched in a field and the entire population turned out to see both them and their "luxurious accommodation," including the gaily embroidered interior of their tents. Standing in the crowd was an archimandrite from a nearby monastery whom they invited for dinner. Asked if the Cypriots had found any improvement in the island since the British takeover, the archimandrite replied: "To tell you the truth, most of them were too ignorant to understand the change."

The population did appreciate, however, that zaptiehs (police) were no longer permitted to demand free food and lodging from the villagers, and that schools had received much-needed grants.

Outside Lefka, their tents went up near some threshing floors where oxen were busy treading out straw for their own consumption, Agnes writes. Cypriot oxen refused to eat straw unless it was chopped up for them into small pieces, she says. Farmers thought this the hardest work which the animals carried out.

"Foolish beasts!" she remarked, but added that humans, after all, were just as fanciful and made more trouble for themselves and for others than is at all necessary.

From the base of a tall lime tree, Agnes looked over the green groves and grassy hills to the bay of Soli, where one of Greece's greatest law-givers, Solon, once lived.

How wonderful it is, she writes, "that we English should, in these latter days, be privileged to bring the blessings of good government to a place which once gave shelter to the aged Solon." The law-giver, she tells us, had been a guest of Cypranor, the king of a town whose site had been identified on the crest of a hill west of Lefka.

The amateur archaeologist, Cesnola, had found the remains of a theatre at Soli, and a circular temple made of limestone blocks quarried from nearby hills. He also discovered fragments of columns and capitals in marble and granite with Greek inscriptions, including the name of Soli itself, she relates.

The day the ladies arrived at Lefka was also the feast of St. George, the name-day of their muleteers, dragoman and the King of Greece as well. It seemed to be a national holiday, with flags flying in surrounding villages. Lefka was inhabited by about

200 families, mostly Moslem, whose children, boys and girls, studied the Koran in Arabic. Officials told Agnes that the children knew the words but not their meaning, as there was no Turkish translation.

HASSAN POULIS

Almost a hundred years after his death, there are Cypriots who can still remember snatches of a song about him.

His name was Hassan Poulis and he is a legend now in Cyprus, a Turkish Cypriot "anti-hero" from Paphos whose exploits as an outlaw captured the imagination and often the sympathy of even law-abiding people throughout the island.

He was as famous here as the outlaws of the old Wild West whose era overlapped his own — Jesse James, Billy the Kid — and he was nine years old when Turkey handed over the island of Cyprus to Britain. He was 31 when he died at the turn of the century and his life and death have been immortalised in folk songs and "pitarides" or rhyming chants, sung at village fairs down through the decades that followed.

In the minds of many, Hassan Bouli or Poulis as he was known to the Greek population who hellenised his last name to mean "bird", was not a real criminal. Given the degree of treachery that the quiet coffee-house keeper often confronted, especially betrayals by his closest friends, his actions might even be justified, they felt. Like the Wild West, his epoch was filled with revenge killings, sheep and cattle rustling, and "stagecoach" raids against passing travellers.

Women were either "good" or "bad" in those days, but there seemed to be more good ones than bad ones and even outlaws had their romances. Hassan Poulis was no exception and he was to fall passionately in love with a young Turkish Cypriot girl called Emette who was from the same village, Mamonia, in the Paphos district hills. She also happened to be his uncle's wife and Hassan loved her all of his short life.

When Hassan was 20, he was "nice looking, about 5' 10" with a slim, strong figure and quiet disposition," according to a former Paphos police commandant, M. Ch. Kareklas, MBE, who wrote a book about the anti-hero and his era.

One of Hassan's friends was a known outlaw called Hairedden, also a Turkish Cypriot and owner of a large flock of goats which he kept near the village. According to the Commandant, Hairedden made an indecent proposal to Emette and justice was swift. An enraged Hassan, vowing revenge, shot at him from ambush on three occasions and in each case missed.

Fearing for his life, Hairedden then found witnesses to "frame" Hassan whom they accused of raiding the former's goat herd with the help of his uncle. Although Hassan claimed that he was asleep in the village when the theft occured, the result was a seven-year prison sentence.

Escaping almost immediately from custody, Hassan fled to the Paphos hills where he spent 1½ years as a fugitive either camped out in the mountains or in safe houses. He "never annoyed anybody there, was very honest and protected women," the author relates, and when meeting them seemed only interested in the latest news and police movements in the area. Hassan told an ever-growing group of supporters that his sole object was to hunt down Haireddin who in the meantime had fled to Ktima, the district capital, for safety. But Haireddin was uneasy there, especially after hearing that Hassan had "taken revenge" against three villagers from Kalokedara who had stolen his father's cattle, relates Kareklas.

Fearing that his turn had come, Haireddin bribed Hassan's best friend, Abdulla of Yerovasa, to invite the outlaw to his "safe" house for dinner and a rest, and there to kill him. Alert to the plot, Hassan's mother warned her son but Hassan went anyway. He kept a loaded gun on his knee throughout dinner, then escaped before dawn through a window after bolting the bedroom door. Along with Haireddin, Abdulla was now on Hassan's target list.

Shortly afterwards, the oulaw again narrowly missed death after falling into a police ambush while visiting Emette. She had moved to a nearby village called Stavrokonnou, which was friendly to Hassan and where their meetings could be better facilitated. Accompanied by a supporter, Hassan approached Emette as she washed clothes at a spring near the village. When police opened fire they hit the wrong man, however, and Hassan Poulis escaped once again, says writer Kareklas.

Assuring villagers in the district that "no honest person" need fear him, Hassan mounted a series of revenge attacks against his enemies, murdering informers as police pursued him through the Paphos hills. His aim had apparently improved since his three abortive attempts against old enemy, Haireddin, for his targets "never left the safety of their home villages when news reached them of the outlaw's wrath." In the meantime, Hassan steadily depleted their sheep and goat herds during nightime raids.

Six weeks before his arrest, Hassan Poulis fell ill with malaria and stayed in an abandoned house at Mamonia village to recuperate. Although nobody had informed against him, and for reasons which are still unclear, the oulaw gave himself up to police without a fight. Perhaps he was too weakened by malaria to run anymore, perhaps he saw no further point in outlawry.

Hassan Poulis was convicted of murder and gaoled in the Nicosia Central Prison where, according to Commandant Kareklas, he was well-liked by other prisoners, learned to read and write, said his prayers five times a day and was so cooperative that prison warders permitted him to work alongside other trustees in the grounds just outside the prison gates.

A few years later, word reached him of the arrest in Paphos of two brothers, Mehmet Kaimakam and Hassan Kavounis, also outlaws who were known as "Hassanpoulies" — Hassan birds. They had been betrayed by certain villagers from Kydassi, and Hassan made plans to escape and burn down the village.

His chance came while working outside the prison's east gate, but the attempt ended abruptly when a prison warder "cut him across the neck with a sword after he refused to stop when called upon." Together with another escaping prisoner, the wounded Hassan Poulis was then shot dead.

But he still lives in the Paphos hills, his exploits immortalised through song and chant almost a century after his death.

FATHER POSSOT'S PONDERINGS

One of the more unusual features of late medieval life in Cyprus was the number of strange-looking animals about.

Overlooked by most visitor-commentators of the time, and later by their archivist friends, the animal world was generally consigned to brief descriptions or footnotes, or otherwise not mentioned at all except perhaps by those who used ox-carts as a mode of travel. Chroniclers rather concentrated on the gluttony of some of the Frankish kings, the strength of local red wine, or the proximity of the Saracens.

We are aware of the prevalence of unusual looking creatures largely because of accounts left behind by a few traveller-pilgrims, who stopped over in Cyprus enroute to the Holy Land or elsewhere between the 12th and 16th century.

One such chronicler was an alert visitor called Maistre Denis Possot, a priest of Coulommiers in Brie, who had left home with friends in 1532 on a pilgrimage to the Holy Sepulchre and came to the island to take on stores. His report was included, along with others mentioned below, in "Excerpta Cypria", a collection of writings about Cyprus compiled early this century by a former British commissioner here called Claude Cobham.

The 16th century priest-visitor, Possot, records seeing camels with big tails and tall bodies, long necks, small nails and little furry ears like a hare. These ships of the desert with furry ears and tiny nails had been transplanted into Cyprus in the dim long ago and were used well into the 20th century to carry produce into the island's more inaccessible regions.

(Cyprus was under Venice at the time of Possot's visit, "hot, rich, fertile and cheap" and full of stony hills, he says.)

He also tells of plentiful fowls, doves, partridges and hares, the last being very large "with big, broad and thick tails which make them sway and waddle." He noticed certain sheep with "six or seven horns" but whose flesh was unpleasant, other wild sheep with the hair of deer and who "run in the country like wild animals," and still more domesticated sheep in one village with "tails as big as their bellies." Then there were the bees, the "good flies", who live inside the houses and come and go at will through holes in the walls. The wax and honey was thus accessible from inside the houses. Venomous snakes, vipers, serpents and scorpions were abundant.

Cotton was widely grown and water wheels were turned by blindfolded horses. Stout pots fastened to chains or long ropes were lowered into deep cisterns, and as they "came up and went down again poured water into a large trough." This was spread over adjoining fields guided by channels and drains and two acres of land could be watered in an hour.

Wheat was heaped into fields and arranged into sheaves. The farmers then stood on fine harrows set with sharp flints and were pulled along by a horse, ass or mule, he writes. With this method, straw was cut up into small pieces and given to the cattle. Between tasks the animals were let loose in the fields.

Father Possot also noticed that Cyprus spring water was clean and healthy and that the island had several clear rivers which watered the countryside. In summer, inhabitants lived by day in small houses covered with earth in which their wheat was also stored, but at night slept on beds in their courts or gardens. There were many earthquakes, he said, one reason why houses were built close to the ground. Sadly, Father Possot died at home six months after his visit to Cyprus, but in the meantime "had confided his notes to another."

The great Dante Alighieri was to mention another type of "beast" in Cyprus in a "mystical passage" of the Paradiso, according to a commentator called Benvenuto da Imola, also recorded in the "Excerpta." On this occasion, the beast referred to was a lewd and selfish king of Cyprus called Henry II of

Lusigna (1285-1310) who also ate too much (and outlived most of his contemporaries).

Those "wailings and groans" in the streets of Famagusta and Nicosia had been caused by this king, according to Dante, who also predicted the day when "injustice and vice shall meet their doom."

Dante wrote:

> "In earnest of that day, e'en now are heard
> wailings and groans in Famagusta's streets
> and Nicosia's, grudging at their beast,Who
> keepeth even footing with the rest."

What Dante meant, says da Imola, was that Henry had exceeded every other Christian ruler elsewhere in "luxury, gluttony, effeminacy and every kind of pleasure -- feasts, sumptuousness, variety and superfluities too tiresome to tell or write about, and harmful to hear." Thank God the Genoese had invaded Cyprus, added da Imola. (Genoa invaded the island in 1372, finally occupying only Famagusta, and was driven out in 1464. Following the fall of Acre in 1241, Famagusta had become one of the richest cities of the Levant after Henry II had offered Cyprus as an asylum for Christian refugees. Most settled in Famagusta.)

Within a few decades of Henry's reign, when Hugh IV was king, the city had also become a refuge for about 1500 Armenians - old men, children, women and orphans who had fled to Cyprus.

More than 12,000 persons in Armenia had been captured or carried off, and invaders had "burnt all the plain and killed many with the sword," according to an Augustinian monk called J. de Verona, who saw them on their arrival in 1335 in Cyprus. They had gathered in a Famagusta square, "children crying and moaning, old men and starving dogs howling..Hear it, ye Christians," de Verona said.

During his three weeks in Cyprus, the writer also attended the funeral of a rich citizen, where two women "sang sweetly" at the corpse's head and two others wailed piously at his feet. "They were singing in the Greek tongue, because all men in Cyprus speak Greek. They understand well the Saracen and Frankish tongues, but chiefly use Greek... they were praising the dead man for his beauty and thrift."

He also attended the wedding of a bride who was carried on horseback to the bridegroom's home with her eyebrows and fore-head painted. She was accompanied by 40 or more ladies, all dressed in black cloaks from head to foot, showing nothing except the eyes. Since the fall of Acre in 1291, almost 40 years before, all the ladies of Cyprus wore black cloaks in mourning, he added.

Famagusta was full of several sects at the time, first the "true Christians" (he meant the Latins), secondly the Greeks who consecrate with leavened bread, the Jacobites who circumcised and baptised in the Greek rites, the Armenians who said their service in Greek, the Georgians and Maronites and finally the Nestorians (who say Christ was a mere man), comments de Verona.

Later in the same century, another visitor called Nicolai de Martoni, a notary of Campania, cites the black mantle worn by local women because of the fall of Acre and "other cities of Syria." De Martoni was "small of stature, shortsighted and could not swim," remarks Cobham. Because of this he ran consider-able risks during his visit here in 1394, which he "naively" related.

There was one particularly nasty encounter with his cart dri-ver whom he had engaged to carry him from Famagusta to Nicosia on arrival. Having hired the cart, the Greek owner then made him drive the oxen and criticised him for poor driving and for beating the animals too much. De Martoni finally got out and walked because he couldn't bear the incessant "squabbling". Dur-ing an overnight stay at a village enroute, he was obliged to sleep on the ground on a rug - "no beds could be found even for money." There was an abundance of fleas in Cyprus, which were "brought by pigs who slept in the houses."

He describes the king's palace in Nicosia, a fine house, with a courtyard "as large as that of the new castle at Naples, and many fine apartments round it and a large hall.

"At one end of the hall is a beautiful throne with many fair columns and ornaments, and around the hall runs a beautifully adorned arcade with columns. I went right up to the entrance to the king's room and had it been open I would have entered and talked to him." Many nearby inhabitants drew water from a fountain in the courtyard, he said, adding that since the king had lost the city of Famagusta he kept great state in Nicosia, "hunting with cheetahs and 300 hawks of all kinds." When de Martoni returned home, he learned of the death of his wife which had been hastened by anxiety for his safety while abroad, according to reports.

Famagusta was to attract settlers well into the Venetian occupation of Cyprus in 1489 and they included about 25 Jewish families. One was headed by Elias of Pesaro who had hoped to emigrate from Italy to Syria with his wife and children. Because of plague there, however, they had remained in Cyprus. In a letter in Hebrew to a relative or friend back home, he had described circumstances here at the time.

Jewish settlers during Venetian rule were made to wear yellow head coverings, he said, as was the regulation in Venice itself. The only exceptions were two Jewish doctors held in such high esteem that they were permitted black hats adorned with a tiny yellow badge. "A man is lucky if he knows medicine," wrote Elias, "for the Greeks respect the Jews as good doctors, and trust them."

Famagusta townsfolk were well-behaved and clean, and were careful to protect themselves from the plague. Visitors were quarantined for 40 days at the port before being permitted entry, he goes on. Meanwhile, Elias had hired a house with two large and handsome rooms and kitchen upstairs, and with storage rooms downstairs for wine, oil and wood. There was also a poultry yard.

There was a fine synagogue supported by the small Jewish

community which lived on the interest of their capital, or through trade or money lending, he writes. Sound security was offered because "every mechanic, every labourer has vessels of silver or jewels in his house." Many Christians also were asking for loans.

Vegetables were plentiful, olives were as big as walnuts, and fruit ripened a month earlier than in Italy. Goods and money were transported in carts pulled by great spotted oxen of all colours... . "One would think the Patriarch Jacob fed his herds here."

BYZANTINE DIMENSIONS

When the mountain winter comes and fog curls round the monastery, Kykko is once again a 12th century creation.

The air-conditioned buses carrying thousands of pilgrims and other visitors annually up the mountain roads have dwindled to a manageable trickle and the wilderness again imposes its monastic rhythm for another season.

Kykko was built by a saintly Cypriot hermit called Isaiah, who was manhandled by a short-tempered Byzantine duke on a hunting expedition 900 years ago. The duke, later contrite, was also the island's governor and helped Isaiah to obtain for Cyprus a miracle-working icon of the Holy Virgin, lodged at the time in Constantinople's imperial palace.

Both monastery and church were built to house it, and the Troodos mountain site soon became one to the most important centres in the Greek Orthodox world. For centuries, pilgrims from all over the East, including Russia, climbed the tortuous paths for days to reach the famed monastery and perhaps glimpse a corner of its veiled, miracle-working icon. Hundreds of hermits and anchorites lived in shelters or caves in the surrounding forest, striving for the salvation of their souls as wild animals roamed nearby and snow banked along the rivers.

The icon, called Panayia Eleousa (Holy Virgin of Mercy) or Panayia Kykkotissa (Holy Virgin of Kykko) is said to ease human suffering, cure serious illness and relieve drought. It is generally attributed to St. Luke, a contemporary of the mother of Christ, and according to Orthodox belief is one of three icons painted of her on special wood, from life, and with her consent.

She is shown holding the Christ Child on her right arm. For centuries, no one has been permitted to view the Kykko Virgin's face, including Church leaders or monks. One 17th century Patriarch suddenly went blind when he attempted to uncover the icon, and another visitor, who drew away the thick veil for a furtive peek, found his hand had withered, tradition says.

Kykko lies in otherwise friendly majesty on a wedge of mountain deep in the Myrhianthoussa region, about 18 kilometres from Mount Olympus. It is a hodgepodge of architectural styles, additions and subtractions, as buildings were added over time when finances permitted, or re-built after several disastrous fires flattened large portions of its former wooden structure and destroyed precious objects and manuscripts. In all cases, the icon escaped damage.

The monastery was already functioning a hundred years before Richard the Lionheart and his crusader fleet made an unplanned landing at Limassol enroute to Acre and holy war. During his brief stay here, Richard drove out the last Byzantine ruler of Cyprus, an upstart governor who had threatened Richard's knights and insulted his bride-to-be. With Richard's brief stay came the long-lasting Lusignan dynasty and the Catholic rule of the Franks.

Today, with its red-tiled roof and towering stone facade, Kykko seems both a storybook structure and a Byzantine Orthodox stronghold, safe from enemy menace from within and without.

Recently renovated in parts, some find its granite-floored reception areas a bit unharmonious, but generally the faithful have not complained.

Its remoteness has usually protected it through the centuries from frequent incursions during foreign rule or invasion, including the early period of Ottoman occupation.

But later it was plundered and many of its priceless treasures, religious artifacts, documents and vestments were carried off.

Its Abbot, Iosif, was executed along with the Archbishop and other Cypriot clerics during the 1821 mainland Greek revolution after being accused by the Ottomans of complicity. Over 150 years later, the former President of Cyprus, Archbishop Makarios, sought temporary refuge there while pursued by Greek mainland putchists during the 1974 coup d'etat here.

According to various accounts, the monastery may have been named after ancient birdsong citing a "golden lady" who would never leave the monastery — meaning the holy icon — or perhaps after a locally-grown bush. At one point in history, the icon had fallen into Saracen hands, but was rescued on the high seas by Byzantine ships which carried it to Constantinople along with Saracen prisoners.

It remained in the imperial palace until promised to the hermit Isaiah after the daughter of Emperor Alexios II Comnenos was miraculously cured of a life-threatening illness.

The Emperor temporarily reneged on the deal and attempted to ship a false copy over to the island. He was then struck down by the same illness, but recovered after the true painting was put on board ship. Tradition says that all the tree-tops near the Limassol shoreline bowed as the icon was carried toward Kykko.

For centuries previously, Cyprus had been either a wholly Byzantine outpost or a disputed province between Arab invaders and Constantinople as they clashed in ongoing power struggles for control of the East and the Mediterranean. Both claimed the loyalty of the local islanders and expected them to report on the movements of whoever was in control at the time.

For 300 years, Arab armies carried out 24 invasions of the island, some punitive and one being led by Haroun Al Rashid himself, of Arabian Nights fame. Others were hit-and-run raids and often the islanders found themselves paying tribute to both sides at the same time. Finally, Cyprus was recovered for Byzantium when Emperor Nikiphoros Phocas expelled the Arabs from Asia Minor in the 10th century.

Kykko monastery was built during the next 200 years of peace and was to become the "pride and salvation of the Cypriots," according to one historian.

Ephraim the Athenian, the "great teacher of the Greek nation" and a learned churchmen, published a narrative of Kykko's origin based on monastic records and early manuscripts. To sustain the monastery, he wrote, the Duke of Cyprus gave it three villages — Milikouri, Peristerona and Milon. The last is one of seven villages between Milikouri and Kaminaria. The duke, incidentally, was the same personage, Manuel Boutomites, who had earlier ill-treated the hermit Isaiah with kicks and shoves for his refusal to speak when they had met on a mountain pass.

From its beginnings, Kykko was known as a "royal" monastery because it had been constructed with imperial money, according to the "Handbook of Kykkos Monastery," published by the monastery's own research centre in Nicosia. The Centre was founded a decade ago on the initiative of its new abbot, Nikiphoros.

Along with scores of other works and research papers, it also published a bi-lingual edition of Ephraim the Athenian's account which originally appeared in Venice in 1751. He had spent 19 years on the island.

Kykko is also known as a "Stavropegic" monastery because a cross had been placed in its foundation stone. In the language of ecclesiastical administration, according to the "Handbook," this translates into meaning that the monastery is self-governing but within, of course, the wider framework of the Cyprus Church.

Throughout its history, chroniclers say, the monastery and its "metochions" or annexes in other areas in the island and previously even abroad, have been a refuge for the persecuted and an important keeper of the Orthodox and ethnic flame through invasions, occupations and long centuries of Frankish and Ottoman rule. Like its Western monastic counterparts in darker ages, it kept learning, and the Church, alive through study, research and the establishment of local schools in towns and villages, and at the monastery itself for area children.

During Ottoman rule, says the "Handbook," when religious faith was equivalent to national identity, the monastery protected religious consciousness and was a breakwater against

Islamisation.

To support the monastery and its annexes during the Ottoman occupation, the impoverished monks literally laboured in the vineyards. Slowly, the monastery acquired mills, land for cultivation, wine presses, houses, olive and carob trees, and farm animals. Its Nicosia annex was saved from financial ruin when its abbot bought the Turkish farms of Ayios Dhometios, Engomi and Lakatamia, the "Handbook" relates.

One of Kykko's better known visitors during this period was a distinguished 18th century Russian monk called Vasilios Barsky.

Author and chronicler of holy places for 24 years, Kiev-born Barsky visited Cyprus three times, first as a mendicant who walked round the island for three months begging for alms and recording facts about local monasteries and churches, later as a learned monk under the Patriarch's protection.

His original manuscript, written in Old Church Slavonic and in diary form, has been lately corrected against earlier translations and its illegible parts deciphered by an Australian academic called Alexander Grishin. He had studied the manuscript at Harvard University for several months where it had been sent by the Ukrainian government for cleaning and conservation.

Although Barsky was a great admirer of the monastery and spent several weeks there after an earthquake had devastated Nicosia, the scholar-monk did not think that the holy icon was one of the original three painted by St. Luke, according to Grishin. Rather, he thought it a later work, although also possibly done by the saint.

Today, 20 monks reside at the main mountain monastery under an "ephoros" or abbot's representative. Almost all have university degrees and all carry out both spiritual and temporal duties beginning with pre-dawn attendance at church services and again in the evening. Others are assigned to annexes or other religious centres. (Note: there are a total of 200 Cypriot monks at Ayion Oros in Greece, according to Kykko Research Centre's Costis

Kokkinoftas. Both he and Ioannis Theocharides produced the 1995 "Handbook," a survey of monastery history and structure.) Kykko's youthful abbot for over a decade, the Archimandrite Nikiphoros, handles the vast task of administering the monastery and its holdings and overseeing a number of other projects. He has also been winching the monastery into the new millennium, at least on the temporal side, and divides his time between the mountain centre and his base at the Nicosia metochion at Engomi.

Besides the Research Centre founded at his behest at a recently restored 16th century annex near Lakatamia, he has also spearheaded the organisation of an awesome new ecclesiastical museum at the mountain monastery. Now opened officially, it houses a priceless collection of historical and religious treasures, either accummulated through centuries or recovered at overseas auctions. Some had been stolen or sold years or even centuries before.

Then, there are monastery-financed computer centres at various schools, a special workshop for preservation of old icons and manuscripts, a school for Byzantine music at the monastery and a well trained choir, child care and youth centres, and retirement homes for the aged.

Two years ago, the monastery began producing and bottling wine and other alcoholic beverages at its mountain factory — if the Benedictines could do it why not Kykko? The result is a series of gentle wines as well as some powerhouse aperitifs, sweet and dry, and some liberally laced with zivania. All are marketed in well-designed, somehow monastic-looking bottles.

Some drinks contain over 40 vol. alcohol and the label of one dry aperitif discreetly reminds anyone who reads the backs of bottles that "this aperitif was made of old in the Holy Monastery of Kykkos and was offered to visitors in brotherly love." Although historians won't say so, this may be one of the reasons why so many visitors clawed their way up the steep mountainside paths in the past.

One drink is called Genevrier and another simply Dry Aperitif. A third is called Zoukki and contains zivania, anise, fennel and citrus blossoms.

All are serious brews with Byzantine dimensions, strong enough to floor a Saracen, but polite enough for a pilgrim's palate.

FELIX FABER

A Latin bishop from Paphos made a rude, 15th century gesture at an outraged knight and the priest who defended him during a dispute over extra legroom aboard a crowded pilgrims' galley bound for the Holy Land, according to records of the time.

As shocked passengers looked on, an unseemly scuffle and "clamour" then broke out as other knights aboard joined the fray while the ship lay becalmed off Cyprus. The bishop then fled aloft to the captain's cabin where he remained throughout the voyage.

It all happened about 500 years ago when that tragic queen, Caterina Cornaro, still reigned in Cyprus and the "gesture" was something which "Italians do with their thumb when they wish to insult anyone," according to a Dominican monk from Germany called Felix Faber who had witnessed the incident aboard the galley.

He later included the story in a lengthy record of his two visits to Cyprus in 1480 and 1483 where he stayed for a considerable time despite warnings that the "air was pestiforous for Germans."

In general, it was a period of great Christian piety, considerable superstition and arduous pilgrimages to the Holy Land by both nobles and commoners from Europe. Enroute, there was always the chance that if the pestilence didn't get you at a local port of call, a Turk, Saracen or Tartar could do so on the high seas. Then, there was the possibility of being unable to sail at all for days as "foul winds" tossed the galleys aimlessly along the coastline or back on to shore.

Some of Faber's own companions had died at sea, including two knights who were wrapped in sheets and weighted with stones for burial amidst "much weeping" and far from home.

At the time, Cyprus, especially Nicosia, was a thriving trade centre and the island in general a convenient jumping-off point for Holy Land pilgrimages. During his sojourns here, Faber also visited the main towns and cathedrals, important monasteries such as the Holy Cross (Stavrovouni) and seemed to have ample time to study the workings of both the Latin and Orthodox churches.

Always on the lookout for signs of worldliness amongst fellow ecclesiastics, Faber had already found a certain number of the Latin clergy in Cyprus disappointingly lax in the rules of poverty, chastity and obedience. Althrough the position of the Latins in Cyprus called for great unity of purpose and the urge to close ranks, the case of the ill-mannered Latin bishop from Paphos, albeit a "beardless" one with a long train, a "womanish" face and bejewelled fingers, was indeed shocking.

Faber was already reeling from other, earlier incidents which smacked of laxness, such as the occasion in Nicosia when, visiting his own Order's monastery adjacent to the magnificent royal palace grounds, he had inadvertently opened a cupboard door while snooping round a second floor dormitory. Instead of priestly garments or edifying missives, he encountered an angry swarm of bees which chased him downstairs and out through the garden. They had constructed their hive unhindered in a monastic closet with access to the outside through a hole in the wall.

Then, there were the cases in certain remote areas of Cyprus where he found clerics holding both Latin and Greek Orthodox services on the same day, switching churches, languages and leavened and unleavened bread as the case may be. The object was financial, he thought. One monk, who was a curate of both Greek and Latin churches, took Faber's group to the Latin church where the arm of St. Anne, mother of the Blessed Virgin, was sheathed in silver. It also contained a nail from the Holy Cross.

"I regarded him as a heretic of the worst kind, deceiving people of both rites," Faber commented. "The Latins condemn them as schismatics and heretics and the Greeks themselves believe the Latins are excommunicated.

"They hate us Latins with a mortal hatred. Such men take on themselves what in each rite catches their fancy, but reject what is hard and burdensome in both... "Many go over to the Greek rite and presume to take wives... ."

Faber's account of his Cyprus visit was uncovered almost 400 years after it was written and found deposited at the Bavarian Library of Ulm by a former British Commissioner at Larnaca called Claude Cobham, who included it in his book, "Excerpta Cypria", published in 1908. The "Excerpta" is a collection of passages, sometimes lengthy, from all known books about the island from the time of Strabo to the late 19th century, spanning almost 2,000 years. Cobham also did most of the translations.

After his initial disappointment, Faber must have found great comfort in an exciting story from the past told him by a Latin churchman — that many Cypriot merchants and traders had met and talked with Jesus during their regular visits at the time to the Holy Land. After hearing Him preach and witnessing His miracles, the merchants had begged Jesus to sail with them to Cyprus to "shower his blessings on the people" here, Faber recorded.

But Christ had explained to them that "first of all He must suffer the cross and die, and on the third day rise again." Then He would send His apostles to Cyprus.

Faber heard the story from a canon at St. Sophia, the metropolitan church of Nicosia, during a visit to the famed cathedral. In a nearby chapel dedicated to St. Thomas Aquinas, he had noticed a magnificent, empty sarcophagus made of solid jasper, and had asked its origin. This was the very sarcophagus, he was told, which the Cypriot merchants in the time of Christ had carved to contain the crucified body of the Lord. (Jasper was more precious than gold, and had been chosen by the dying Alexander the Great for his own tomb, according to legend.)

After their return to Cyprus, Faber relates, the merchants had agreed to bring his body to Cyprus rather than having it "thrown out as a condemned criminal's" in the event of his execution. "But when the Lord was dead and honourably buried (in the Holy Land), the Cypriots were appeased and preserved his sarcophagus even today. Nor would they sell it to anyone, nor suffer any man to be buried therein."

In Faber's time, the precious jasperstone was believed to drive away fever, check phantoms, help women in childbed, protect a man in danger, stanch blood, repress passion, cure ulcers and purge the eyes. It was also a proof against witchery and spells. The stone was found only in Scythia, Faber heard, where it was guarded by gryphons - fierce creatures with the heads of eagles and bodies of lions who would attack armed horsemen and carry off both horse and rider. These beasts were never found except near mountains which "teemed with gold and precious stones," and could only be defeated by Cyclops, the giant savages with a single eye in their forehead.

From the church canon he heard a pleasant story concerning the immense stone's early, pagan use. It seems that Venus, the queen and goddess of Cypriots, had thrown aside all modesty and entertained a number of lovers, including Mars, at her temple. The jealous god then drove his chariot to the hill of Jasper, tore away a huge stone and "set the stone for her bed to temper and subdue her appetite." When she died it was forbidden to carve her image, and the "rude, unpolished block of jasper" stood in place of her effigy. As Virgil wrote, the "image of Venus bore no human likeness."

Faber was to hear another tale of Venus during a visit to the monastery of St. Croce (present day Stavrovouni) where a piece of the Holy Cross was venerated along with the cross of the good thief who had died to His right.

Accompanied by some knights, an archdeacon, and a Swiss and Flemish merchant, Faber and the group set off on muleback for the monastery. "We were eight picked friends, the weather was fine, the country famous and the road good," he wrote. "The bushes gave out a sweet smell - nearly all plants in Cyprus are aromatic and particularly fragrant at night" — and enroute the men ate bread, cheese and drank wine.

They rode all night until reaching the village of Santa Croce, he relates, where he said Matins and abstained from food as he intended to celebrate Mass on the mountain. It was high and precipitous, he said, and they shuddered somewhat at its height as they toiled up on foot, perspiring freely. It resembled exactly Mt. Thabor in the Holy Land, he recorded, "on which our Lord was transfigured." But Faber urged the group not to expect a miracle, or to "pry too curiously" when seeing the Holy Cross.

"We observed it before and behind. We looked at it carefully." It was fairly large, covered with silver gilt plates. It was bare on the wall side, of a wood like cypress, and was said to be the cross of the good thief, Dysmas.

This was the one that St. Helena, founder of the monastery, had kept after finding all three under Mt. Calvary. She had carried the good thief's cross intact from Jerusalem to this mountain where she built a monastery of monks and a church, with a shrine or niche near the altar for the cross.

There it remains, untouched until this day, in a dimly lighted niche and apparently free standing, Faber says. "I might have examined it more closely but feared God." A small piece of the true cross had been set in for purposes of additional veneration.

Why had St. Helena chosen this particular mountain for her monastery? Nearby had stood a temple to Venus who had "left marks of her wantonness throughout the island." St. Helena destroyed the shrine and set up a cross "for the rule of chastity and bid religious men, vowed to chastity, to live here and give the lie to Venus," Faber wrote. Remnants of the thick temple walls were still visible.

The place had been called "Ydolius", and it was thought

that Perseus had flown from this mountain to free Andromeda, bound to a rock at Joppa (Jaffa) and left to be devoured by a sea monster.

In a certain part of the mountain was also a cleft where the rumblings and a roar of wind are heard. "This was said to be the way down to hell." The Cypriots feared hell the more when they saw the entrance, and "to meet this vain fear, the holy woman set up the cross." On clear days, a visitor to the mountaintop could see the Holy Land, Armenia, Cappadocia and Galilee.

Hoping to be offered refreshments, Faber and his companions entered the Orthodox chaplain's cell but "the room was bare and empty, with neither water nor biscuits." He thought this was because Orthodox churchmen disliked the Latins.

Only two Cyprus towns had impressed Faber — Nicosia with its royal palace and numerous churches and convents, and the Salines, near present-day Larnaca, whose yield from the Salt Lake helped to enrich the Queen of Cyprus.

Nicosia, the capital and a great city, was surrounded by fertile and pleasant hills, and a torrent ran through the town at certain times of the year. Merchants from every part of the world gathered here, Christians and infidels, he said, to buy or sell the precious aromatic herbs from the East which were kept in great stores in the capital. Nicosia abounded in dyes and perfumes and in great structures such as the Archbishop's palace near the main church and the high, thick walls where the kings of Cyprus were buried.

At the monastery church of St. Augustine built in sugar cane gardens was the tomb of the German noble, John Montfort, whom Cypriots consider a saint. His body "lies whole, though the flesh, muscles and skin have shrivelled," the writer says.

Limassol, or "Nimona" was once a great city facing Tyre and Sidon with the best harbour in the world for trade with Armenia, Cilicia, Antioch, Laodicaea and other Mediterranean centres. But only one church survived of all the great ones then existing, "a wretched church without bells." A few Latin clergy lived there, but their habits were "not edifying." The city had been striken by earthquakes in the past, the wrath of the Saracens, and floods from the mountains behind.

Above Nimona was a certain spot full of serpents and noxious animals. A convent had been built there by "ancient fathers" to be less exposed to the visits of "worldlings." There they kept a number of cats who remained inside at night but roamed the area by day, hunting. When summoned by a bell to dinner, the cats hurried inside the walls.

He found Famagusta a town of ruins and with a corrupt air, while Paphos, once a great, vast city with stately churches, was now a desolate, miserable village with an abandoned harbour.

It had been laid low by earthquake and "so it lies still," he said, "with no king or bishop giving a hand to raise it up again."

In the meantime, Faber urged that bishops of ripe age and strong character — "I must lift up my voice to heaven" — be sent to countries like Cyprus. Their learning and example would bring not only their own flocks, but the Greeks, Armenians and other "Eastern heretics and schismatics" to love the Roman church. It would even provoke the Saracens and Turks to admiration of their striking virtues, he thought.

Holiness was more necessary here than at Rome, and excess more pardonable there than an evil example here, he cautioned. In the early days of the church there had been apostles such as Peter and John. "Now, who are the men sent to be bishops in these remote places?"

He had just encountered one example, he said -- he of the arrogant manner and long train who had flashed a vulgar sign at a "pilgrim knight" as their galley made for the Holy Land and the salvation of their souls. "I wonder that the name of Christ has not been uprooted from Cyprus, lying as it does among the Turks and the Saracens."

COMING OF THE BRITISH

The British army came ashore in Cyprus, at Larnaca, in July, 1878, in full military regalia, their officers in plumed hats and spurs and with the ink barely dry on a new defence treaty with Turkey. Signed only a month before, it was perhaps thought prudent to hasten its implementation before the Sultan suggested any more annexes.

Under the treaty terms, the administration and occupation of Cyprus was handed over immediately to Britain.

In return, Her Majesty would defend Turkey militarily against any further Russian encroachments on Turkish territory in Asia, an eventuality which, according to Lord Salisbury, would "deeply affect the interests of England."

In a letter from Salisbury to Britain's ambassador to the Porte, still preserved in the achives of the Cyprus parliament along with volumes of other reports and dispatches of the time, Salisbury outlines the purposes behind the treaty from Britain's viewpoint. A British presence in Cyprus, he points out, would not only be a springboard for quick assistance to the Sultan should Russia annex more Ottoman territory, but would also stabilise Ottoman rule in provinces that Turkey still retained. These included Syria, Asia Minor and Mesopotamia at the time.

By propping up the ailing Ottomans, Salisbury hoped to quash any ideas amongst it population of "speedy political change" provoked by Turkey's recent defeat in the war and what he termed the "known embarrassments" of that government. "If the population of Syria, Asia Minor and Mesopotamia see that the Porte has no guarantee for its continued existence but its own strength, they will, after the evidence which recent events have furnished of the frailty of that reliance, begin to calculate upon the speedy fall of the Ottoman domination..." wrote Salisbury.

Since proximity would play a vital role in fulfilling the treaty terms, he continued, Britain should occupy a position near the coast of Asia Minor and Syria... "the island of Cyprus appears to them to be in all respects the most available for this object."

Cyprus was not to become a British colony, Salisbury wrote, but would remain under the Sultan's sovereignty. Britain would collect the taxes from the Cypriots and any excess of revenue over expenditure would be paid over annually to the Sultan's treasury. (Later, an ongoing row was to erupt with the Cypriots who claimed that when Britain finally assumed full control over the island, special taxes collected annually for the "tribute" continued to be levied, but that the amount remained in the island with the authorities.)

Further, should the Russian threat recede, England would withdraw altogether from Cyprus. On paper, the agreement seemed beneficial to all sides. Britain had a firm foothold in the Eastern Mediterranean, Turkey had big-power backing against Russian expansionism and possible revolt in her provinces, and the Cypriots, the majority being Christian, were released from almost 300 years of Ottoman rule, commentators pointed out.

British intelligence reports as early as the 1830's had called Ottoman rule in Cyprus "corrupt or non-existent," and pointed out that the accountant-general, who was responsible for the Sultan's treasure chests, was the most important man next to the governor on "this sandjak in the Vilayet of the Isles of the White Sea." Moreover, the main function of Ottoman government offices had been account-keeping, land registry and transfers, and tax collection.

Along with the British troops that first summer of the new regime came the first British civil servants under Sir Garnet Wolseley, the new Governor.

They had come to do what they did best — to administer. Firmness tempered with justice was to be the policy and the orderly collection of taxes would go hand in hand with steady agricultural growth and all-round improvement. There would be a British commissioner in every district and an Englishman in every court. The annual tribute to the Sultan would be easily paid and sure-handed administration would rescue the island from the shambles into which it had fallen. (It was to be a drought year in Cyprus and bad harvests two years out of every five due to water shortages.)

Meanwhile British officials made innumerable trips through their districts, meeting the population and studying local problems. They pressed for monetary reform, mass irrigation projects, and replanting of impoverished forests. They called for two crops a year, an overhaul of the court and prison system, and yelled for interpreters.

The men of the new administration appeared in countless etchings -- well-pressed civil servants of the Crown in pith helmets, earnestlly addressing a peasant assembly.

(It was not yet generaly known that pith helmets made bald empire-builders. There is some scientific evidence that the pith in the helmet prevents free circulation of air and eventually causes the roots of the hair to rot.)

The locals usually "carried something" on their backs and wore sensible cloth headgear, according to reports; the men sometimes equipped themselves with long, pointed knives as a precaution against highway robbery or personal insult. In paintings or engravings of the time, Cypriots are often shown pausing at their tasks in field or quayside, listening to the wind of change in a language that they didn't understand.

THE BLACK WATCH

Sometimes empire-builders didn't have much fun either, especially if they were ordinary soldiers newly arrived in Cyprus 118 years ago and were encamped in one of the hottest and unhealthiest places on the island.

This is what happened to 900 men of the famed Black Watch Regiment, one of the first off the boat that July after Britain took over by agreement the administration and occupation of Cyprus from Ottoman Turkey in 1878.

They were among some 10.000 troops who had come to secure the island. For the first three months they lay all day in thin "bell" tents at Larnaca, the canvas blocking any air as the "poor tortured men gasped for air in the intolerable heat."

The soldiers were encamped at Chifflik Pasha, the hottest site that could possibly have been selected, according to accounts of the time. This was near the Larnaca coast and its Salt Lake, with its then "noxious vapours arising from these stagnant pools." As a result, the troops "suffered such shock to their constitutions" that they were left vulnerable later to fevers and other illnesses.

One account of their trials comes from a sympathetic and very irate army officer's wife married to a captain in the 42nd Royal Highlanders (The Black Watch). She blamed poor management and bad logistics for the unnecessary suffering caused to the Other Ranks. She was Mrs Esme Scott-Stevenson, whose book, "Our Home in Cyprus" was published in 1880 by Chapman Hall. Her husband, Captain Andrew Scott-Stevenson, was later to become Commissioner of Kyrenia.

At Larnaca, according to the author, the nights had been cold and chilly in comparison to the all-day heat, and the troops, having no mattresses, had slept on the bare ground "with only a blanket to cover them."

Things had gone wrong from the day that they landed. "The

commissariat arrangements were so bad that no food was to be had for the troops till many hours afterwards. The officers had to go and forage for themselves, and had nothing for dinner that night but eggs and champagne." Water was not available.

When the regiment was finally transferred to Kyrenia, the situation did not improve. Instead of camping on one of the many higher plateaux at 1,000 feet which caught cool winds from the sea, she tells us, they were billeted on a flat plain only 20 feet above sea level and too distant from the shore to benefit from any sea breezes.

"I earnestly think whoever selected that spot as a camping-ground for the 42nd is, to a certain extent, responsible for all that they suffered later." The authorities, she went on, had miles of good table-land to choose from, not farther off than one or two miles... how could sane people have kept 900 men roasting on the plain? ...It was like the tropical heat of Africa. There was no tree of any kind to shelter them in the daytime, and they were forbidden to go a mile beyond the camp."

Eventually, she went on, many of the men went sick having "sensibly come to the conclusion that it was much better to be sick and sent to the cool hospital tent with plenty of luxuries, even beer and pipes, than to lie idle in their shelterless tents." Hospital, she tells us, was the only relief for them and from the intolerable monotony of their lives.

There were no occupations or recreations for the miserable men, it was too hot to parade, and "nothing to do in camp but lie dozing on their backs under the canvas, shifting their knapsacks occasionally to save their heads being blistered." Some became genuinely ill with fever, which was believed at the time to come from exposure to heat, swamps and "miasma" and was technically called malaria.

"But there is no marshy ground in Kyrenia," Mrs Scott-Stevenson points out. She had her own theory about the fever — "as long as the sun and bodily exhaustion through fatigue or fasting be avoided, one will escape it." Quinine, she says, is "par excellence" the remedy, the fever yielding rapidly to its action. A preventive dose ranged from two to four grains daily — "on the other hand Sir Garnet Wolseley (High Commissioner) has for some years taken a two-grain pill every morning."

In Alexandria she had heard of another cure called Warburgs Tincture containing an enormous amount of "peculiarly prepared quinine." But it was too expensive for general use. Every soldier in her husband's regiment was given three grains of quinine daily, and usually remained no more than four days in hospital if the fever struck. Relapses often occurred, however. One-fourth of the regiment were in hospital at one time from malaria and although it was seldom fatal, three men had already died.

Their remains lay in a little graveyard situated above the encampment in the foothills shaded by olives and carob trees. The army had purchased the small site and a wall and gate were built round it. Her husband, she said, "knew that these poor men's lives had been just as much sacrificed for their country as if they had been killed in battle." The bodies of dead comrades could not be allowed to lie on a waste spot, to be disentombed by dogs or ploughed over by oxen, she stressed.

Amongst the Cypriots, the most frequent disease was fever, which was not regarded by them as fatal or even dangerous, although the liver or spleen was affected. The effects were distressing to see, she reports. When later she visited the poorer villages, she often saw young children from three years upwards so swollen as hardly able to walk.

Many of the women had a sallow, unhealthy look, she said, but seemed quite fit for ordinary occupations, adding that eye diseases were very frequent and the number of blind or partially blind Cypriots was large. But as a rule, people live a to a very old age here, and more than once she had met old men said to be over 100.

Mrs Scott-Stevenson, an educated upper-class officer's wife who said that she had left her English maid at home and travelled round Cyprus on horseback with her husband, often referred to the island's inhabitants as "natives." She writes that she had "never enjoyed better health or happiness than here. I have lived amongst the people and grown to love them."

APHRODITE'S TOWN

Loose change over 2,000 years old lay wedged between the stone seats of an ancient Paphos theatre not far from the old port — dropped carelessly, perhaps, from the voluminous pockets of some Hellenistic garment?

Other sudden glimpses into antiquity — the potter's faint thumb print on a family bowl, the lingering stench from an ancient latrine as diggers pry up giant slabs from a public walkway, the excitement when a bronze figurine of Athena with helmet and raised hand is unearthed nearby.

Where is her sword and how can unpleasant odours over 2,000-years-old persist for so long?

Paphos is Aphrodite's town and the archaeologist is devoted to his trenches and the way tiny fragments of information can be coaxed from the chaos of the earth, say the scientists. It's all recorded at the end of the day in minute descriptions and measured words and logical connections; measurements and depths and objects — careful scientific accuracy and little room for lyricism.

There is no mention of personal, emotional reactions — the unexpected grief for the ancient dead suddenly alive for moments, or for the site, somehow, and the leaving of it, or the surprise when flowers re-appear each archaeological season on a cleaned and swept site, of a startling insight into how people may once have lived, perhaps, because on old women in black sits silently in the doorway of her house just now, a single dim light behind her.

Cyclamens flower amongst the stones.

"The people are gone but the flowers come up every year," says the woman archaeologist from Australia, Diana Wood Conroy, in her evocative diary of an excavation overlooking Kato Paphos. She is a member of an Australian team excavating a Hellenistic theatre there, led by Dr. Richard Green.

Today, archaeologists no longer carelessly "grope among the tombs of the dead" ("Eothen," 1845) or hustle hastily piled finds aboard waiting vessels. They now "read the earth," supported by other trained specialists, "unstitching and unpicking" the fibrous soil for facts and leads, she says. This is the only way to decipher the layers and debris. Meticulous excavation, like breaking a code.

With shovel, trowel and whisk, and the almightly grid, the earth's secrets can, hopefully, be winkled out. The grid, "large ones of metres to tiny grids of millimeters" is the archaeologists net which holds it all together, she points out. It is the outdoor workroom with invisible walls offering form and structure to an excavation and prevents it from splaying out into slipshod amateurism and overlooked data. A careless dig can hide a major sanctuary.

But it is not all tholoi and dromoi and the emerging, grinning countenance of a half-shattered figurine. How do archaeologists themeselves react during the off-guard moments when scientific pragmatism gives way to simple wonder?

Archaeologist Conroy tells us something of her own thoughts in her recent contribution called "From an Excavation Diary", which appeared in an Australian literary magazine called "Heat."

In it, she records her impressions as a member of a two-month dig in 1998 on a Paphos hillside called Fabrika, where a team of 35 experts and their assistants worked to uncover the ancient theatre. Maybe, just maybe, another sanctuary to Aphrodite lies buried nearby. (Her birthplace on the coast attracts hundreds of tourists.)

Here is part of Conroy's diary, which begins on 19 March when the asphodels have finished but the daisies, poppies and wild grasses are abundant, and tiny purple irises too - "I've noticed how ruins attract flowers as if the debris of so much past life formed a kind of natural fertiliser.

..."The process of excavation could appear like a kind of ceremony. The site is approached with reverence and hope, the soil and stones scrutinised for signs that may reveal what is beneath.

"A beautiful old terebinth tree grows in the middle of what may have been the theatre's stage area... in pits and trenches the diggers scrape and shovel.

"Indigenous people in Australia make large clearings on the ground and construct ditches and mounds around which they spend a great deal of time performing various rituals whose intensity forms a curious parallel to the devotion of archaeologists to their sites."

Six trenches are being dug, and some new ones being started - how much seating was there actually in the theatre? (Conroy visited the top trench with a venerable archaeologist who has worked in Cyprus since the 1930's, she writes. Just beyond the top of the hill where there is a magnificent view of Paphos, large cuttings in the rock form a rectangle and are supposed to belong to a temple of Aphrodite. But it's a thousand years too late, the venerable visitor points out. The hill has been washed away by earthquake and rain and the great stones of Greek and Roman temples were long ago quarried for other buildings. During World War II, the vast underground tombs and quarries were used as military hospitals.)

"The trenches are like wounds, revealing bony depths and inarticulate bedrock.There is a colourful layer of flowers. Paphos has beautiful skies and sunsets, and a clarity of air.

... "The issue of philosophical meaning is not really discussed amongst archaelogists. What is important is logical connections across the site in the process of excavation and analysis.

"Beautiful and accurate description can result from this emphasis on material and factual evidence. But the rigid discipline now includes elements from literature and poetry.

... "To understand the place of the theatre is to re-evaluate the importance of festivals in Greek life, particularly the element of sacrifice."

In the great ceremony of leading the animal to sacrifice, the animals must consent, she goes on, must nod its head in assent in order to be killed. Various devices were used, such as water thrown gently, to make the beast nod.

Conroy set up her storeroom at the dig in a room smelling of cat, she writes. The animal had been locked in there inadvertently for a week and Conroy had used harpic and bleach to banish the cat smell. It had been a kitchen in an old dwelling that was now the "dig house" or excavation headquarters. The walls are disintegrating and stained and rain comes down the chimney. "An old woman who made yoghurt for the whole village used to live here — a nice spirit to have around."

All finds from last season are in boxes on the other side and kept by a volunteer who comes to archaeology after a career as a forensic scientist, she continues. The finds have been interesting... yesterday a bit of terracotta dog figurine. "But the lingua franca of the site is red unglazed earthenware from late Roman to medieval times - a span of almost 800 years."

The theatre itself was used from before the time of Christ, from 320 B.C. to possibly 500 A.D. —an enormous length of time, she writes.

... "The Byzantine period is the longest. Remember, as in Greece, there's been no Renaissance but rather a medieval period that extended to the 19th century. "As I write, the long drawn out chant wafts over the town from the basilica church, St. Mary Covered with Cloud, a block away. The round domes and curves in these Greek Orthodox churches seem to relate them closely to mosques, which must have inhabited the same town...."

An ancient coin has been found in the trench on the side of the seats (of the theatre) as yet unidentified. "So many textures and colours of soil. What must it contain. Someone paints a flower, like an asphodel but smaller...

"A small bronze figurine of Athena turned up in the garden

trench...marvellous to see them being lifted from the soil. The gems of the unconscious earth... .

"Relationships in this team of diverse people are complex...this very strange activity of stripping back the earth...an enormous richness of vision, looking goes from the wide view, the big picture, to the tiny detail. Vision is as complex as language... .

"I compiled a list of known earthquakes over a thousand years so we can see if our fallen walls and tumbles of fragments are related...lots of earth-moving and lifting of rocks and column fragments... .

"So nice to get out of Paphos to the village of Fiti... patterned with terraces and twisted vines. Small with winding streets and many empty houses. Found a hill with a vast view over mountains to a distant snow-covered peak and had a delicious lunch of horiatico (village) bread, fetta, olives from Athens, tomatoes and cucumbers.

... "The deep silence of that profound space was a relief. But so many terraces abandoned, the intimacy of this once fervently cultivated landscape is going back to asphodel and thistle... .

"We looked at an abandoned farmstead... a roof had collapsed, a loom still strong lay rotting outside a barn, a piece of fine cotton still tied to the upright."

There were only a few old women weaving now - it wasn't being passed on. "Only pensioners in Fiti," said a cafe owner returned from South Africa after 40 years. "Only a few old people out of a town of formerly 600. All the young ones gone... .

"In the workspaces of our HQ, the old peasant house, I love the continually shifting tables of sherds...glints of colour and whole forms. A loom weight, a bowl from a Turkish pipe, a handle. Minute variations in colour in the fabric of a clay, whether the mica atoms are silvery gold or gold coloured, indicating a different origin."

From such detail archaeologists reach conclusions.

She continues: "I walked on Fabrika hill (site of the excavation), radiant with flowers. The animals on the site are somehow poignant... A camel staring out morosely from the barrier, longfaced sheep...the same colour as the battered rocks.

..."so much untidiness, things left anywhere in the growing tourist areas. But also blocky old houses enshrouded in almonds and figs, huge artichokes. They are the homes of the old women in black, still around, still entrenched in old traditions... Open doors reveal pictures of saints, rows of rushbottomed chairs, plastic-covered tables. They must be the ones who keep the candles burning in the tiny churches...fragments of another life like the Turkish fountains and odd bits of Frankish walls... .

"I saw a party of English birdwatchers staring at the empty sea. They carried very complicated equipment. The landscape was desolate with thorn bushes and heaps of old stones... .

"The scene evokes early 19th century drawings - the melancholy pleasure of ruins!"

The new desolation is the endless unplanned streets of concrete hotels and tourist shops, so much larger in scale than anything in antiquity that has survived, Conroy goes on. Further, "the pattern of earthquakes is so consistent over the past 2,000 years...the same cycle could just conceivably occur...new heaps of rubble to be built over.

"How transient our individuality is, looking at the depths of the past in newly-opened trenches. The great commonplaces are really all that we will be remembered for; being born, doing some particular activity, having families, dying at a particular time."

Conroy also visited Palepaphos (old Paphos) 15 kilometers away from the modern town, where the temple of Aphrodite once stood, visible from far out to sea. The ancient conical stone representing the goddess is still on the old site. "St. Paul had it in for Aphrodite - he harried the Paphoits as he did the Corinthians because of rumours, or truths, about temple prostitution."

The team is getting stressed by the amount to be done in the next two weeks... "Conservation is stripping the encrustations from several coins and strong images are emerging. An arrogant profile, a deity seated with a lyre. Then a cross on a cylindrical stone found in a new trench. I am moved by the innumerable boxes of small finds, the crusty bone, the glinting and tarnished glass of such fineness... the little bronze Athena fizzes in her electric cleansing bath."

Each day Conroy passed the little solid chapel in the main square. "It's a mess inside, old candle wax, bottles of fuel for lamps, and icons covered with lace curtains. The Panayia, the Virgin, is an old 19th century print. A charming face, holding a little man somewhat apart on her lap... the heavy smell of incense which reminds me of being young."

Another church — St. Mary Covered with Cloud, miraculously saved by the Lord from Arab invaders in the 7th century by being covered in thick mist. "Heavy rain, bleak east wind...the digging has stopped for the season and the site is frozen and static as we prepared to leave." Despite the grid, she says, "the past here comes to light as elusive fragments, tantalising, without completion, or any final ordering."

Here, the diary of an archaeologist ends.

WHAT CYPRUS ATE

Sometimes things were looking good in Cyprus. There were little luxuries like the dates that the villagers wrapped in soft straw to protect them from the ravens, or the sweet lemons that looked like oranges and that even the poor could afford.

Game was abundant, the rains came, and the wallop of a good grape-based zivania in a farmhouse kitchen could almost always blunt the "weltschmerz" of an honest vrakaman.

"In all the world there are no greater or better drinkers than in Cyprus," a 14th century visitor to the island called Ludwig von Suchen had written gleefully. At some point in the past, the home-made bread of Cyprus was pronounced the finest in the Levant — even the Sultan in his palace at Constantinople had no better, it was said. It was also well-known that Aphrodite herself had planted the first pomegranate in Cyprus after the seaform carried her ashore.

For the past 300 years at least, through both Ottoman and British rule, most Greek and Turkish Cypriots have clung to an almost unchanging diet, unwilling or unable to vary their traditional fare except for the occasional oriental culinary intrusion, according to reports of the times. All but the rich were unvaryingly dependent for their diet upon bread, pourgouri (cracked wheat), beans, olives, olive oil, fruit when available, cheese and the occasional boiled chicken.

Even these basics were not on the table during long, disastrous periods of drought or famine, however, and there were times when entire villages survived on roots or on bread and olives with the last being carefully counted out.

So significant had nutrition become in the national consciousness that foodstuffs were included in the list of a dead man's personal property, along with kitchen utensils and the number of wine jars left in the household stores.

The contents of a person's larder was also an accurate indication of his social and economic standing; you were what you ate in more ways than one.

Nutrition is a cultural phenomenon and it should be studied as such, says Dr. Frosso Egoumenidou, an archaeologist with the University of Cyprus' Archaeological Research Unit.

Traditional forms of nutrition, she says, reflect the living standards of an era, while social differentiation can be seen in the use of more sophisticated and refined food habits as compared with simpler ones.

Although sufficient evidence is lacking, there are indications that the rich, both Moslems and Christians, ate a refined and sophisticated diet, with clues including the variety of plates and dishes, glasses, silver cutlery, special desertware and other accessories found in the property lists of such well-known Nicosia figures as a dragoman called Hadjigeorgakis.

Similar lists, with some exceptions, were found amongst the belongings of rich Larnaca merchants and included skewers, casserole sets, faience cups from China, mustard pots, punch spoons and liqueur glasses.

Dr. Egoumenidou was a guest speaker in 1997 at CAARI, the Cyprus-American Archaeological Research Institute in Nicosia. (Note: CAARI is headed by Dr. Nancy Serwint, archaeologist and also deputy director of annual excavations at Marion-Arsinoe, which lies under or near the modern town of Polis tis Chrysochou in Paphos. Throughout the year, CAARI sponsors a series of lectures and seminars on archaeology and related topics.)

Dr. Egoumenidou's subject was "Traditional Forms of Nutrition in Cyprus from the 18th to the early 20th Centuries," and her lecture spanned a period when the local economy relied mainly on farming, stockbreeding and later, agricultural exports. There were times, she says, when the average Cypriot had to survive on a bare minumum, exploiting the natural environment to the maximum to satisfy his family's basic needs. This kind of subsistence economy, she adds, survived in some areas of Cyprus until the mid-20th century.

What of the past with its great nutritional gap between rich and poor? By the early 19th century, there were already extensive private gardens within Nicosia's walls, filled with figs, mulberry, orange, lemon, pomegranate, palm and apricot trees. Public gardens occupied more than half the town's extent. She noted that date palms have been in Cyprus since antiquity, more recently in urban areas or large villages and mainly associated with Moslems.

For most of the population, the 18th and early 19th centuries were ongoing battles to survive, with the fate of most rural Cypriots see-sawing between a sustaining but monotonous diet in a no-frills lifestyle, and long periods of deprivation when rivers and streams dried up and the wheat crops withered.

There were also earthquakes, locust attacks and upheavals against heavy taxation, according to Archimandrite Kyprianos in his "Chronological History of the Island of Cyprus, 1788."

Food had been so scarce a few years before, he wrote, that residents depended for survival upon a "noxious" root which they cooked and ate with wild herbs.

During the first 50 years of British administration, Dr. Egoumenidou points out, farmers were still being heavily taxed and agriculture faced serious problems, with indebtedness and exploitation by local money-lenders persisting into the 1950's.

Information on past food habits is still relatively scanty, and relies mainly on sometimes contradictory travellers' accounts, consular reports, historical documents, scholarly studies, monastic records and oral tradition. Her own address drew on 32 sources. (Variation in traveller's accounts could be due to the time-frame, area visited and a particular host's status.)

Visitors to Greek and Turkish houses in Nicosia, writes S.Salvator in 1893, always received jam made of melons, quince, cherries, apricots or rose leaves. With this "sweet stuff" called "tatli" in Turkish and "glikon" in Greek, the servants bring little baskets of silverwire with small ornamental spoons, he relates. ..."After that comes the coffee, as a sort of invitation to leave, especially with the Turks. After coffee, cigarettes are usually offered." Today, "glikon" and "tatli" are still prepared and served by many house-wives.

Another visitor, Magda Ohnefalsch-Richter, tells an exceptional story of early 20th century hospitality when she and her husband, losing their way in the middle of a winter's night, arrived unexpectedly at the home of a rich Messaoria villager.

The entire family sprang from their beds, initially offered water, fruit, brandy and Turkish coffee, then sent a son round to the local priest for a gourd of wine, sausages and cheese. The eldest daughter was ordered to grind corn with a hand mill to make fresh bread, while the youngest, aged 8, burnt olive leaves in an incense burner to ward off the evil eye. The best table-cloth was taken from the chest and guests washed their hands with water poured from a special jug. (Homer describes in the "Odyssey" a similar custom and it was also common practice during the Byzantine period.)

Only the host joined the guests; his wife and the rest of the family were only present to serve food. (This habit had been strongly criticised by another visitor to Cyprus almost 200 years earlier called Pococke. He pronounced it a "barbarous" custom of the Eastern nations of "treating their wives as servants.")

Dinner ended at 3 a.m. with a hot soup called "trachanas" made of dried crushed wheat, milk and salt, enriched with pieces of "halloumi" cheese, and sausages fried with eggs in olive oil and pig's fat. Later that morning, the strangers were given a "rich lunch" of soup, grilled meat, potatoes and colocassi, with fruit and flowers offered on their departure.

A century before, visitors were already praising the quality of Cyprus bread, with a Dr. Hume in 1802 calling it unequalled and made with the purest part of the wheat called "fiore di fari-na". A decade later another traveller described it as "white as snow and baked with milk instead of water." Offered at a dinner given by the Archbishop, he calls it the best he remembers to have tasted.

During the same period, visitor Turner describes the average Cypriot's diet — coarse wheatbread and herbs, at rare intervals an occasional home-fed chicken, and the wine of the country bought very cheaply.

Other reports stress the islands fertility — the "Macaria" or Happy Land.

Yet another account reads "agriculture neglected...inhabitants oppressed...population destroyed...pestiferous air...contagion... poverty...indolence...desolation" (Clarke, 1801). As late as pre-war 1939, Dr. Egoumenidou said, a considerable number of rural Cypriots were underfed and thus liable to tuberculosis, colds, infectious diseases and epidemic ophthalmia. Poverty was the main cause of diet deficiencies, both in town and countryside.

Throughout the 1920's and '30's, according to oral tradition, the local diet was mainly the inevitable bread, olives, beans, cheese and milk, with eggs and meat occasionally. All were in restricted quantities. Pig's fat or lard was spread on bread because butter was unavailable.

"We can understand why children, and adults as well, eagerly awaited Sundays and religious feasts; these days not only meant rest and play, but better clothes and mainly good food. It is not by chance that the best traditional Cypriot dishes are connected with popular religious feasts and specific traditional customs."

Christmas is the main winter religious feast. Rural households, she said, used to buy a piglet at a fair and after fattening it for a year, slaughtered it at Christmas time. Part was consumed during the holiday, most was used for making sausages, smoked ham, or "zelatina" (brawn); pieces of fried pork meat first soaked in wine were preserved in jars filled with pig's fat. This treat lasted the whole year. To this day, a soup called "avgolemoni" made of chicken broth, rice, eggs and lemon juice is eaten after church on Christmas morning.

To appease the "kalikandjari," cackling, goblin-like beings which roam the earth for 12 days between Christmas and Epiphany, housewives tossed homemade honey cakes and sausages onto the rooftops for the waiting creatures, believed to be children who had died unbaptised.

What else did the average Cypriot eat? Second in importance after bread and home-baked "arkatena" (made with flour, broad beans and chickpeas) came olive oil and olives — the main meal of peasants and shepherds in the fields. In Paphos, residents boiled, then crushed and pressed their olives and used the thick black oil for cooking or seasoning boiled pulses and vegetables. A popular snack is still olive cakes.

Other treats -- "black honey" made from carobs (which replaced sugar) grapes, raisins and a must-jelly called "palouzes", and other sweetmeats from apples, pears, nuts and almonds.

Wine was the vineyards' main product, and Cyprus wine had become so famous over centuries that it was "said to possess the power of restoring youth to age and animation to those who were at the point of death." It was so strong, that twice as much water as wine was added to make it drinkable. The best and oldest was kept for weddings and funerals.

As early as Frankish rule, there were pears, apples, cherries and plums in great variety, and one writer in 1598 mentions bananas that were picked unripe, buried in the sand, then hung up in bedrooms or exposed to the sun to ripen. Other fruits were sun-dried and eaten in winter. A tuber called "colocassi" has been known in Cyprus since the Frankish period, and tradition says it was served at the wedding feast of Richard the Lionheart and Berengaria at Limassol. It is traditionally cooked with celery and pork.

Fish was uncommon here due to the scarcity of rivers, but salted fish and sardines were imported from Turkey and Europe last century. Eels were caught locally with wooden tongs fitted with nails, and octopus, scallops and small shellfish were also available locally. Land snails cooked with tomatoes and rice are still popular.

Hunting in the early 18th century was described as "delightful" -- francolins, partridges, pheasant, quail, snipes, thrushes, waterfowl. Most travellers, says Dr. Egoumenidou, were impressed by the numerous vine-birds, the tiny "beccafici" whose capture today is illegal.

During Venetian rule here, "infinite numbers" were preserved in jars and sent for sale to Venice, making "a dainty dish greatly in request with princes and lords throughout Italy" (Locke, 1553).

Two centuries ago, according to writer G. Mariti, "the sale of these little birds was in the hands of the Europeans at Larnaca. Some were sold fresh, most were scalded and placed in vinegar and herbs. They are still eaten in Cyprus today, caught illegally and surreptitiously and served with crushed wheat cooked in their broth, or pickled in vinegar. Boar and moufflon were once abundant, but the hare was the ancient and modern favourite "owing to the aromatic food upon which they live," a visitor related.

Chickens were kept by most rural families, with the hardy black breed thought the best egg-layers. Most fowl was reserved for feasts or cooked for guests or a sick family member. Animal meat, when eaten, was provided by pigs, sheep and goats. Cypriots were reluctant to slaughter the last because of their milk and cheese-producing qualities. Devout moslems in the Turkish community shunned pork, but others ate pig meat along with the Greeks.

Cypriots did not eat oxen or calves, and avoided cows milk. "These animals were so important in agriculture that in poor areas people lived with them in the single room of their house... oxen were given extra food during ploughing.

"They plough with their cows, which they do not milk, looking on it as cruel to milk and work the same beast," another visitor in 1738 writes. "But perhaps they may rather have regard to the young that are nourished by them." Yet another says, "There is no such thing as cows milk to be had on the island... there is no summer grass."

Local cheese has been renowned since Roman times, and halloumi in the 18th century was described as "small and thick, much in the shape of ancient weights and traditionally produced at home by the womenfolk."

Most Greek and Turkish dishes were similar in Cyprus, with a good deal of yoghourt and other sheeps-milk products. Pilav was a Turkish favourite, and during weddings and the first Bairam it was cooked with lamb, chickpeas and onions. Another specialty was "molohiya" the dried leaves of a plant popular in Egypt and cooked by Turkish Cypriot housewives with meat, onions, green peppers and lemon juice.

But Cypriots in general seemed to resist innovation in nutrition habits until recently. As late as 1939, the British Commission on Nutrition was reporting that "the Cypriot is tenacious of his food habits and is suspicious of change." But World War II, independence and higher living standards have changed all that, with many of the old traditional dishes being put aside for European or sometimes Levantine and even Chinese recipes.

While enriching the Cypriot kitchen, perhaps, Dr. Egoumenidou fears that many cultural aspects connected with traditional food may die out, gone forever unless carefully and systematically recorded.

Will the eggroll replace the "flaouna"? And what will happen to honey cakes and halloumi and souvla and those ladies' fingers covered with honey and nuts? And what will the "kalikandjari" say?

WOLSELEY

The man who led the bloodless takeover of Cyprus in the late 19th century, Sir Garnet Wolseley, was intolerant, grumpy and disliked foreigners.

In daily, often peevish letters to his wife back in England, Wolseley grumbled about the heat, the "filth of centuries" accumulated in some Cyprus towns, and the selfishness of certain "royalties" whom he wished would "keep out of his way."

The distinguished Lt. General had barely time to pack his kit before being catapulted out of England to occupy and administer Cyprus that July in 1878 in the name of the Queen.

He was not a man to suffer fools gladly, and in his opinion his path was littered with plenty of them. They included a number of his fellow officers, his own chief of police, his supplies officer, the governor of Malta and that "infernal Italian" Cesnola, whom he threatened to arrest along with his "organ grinder" of a brother for illegal archaeological dealings.

Wolseley also had a low opinion, often unjustified, of many civilian guests whom he was obliged to entertain either at camp or on the HMS Himalaya which had brought him to Larnaca.

One of the few persons he seemed genuinely fond of was the Abbot Sophronios of Kykko monastery annex near Nicosia, the benign-looking churchman "with the long white beard" who lent Wolseley his room during the day to escape the torrid heat of the tents. The abbot had agreed that temporary military headquarters be set up on monastery grounds. Wolseley had also debated whether to ask for the small church there as a private retreat but finally thought better of it.

In the abbot's quarters the new High Commissioner was often to write his dispatches, his orders of the day, the guidelines for the new administration, and his daily letters back home to his beloved wife, Louise," whom he called "Loo." These letters were later to become his "Cyprus Journal," a private and candid account of his adminstrative and personal worries during his first months as Cyprus' first British High Commissioner.

The original journal is now in the Records Office at Kew, England, but was republished in 1991 by the cultural arm of the Popular Bank of Cyprus. The publication was edited by Mrs. Anne Cavendish and is now in its second reprint. It includes illustrations of the time, and has been put together with care and sympathy; its footnotes sometimes take issue with Wolseley's jarring criticism of people and places.

The letters had been meant for his wife's eyes only, Mrs. Cavendish points out, and ceased when she joined him here five months later, a few days before Christmas. Besides recounting his official frustrations and reactions, along with the devastating effects of malaria on his troops, he also wrote details about army life, humidity and the number of blankets he needed when evenings became chilly.

"I hung up my flannel waistcoat between the two doors (presumably by then a hut) and in the morning it was saturated...a plumbago vine was sent to me from Limassol."

She also heard about his impressions of Cypriots and their countryside during tours of the island. He thought Mathiati village an ideal place for a camp if only he could persuade the few Turkish villagers living there to move out. Wolseley was a paternalistic Victorian and a dedicated imperialist, and while appreciating his integrity and honesty, his wife often teased him for his more outrageous remarks and prejudices.

When her return letters were delayed, he could barely conceal his disappointment and in one case wanted to thrash the official back home who had caused her to miss the outbound military post.

Throughout his stay in Cyprus, for just under a year, he mourned for active service in Afghanistan or elsewhere, but in the meantime visited almost daily the site outside Nicosia where foundations for the new, wooden Government House were being laid.

It was to be shipped in parts from England, and he hoped to have Christmas lunch there when "Loo" joined him finally. (As it happened, high winds blew in many of the windows just before the holidays and the couple closed off most rooms. It was only partly furnished, and rather bleak). In the meantime he sent her a pencilled plan of the one-story building, remarking that the bedrooms seemed rather small. According to the Journal's editor, Wolseley was opposed to families arriving before suitable accommodation was found.

As an administrator here, Wolseley had expected to have almost "carte blanche" in the little-known island which the alarmed Ottomans had been prepared to vacate so quickly. This was in return for British protection against the Tsar whose troops only a few months before had been massing outside the gates of Constantinople with unconcealed anticipation. Disraeli was also worried about the balance of power under threat in the area.

By July, 1878, the British were landing troops, supplies and horses in the punishing heat at Larnaca, with Wolseley at the head and an impoverished, heavily-taxed local population already preparing petitions for quick reforms after 300 years of Ottoman rule. One of the first was a demand, quickly rejected by Wolseley, that Greek be the island's official language.

In addition, the "selfish" Duke of Edinburgh was also on site at Larnaca in charge of unloading troops and equipment. According to Wolseley, he bothered him at every turn with trifles and unnecessary detail, tasks usually handled by Greaves, his Chief of Staff from the Ashanti war.

Then there was a dolt of a supplies officer, according to Wolseley, who had bought ninety mule carts from Malta stacked in pieces and had forgotten their link-pins. "The mules were sent to camp but Downes didn't know why he couldn't use them with pack saddles. The idea seemed a new one to him. Nor did he know if he even had pack saddles."

The presence of the Duke of Edinburgh aboard the "Black Prince" off Larnaca continued to disappoint him. "No one likes this Edinburgh. His laugh is the most unpleasant thing I ever heard. No man could have a good heart who laughed as he does."

The Duke was the second son of Queen Victoria and married to the daughter of Emperor Alexander II of Russia. Wolseley was "glad to say he is soon to go away...to be present with his wife at her confinement... I wish these royalties would keep out of my way." (Five years later, Cavendish tells us, Wolseley was to accompany the Duke and Duchess to Russia for the Emperor's coronation and they became firm, lifelong friends.)

Of Lord John Hay, who had taken over the island in the name of the Queen less than a fortnight before and thus perhaps upstaged Wolseley somewhat, he had this to say: "He is the devil to talk and talk such nonsense. I thought generals were far from brilliant, but they are Solons compared to the pompous ignorance of such men as the Admiral Lord John Hay.

"...He talks as if he had arranged all the affairs of the island before I arrived." Wolseley felt himself lucky to have Evelyn Baring's brother from the diplomatic service on hand to keep Hay from"great follies."

(In one footnote, it is remarked that Wolseley's stream of peevish complaints may have been provoked by the intense heat, along with other accumulated irritations and frustrations. His Indian troops whom he had relied upon to help garrison the island, for example, had barely disembarked when there were orders to send them to Bombay immediately. He suspected that his government was cost-cutting.)

Wolseley lived on board ship during his first week here, except for brief visits to Limassol and Famagusta, again by sea. He described Limassol as a "small but clean place," very different from Larnaca which looks "a pesthouse of dirt and fever. If cholera takes hold of the people of Larnaca, it will decimate the population. I never saw a filthier spot. Limassol, on the other hand is well kept, with streets tolerably paved and houses of better condition and type."

Soon he intended to send an officer to each of the "keimak-lianatsi" or districts into which the island was divided, who would eventually take the Ottoman representative's place, he told his wife.

Wolseley and a few of his officers also steamed round the coast to Famagusta where the Turkish garrison fired a salute and he toured the ruined town. There he found the remains of fine old palaces, churches and one "very grand church, now a mosque," but there was an "air of decay about the place."

Another footnote points out that "the occupiers were uncertain of their welcome and were even prepared to meet some armed resistance from the Turkish garrison."

A far more dangerous enemy awaited them than a few hundred ill-disciplined and ill-equipped Turkish soldiers, continues the comment, and that was the devastating heat. It had already killed a 40-year-old British sergeant called Samuel McGaw as he marched to camp outside Larnaca on the first day of the landing.

A week after his arrival in Cyprus, Wolseley made his triumphant entry into Nicosia with mounted escort and a crowd of officials and civilians awaiting him. But even that did not go as smoothly as intended. The party left Larnaca by the wrong road, and "wandered about in a helpless state at first (in dreadful heat) for some time until we found the made-road with its accompanying telegraph poles."

The countryside there was arid, with soft, white-looking rock, and he saw a woman driving bullocks as she threshed corn, he said, with her baby seated behind her on a chair. Corn and wheat were threshed in Cyprus by bullocks dragging a sledge upon which the driver sat or stood. Its underside was studded with sharp flints. Wolseley also wondered where all the forests were, as Cyprus had been famed for them at one time.

The party's baggage had been sent ahead the night before by camels or in native carts with high wheels and iron tyres and drawn by bullocks. He thought the camels well-bred and much finer and better than those of India. The donkeys and mules were also "nice looking brutes."

He was not so complimentary about the appearance of the Cypriot women he had seen — "plain looking lot who do Venus no credit. (Yet another footnote points out that it was no wonder, as Cypriot women had been used as beasts of burden for centuries.)

Nicosia had only three entry gates, Wolseley told his wife, with a number of old guns on the ramparts including some fine old bronze pieces from Venetian times. Some of the others looked like 32 pounders.

He thought the city view uninspiring, although on one of the bastions a little mosque stood surrounded by a garden of trees (Bairaktar?).

The streets were narrow, dirty and badly paved with a gutter running down the middle, but there was a good, clean water supply from three or four aqueducts.

The wells within the walls would surely have been contaminated from cesspits belonging to every house, and which were never cleaned out, he added.

That evening at the Konak (administrative building) he was to meet Samili Pasha, the Ottoman governor who was to remain briefly for the handover, other Turkish officials and the Archbishop. He thought "Sami Pasha" as he called him, pleasing and with a good-humoured face, "fat, my age, and smokes cigarettes continually." The usual compliments were paid all round and "a man entered carrying a tray with sweetmeats and pleasantly flavoured water."

The Konak, he says, was a rambling, tumbledown affair, and underneath the offices were the dens where some of the most dangerous convicts in the Ottoman Empire were kept.

Wolseley was to worry continually in case they broke out. After much urging, Turkey finally agreed to ship them back. The convicts cheerfully walked all the way to Kyrenia laden with heavy irons or carrying pet dogs in their arms. There were no problems although some of the Gurkhas sent to guard them "went down like ninepins," in the heat, Wolseley was to report.

In the meantime, Wolseley could not understand why Sami Pasha lingered on in Cyprus instead of going home. Finally it emerged that the Sultan wished to claim all the local waste lands and that of all intestates in Cyprus as belonging to himself. He also wanted the annual salt production and the 25,000 donums which he had recently purchased at "Khrysokles" and which had been registered in a Constantinople land office but not in Cyprus.

"A swindle!" cried Wolseley, hearing the news. If the Sultan were allowed this property, very little would remain to the island including minerals, forests and other means of revenue. When the Sultan finally announced his intention to sell, the British government agreed to compensate him annually instead.

Meanwhile, "that villain Sami" didn't leave until late August, a week after "the great function in honour of hoisting the English flag." This took the form, Wolseley said, of a church service where "dirty greasy priests" were chanting dreary dirges. Most could not read or write, he said, and wore long, effeminate hair down their backs. "The holy bread was carried aloft in what looked like a silver muffin dish," he added.

Wolseley, with his prejudices and irritations on the rampage, was also having difficulty with his eyesight. One eye had been almost blinded during the Crimea campaign, and now it was worse. ..."some infernal insect must have stung me or bitten me. ...I blacked over the glass of the bad eye with ink and lamp black." And what a blessing, he was to tell his wife, to have a religion that has nothing to do with the stomach (unlike the Moslem Ramadan and the Catholic and Orthodox Lent).

"I am always thirsty. I go about carrying a great paunch full of water in front of me that is supposed to be my stomach...my throat is dry and craving for liquid (it was September)...I am drowsy and long to lie down and sleep." Wolseley was taking quinine and so heavy was the general humidity that the army tents were saturated by morning. "Those who do not slack off their ropes at night are roused by hearing the tent split with a noise like a rifle shot."

For all of his gruffness and seeming dislike of foreigners – he felt that sympathy for foreigners on the part of some British "cosmopolitans" somehow deprived his country of the total loyalty it deserved – he agonised over the necessity for drastic reform to relieve the severe poverty of the Cypriots.

He quarrelled continually with London over the skinny budget he was alloted that year, and their parsimonious budget-cutting moves. There was only £23,000 left to cover the "many changes and improvements" he planned. Later the amount was to be increased.

His immediate priorities were reforms of both the land tax and the legal system, the latter to end bribery in the courts which had reached outrageous proportions. But his insistence on immediate dredging for a new harbour at Famagusta and a minimal road system along with drainage of the malaria-breeding swamps, was to be stalled for lack of funds at the time. He was also deeply concerned for his men, many of whom were miserable because of inadequate housing, debilitating fevers or other illnesses.

In December, the Bishop of Gibraltar arrived on a visit, "a poor miserable little devil who has lived his life at Oxford as a proctor" and talked of his hardships. "It would seem that having badly-cooked food on steamers when moving from place to place were the hardships," Wolseley was to remark.

Two days before Christmas his long-awaited wife arrived. She had been ill throughout the voyage and never left her bed, he said. They "bivouacked" at Government House, still barely habitable, and five months later Wolseley was again on active service as head of British Forces in Zululand, where he captured the King of the Zulus.

Wolseley was 45-years-old when he arrived in Cyprus, and died at the age of 80 with "Loo" at his side. His career had been a long and full one and finally he was to become Commander - in - Chief of the British Army. He was buried next to the Duke of Wellington at St. Paul's.

PASHAS AND PROCTOCOL

Diplomats in Cyprus in the 18th century were splashed with rosewater to signal the end of an audience with the Turkish governor here. This was thought a polite way of indicating that talks were over. Palace servants also sprinkled the hands and face of the provincial ruler.

The farewell ritual followed talks on news of the day and politics, interspersed with black coffee, candied fruit and finally, a kind of sherbert smelling of musk and amber. Previous to the visit, a foreign representative would have sent ahead his own chair on which he was to sit, along with presents for the ruler, often cloth.

A diplomat's arrival for an audience was meant to be impressive, and along with the dragoman and members of his colony, he was led up the palace steps by two of his janissaries who wore a "dolman", a long red gown with black trimmings and topped by a crown-like cap. A corridor lined with attendants and guards led to the audience hall, and when the governor entered there were cries of "ya Allah!" from his staff.

During the talks, the diplomat on his personal chair and the governor on a sumptious divan, Turkish attendants and servants stood round the governor "in a respectful attitude, their hands crossed on their breasts and their eyes fixed on their master, whose least look or sign they understand and obey."

When discussions ended, the visitors were led out amidst the aroma of burning aloe chips set alight by a "chogadar" or courtier-attendant. (Note: By order of the Turkish Sultan, a foreign consul here was called a "beyler-bey," a title equal to an ambassador, although Cyprus was a province. In addition, the consul held letters patent from his own sovereign.)

Visits to the governor were quiet occasions compared to a consul's appearance before a pasha, when a band played throughout the meeting and consisted of kettle drums, cymbals, flutes, obocs, trumpets and hunting horns.

This account was part of a colourful, 18th century report on the life and times of foreign representatives in Ottoman-held Cyprus carefully kept by the Abbe Giovanni Mariti, who spent seven years in the island from 1760 to 1767. His book, "Travels in the Island of Cyprus," was translated from the Italian early in the 20th century by the former British Commisioner at Larnaca, Mr. Claude Cobham. According to Cobham, the Abbe's work relied almost entirely on his own notes of what he had seen and heard — "herein lies its value."

Wherever they went officially, the Abbe tells us, the consuls wore a sword as part of their formal dress; they were accompanied by official dragomen who were employed to translate Eastern languages, either verbally or from documents. All official discussions or negotiations were conducted in Turkish through the dragomen-interpreters, even though a consul may have been himself fluent in the language.

He was also accompanied by two janissaries (Turkish soldiers) whose other duties included guarding the consul's house and walking before him in the streets. "They carried a staff which they kept striking on the ground to warn people to give way."

Strict protocol marked the encounters between high officials and the consuls here, and flags were forever being hoisted or lowered. There were the arrivals or departures of new consuls and other important officials, or of Turkish warships. The flags also went up after the death of another consul, a dragoman, or any other significant person.

There were frequent courtesy calls on officials and envoys, return calls to receive, and visits by nationals in trouble or seeking financial help. The consul's were also responsible for examining ships' bills of lading, issuing clean bills of health for departing merchant vessels, and warning other countries if the dreaded plague had struck in Cyprus too. It was a serious offence to permit a ship with the possibility of plague on board to sail unheeding to a foreign port.

The foreign community was tightly-knit and supportive of its consul, writes the Abbe Mariti. In turn, their representative rallied round when needed, and attended community funerals and other functions.

The consuls usually presented a united front before the Turkish ruler and officials, he points out, and adds his own advice urging "entire unanimity and a common policy... these inspired respect, even fear." When consuls acted in harmony, "their representations against some exaction or injustice on the part of the island's governor are treated with proper consideration."

Included in a consul's main duties was to enhance as much as possible the dignity of the sovereign whom he represents, and to protect to the best of his power not only his subjects but others commended to his care, wrote the Abbe. He had no right, however, to protect one of the "riyah" (Greek orthodox subjects here) unless with the permission of the Sultan.

During the Abbe's stay there were only three consuls in Cyprus — France and Venice who were forbidden along with their staff to engage in trade, and the English consul who was free to do so. All lived and worked in Larnaca.

The French consul, he tells us, had public and private precedence over his colleagues, not only because of his official rank in his homeland but because any commands by him carried the authority of his king. Most foreign nationals without a representative in Cyprus chose him as their surrogate consul.

The Venetian consul, he adds, was also responsible for the coast of Syria from Jaffa to Tripoli, and under letters patent also protected Neopolitans, Sicilians and Swedes.

The English consul, we are told, could inflict trifling punishments, but could not banish a subject except under grave circumstances such as a serious crime, an intention to convert to Islam, or plans to marry an Ottoman subject. "It is expressly forbidden to a European to marry an Ottoman subject," the Abbe writes, and any Frenchman who dared to do so in the Levant would be expelled to France along with his wife.

All newly-arrived Europeans were obliged to visit their consul immediately and explain their purpose in Cyprus. In this way, it was hoped that the vagabonds could be ferreted out and sent home quickly.

The consuls were supported either by fees collected, through personal funds, or in one case by the Levant Company. The main expenses facing a diplomat were for presents he was expected to offer local officials at set times, and the upkeep of dragomans and janissaries.

Then there were ransoms to be paid police for the recovery of destitute subjects, "especially if the honour of the nation were involved." There were also expensive outlays for gifts of cloth to visiting pashas, and presents to the commanders of caravels or Turkish men-of-war anchored off Larnaca.

If the local government held public festivities to celebrate the birth of a son to the Sultan, the consuls illuminated their homes and kept open house for three days, offering coffee to Moslem and Christian alike, relates the Abbe.

When a new consul arrived at Larnaca, he immediately informed his community of the event, while the vice-consul despatched a dragoman to inform other consuls. "These hoist their several ensigns and at the hour appointed for landing, the chancellor, a dragoman and janissaries receive him on shore."

The new consul's subjects then escort him home, "where the dragoman offers him the usual compliments." The governor in Nicosia has in the meantime been already informed of the new arrival and sends his congratulations back to Larnaca. There the letters patent are read and the consul takes over his post officially.

The abbe tells us of another type of dragoman, a more important one, called "beratli, who are always Ottoman subjects, Greeks,

Armenian or Jews, but who become the subjects of the consul to whom they are alloted and fall under his protection. They dress like Turks, but instead of a turban wear a tall cap of marten or other skin.

About 600 merchant vessels under various European flags touched at Cyprus annually, the Abbe continues, and usually sailed in small squadrons. They transported passengers or merchandise from one part of Syria to another or traded with Europe, he tells us. A larger number arrived under the Ottoman flag or were war vessels belonging to the Sultan or other sovereigns.

One reason behind the visits by European men-of-war, the Abbe writes, was not only to see how mercantile houses were carried on, but to give "greater importance to the subjects of their several sovereigns established in the East. The Turks are deeply impressed by the presence in their waters of the war vessels of Christian princes."

BERENGARIA

Almost 800 years after her death in a Cistercian convent, the onetime Queen of Cyprus and wife of crusader-king Richard the Lionheart, is still an enigma.

Was Berengaria of Navarre a wistful wimp who had married the most eligible bachelor in Europe and then went uncomplaining into a life of neglect while her bossy mother-in-law did the royal honours?

Or was she a prudent and dutiful stoic from a minor royal house, whose distillusioned Basque heart slowly mended through religious commitment and the ear of popes, while her warrior husband, an alleged bi-sexual, rode through life on martial and personal encounters of his own?

No known portrait of her exists, and we know her features only from a recumbent effigy over her tomb in a Le Mans abbey in France. "It portrays a beautiful woman, dressed as a bride with long flowing hair," says one historian. Some believe she died a virgin.

She was short, slim and died between the age of 60 and 65, contemporary scientists said after examining the bones. The marks of her crown were still impressed on the skull; she had always signed herself the "humble Queen of England" although she was never officially crowned there, nor did she visit the country or speak the language.

Throughout her life, chroniclers of the time often dismissed her in a phrase, says historian John Gillingham, and "about Berengaria herself we know almost nothing — she moves silently in the background of events." One chronicler had called her a lady of beauty and good sense, another described her as "sensible rather than attractive."

Although Richard's every deed, including his sexual preferences, was carefully recorded or at the least hinted at, and his mother's life detailed, medieval writers "found little either to praise or blame in Berengaria," he adds. If she is mentioned by later historians, caught by the poignancy of her position, much of the original material drawn upon has come from Spanish sources.

After their marriage in Limassol in May, 1911 A.D. and for the rest of their lives, Richard and Berengaria spent very little time together, historians agree, "sometimes because of circumstantces, usually because Richard preferred it that way," says Gillingham in his 1994 publication "Richard Coeur de Lion", Hambleton Press, London and Rio Grande.

The couple rarely corresponded, and even if circumstances took Richard to an area where his wife resided or happened to be, there was often no meeting.

Berengaria had been crowned queen of Cyprus and England during the Limassol ceremony, but Richard's own kingship was re-confirmed during one of his two visits to England in a spectacular coronation rite there.

Like Berengaria, he did not speak English and spent most of his time on the continent either in clashes with local royalty or visiting his own holdings. He was also Duke of Normandy, Count of Anjou and Marne, and Lord of Brittany. After his mother's death he would also inherit other lands.

Berengaria and her contemporaries lived in an era of royal alliances and convenient dynastic marriages arranged with hopes of battlefield support or the acquisition of further lands. In Berengaria's case her father, King Sancho the Wise, was a major figure in the Crusades at the time.

It was an age of royal abandonment and a confusing swirl of marriages, early widowhood and fearful massacres in distant lands, when bedfellows made strange politics and the bastard children of erring nobility were sometimes poisoned before they could stand up and be counted.

It was also the age of chivalry, gallantry and romantic love (and chastity belts) when the defeated enemy could be flayed alive, beheaded in a trice or at the least de-nosed (which may account for the hinged nose-covering on knightly helmets which clanked down when an enemy hove into sight).

Berengaria was 27 when she married the 34-year-old Richard at the glittering chapel ceremony in that "loveliest of cities, Limassol," according to reports of the time.

Richard, in bejewelled flowing robes, rode to church on a magnificent Spanish charger, richly caparisoned with precious metals and tooled saddlebag, according to historian Mairin Mitchell, author of "Berengaria, Enigmatic Queen of England."

Her book was published in 1986 by A. Wright, Pooks Hill, East Sussex. The author was 91 when she finished the final chapters.

Berengaria appeared at her wedding in a simple, unassuming gown, we are told, "probably to ensure that nothing could deflect from the centrepiece" (Richard), she remarks. Both designs had possibly been chosen by Richard's mother, Eleanor of Aquitaine, who had engineered the royal marriage in the first place.

Anxious for a royal heir to the English throne, Eleanor hoped that an understanding mate might guide Richard patiently away from his more "unusual practices" as well as the heterosexual licentiousness so common to a number of knights. (Later, Richard did public penance for his sins after being chastised by the clergy.)

The couple postponed their wedding night until their arrival in Acre where it was again postponed, presumably indefinitely, several sources agree.

Instead, three days of feasting and revelry followed their wedding vows, while Richard distributed goodly sums and presents to the poor and guests dined from gold plate. The plate had been carried all the way across Europe on muleback as a gift from Richard's sister, Joanna, who with his mother had earlier escorted Berengaria to her waiting fiance in Sicily.

Richard and the French King, Phillip II Augustus, were already at Messina, preparing to sail with their massed armies to Acre and the Third Crusade where they planned to drive Saladin and the other Moslems from the Holy Land. From Sicily, Berengaria and Joanna were to join them there in separate ships of the crusader fleet. Instead, the vessel carrying the two ladies, the "Buza de Liuna," lurched ashore in Cyprus during the "worst storm in Mediaeval seafaring annals," says historian Mitchell.

With Richard still at sea, quick to the scene came the local Greek despot in Cyprus, Isaac Comnenus. Made aware of Berengaria's identity, he saw ransom possibilities in the situation and hoped to lure the women ashore. He refused provisions and water to the crew and offered the royal ladies "wine" instead, meanwhile ransacking two other vessels shipwrecked alongside and commandeering Joanna's gold plate as well.

When Richard landed soon after, "axe in hand", he temporarily interrupted a vengeful pursuit of Isaac to celebrate the nuptials. His army later captured both the despot, his young daughter, Beatrice, and finally the entire island in the name of England.In an initial skirmish, they also retrieved the gold plate.

Berengaria was at last the wife of a man who embodied all that stood for chivalry. Yet there had been cliff-hanging moments earlier, when the projected wedding could have been cancelled at any time while Berengaria was making her ardurous, four-month journey on muleback to Richard's Messina camp.

For Richard was already promised to Alice, the sister of his friend and crusader ally, Phillip, the French king sharing Richard's quarters in Sicily at the time. Years before, their respective fathers had betrothed the two children and the agreement had been confirmed on several recent occasions.

Although determined to break the engagement to Alice, Richard was aware that if could "cause an awkward diplomatic situation between Richard and the French king." Such an offence could even jeopardise their alliance, what had been the "pivot of Richard's policy for the past three years," according to Mitchell, and "an essential part of the preparations for the Third Crusade."

But by marrying Berengaria, Richard could also "cut through a thicket of other political problems through an alliance with Navarre." The usefulness of this alliance lasted for some years, at least until Richard gave up hope of an heir and Sancho had died. Berengaria also owned substantial lands.

Richard had met her earlier, during a banquet given by the French monarch at Limoges, when the Navarre princess was 13 and Richard was "tall and dwarfing all other competitors in a joust." She remembered his "red-gold hair and ruddy complexion." On the other hand, Alice "meant nothing" to him, Mitchell adds.

Already suspicious of Richard's intentions, and aware of Berengaria's imminent arrival in Sicily, the wary Phillip had to be made to drop his insistence on his sister's wedding to the Lionheart.

The two kings quarrelled bitterly, but Richard finally produced a stunning and extremely effective excuse. It was also a sordid one. Although he had no wish to discard Alice, he told the French king, he could never marry her because she had once been the mistress of Richard's own father and had borne him a son. This devastating accusation was particularly grim, Mitchell goes on, because Alice had been entrusted as a child to the old king's custody (Henry II, husband of Eleanor).

Richard then claimed that he could summon many witnesses to back up the charge and "in the face of this terrible threat to his sister's honour, Phillip gave up the struggle to save her marriage." In return for 10.000 marks, he released Richard from his promise and left shortly afterwards for Acre without the Lionheart. If Richard's father had, as the gossips said, actually dallied with Alice, Eleanor may have been motivated by both spite and disgust in supporting her son's betrothal to Berengaria instead, and in persuading King Sancho to agree also.

Always the enigma, there is no record of Berengaria's reaction to her position as one of the bartered brides or her impressions when later, enroute to Acre, Richards crusader ships - there were 214 with pennants flying - engaged a large Saracen vessel carrying troops to Saladin.

Again and again part of his fleet rammed the encircled ship, with Richard threatening to crucify his seamen if they let the Saracens escape. Finally, riddled with holes from the iron prows of the Lionheart's vessels, the Saracen boat sank and the injured men with her. Through it all, Berengaria and Joanna looked on.

Richard fell sick almost immediately on reaching Acre, reports say, "and as a bridegroom at this time he couldn't have been a very attractive lover," says Mitchell.

A victim of "arnaldia," his face was raw and badly blotched. The malady, which claimed many fair-skinned crusaders, also caused loss of hair and nails.

"Like many of the rufus type," says Mitchell, "his skin was particularly sensitive to strong sunlight and if he removed his helmet, even for a few moments, it exposed him to ultra violet rays which affected him badly." His skin peeled in strips, one eyewitness had said. He also suffered constantly from fever, but insisted upon being present at sieges even though at times carried on a litter. His men fought in the intense heat in suits of mail lined with wool.

Although the Saracens fighting on the surrounding hills over Acre surrendered after a five-week siege, Saladin failed to fuefill the peace treaty, according to English sources. In response, Richard ordered the horrible butchery of some 2,700 Saracen survivors of the fall of the town.

"They were beheaded in his presence," Mitchell quotes sources as saying, and included women and children. It was August 20, 1191, three months after his marriage to Berengaria. For months she had been kept some distance from the fighting, at the "Tour aux Chevaliers" with only Joanna for company. Already the ladies had become life-long friends.

Richard's cruelty on occasions, says Mitchell, "does not diminish his stature as an outstanding military general," and it was his royal standard with the leopards of England which was accorded precedence. And "through the heat, dust storms and among the corpses of Christians and Moslems alike, Richard had led his men... he had no peer, he shared the sufferings of his followers and won their love."

In the meantime, the French king had withdrawn from the fighting, along with the Duke of Burgundy. Heavily defended, Jerusalem could not be taken finally, although Richard did capture Jaffa and Arsouf. The only record of any visits to Berengaria during the period was at Christmas and on one other occasion.

He did have female company at the time, according to an English annalist called Hoveden, who claimed that the Lionheard was newly infatuated with Beatrice, daughter of the Greek despot, Isaac. She had been entrusted to Berengaria for safekeeping and brought to Acre from Cyprus with the group.

According to Mitchell, Richard had a "flaming temper... sudden storms of passion that swept him... and deviations in his sex life.

"But he had dauntless courage, a fitful liberality and readiness to forgive. But he needed a patient wife who would check his outbursts, his brutality and if possible keep him on a normal path in his sex life.

..."With his physical attraction and personal charm, he endeared himself to both sexes."

Berengaria, that virtuous and gentle princess from Navarre, was hardly an enchantress, it seems, in the eyes of her fairy prince. Nor did she produce an heir.

(Although sadly neglected, Berengaria did not suffer the same degree of humiliation as her contemporary, a young Danish princess called Ingeburg. Her bridegroom, Phillip Augustus, had felt such revulsion for her during their marriage ceremony in Amiens cathedral that he repudiated her immediately and told the Danish ambassador to return her forthwith to Denmark. Ingeburg did not comply and lived to regret it, facing imprisonment and physical hardship thoughout her life.)

Just before the crusaders left Acre, Richard sued for peace with Saladin, unable to capture Jerusalem and with his forces, now disorganised, unruly and outnumbered.

He also suggested that Saladin's brother marry his own sister, Joanna, and that Saladin and Richard rule the Holy City jointly. Joanna, outraged, promptly rejected Richard's "grand design", as did Saladin's brother, Melia al-Adhel.

When Richard returned to England, Berengaria travelled to several European cities, including Rome, Pisa, Genoa, Marseilles and Toulouse, finally settling at Le Mans. There she was "loved by all", chroniclers say, and spent the remainder of her life in good works, embroidery, alms-giving and raising money for a new Cistercian abbey. Eleanor and Joanna were now dead, and Richard died at the age of 42 from an arrow wound that had festered following one of his raids on a castle. The bowman responsible was captured and flayed alive.

When Berengaria died it was the monks with the white habits, the Cistercians, who buried her. She, herself, had dressed in white for years, the colour worn by mourning royal widows.

She had lived frugally, receiving the dower money pledged to her from Richard at their marriage only after a 20-year effort and the Pope's intercession with Richard's successor, King John.

On her tomb, the monks had inscribed: "You have come at last to the place where your heart is".

TALE OF THE DOOMED MALTESE

This is the story of a small band of Maltese farmers who came to Cyprus over a century ago and settled in the swamplands of Kouklia, near Famagusta.

They were to grow cotton and cereals and they brought their wives and children with them; 41 persons in all.

They were to be the pioneers of what both the British government in Malta and the new British government in Cyprus thought would be a quickly expanding colony of Maltese immigrants to the island. Ultimately, it was to have involved the clearing and cultivation by new farmers of thousands of donums of Cyprus wasteland, referred to at the time as acres.

In addition to land reclamation, another objective, equally important, was to relieve the Maltese homeland of part of its own redundant labour force by encouraging emigration. Hundreds of new settlers would surely set sail for Cyprus when word reached home of successful harvests and new-found prosperity once the swamps were drained.

Although not unduly excited about the prospect of more farmers in mainly agricultural Cyprus, with its already severe water shortage and reconstruction problems, the government here had found Malta's request difficult to refuse.

Months of polite haggling followed over terms of stay and the actual areas to be occupied. Several regions had been suggested but finally rejected for various reasons, including prior Cypriot claims in areas such as the Akamas near Polis tis Chryssochou, Pissouri, or Kouklia (Paphos district). Anchorages and good soil for cereals and cotton were available there, as well as pasturage for mules and horses.

Unfortunately for the new settlers, one of the unhealthiest places in the island was finally chosen for the pilot settlement. It was in Kouklia, near Kalopsida in the Famagusta district, an area infamous then for strange summer fevers. The site was known as the "Daoud Chiftlik," a steaming coastal swampland rife with "miasmas" and vague illnesses and where Cypriots refused to stay.

A total of 500 donums of land had been alloted to the Maltese, with each family to be given eight for cotton and corn, according to the Famagusta Commissioner at the time, Mr James Inglis.

The first settlers arrived at a Cyprus port aboard the "Hidma" in March, 1880, almost two years after Ottoman Turkey had handed over the occupation and administration of the island to Britain.

Their arrival and terms of stay had been organised by Mr. Vincenzo Fenech, an enterprising civil servant in the Maltese government's Land Revenue and Public Works department who had been given a two-year leave of absence for the project. It was regarded by both governments as a private venture "at his own risk and expense", but carried out with their approval.

Passage for the 41 new arrivals had cost 16 shillings each, their food during the voyage another 16 shillings eight pence, and the cost of transporting cattle, farm implements and seed was £2/10 shillings and included food for the beasts. All expenses were covered by Mr Fenech, who was to be reimbursed after the first harvest.

The first Maltese died three months later after doctors diagnosed "hard drinking and eating a quantity of unripe fruit."

He left a widow and two children who had been housed in one of several cottages at Kouklia along with the rest of the group and where the new colonists had begun cultivation.

Soon after, other Maltese reported suffering from "a kind of local fever," according to Mr Inglis who visited them with a medical officer. Within the next two months, almost the entire community became ill and were finally found in four rooms of a Larnaca poorhouse, lying on the floor in their own excreta and too weak to move. Several were dying or near death from what was finally diagnosed as malaria or typhoid fever.

Although almost destitute, the pitiful little group had paid their own fare from Kouklia to Larnaca. Now they wished only to return to Malta. The project which might have been the foundation of a sizeable Maltese community in Cyprus today, had collapsed in only six months.

Perhaps the most graphic account of those last days was included in the 1880 report of the new High Commissioner, Major General Biddulph, who had succeeded Sir Garnet Wolseley. In it, Mr Inglis himself tells the drab, tragic story of how hopeful new immigrants in a strange land who knew no language except their own and lived on fat pork and fruit went from good to bad to destitute in six short, work-filled months.

After the first death in June, the report says, Mr Fenech had begun issuing the settlers with quinine. In the meantime he was also constructing water wheels - there was water only 15 feet below the surface in some parts - and was making plans for new houses and a church for 100 people. Only 40 donums had been ploughed and sown until June, and locusts had destroyed the vegetable crop.

There were plans to sow again in October.

The families were to stay eight years with an option to stay another eight. Each family of five received £21/10 shillings annually, as well as a pair of oxen, a mule, and a cart. This was debited to their accounts and would be paid off after the harvest. Mr Fenech also provided implements and seed in return for half the crop. "All seem contented," Mr Inglis reports, "but all seem to catch the local fever." He added that Mr Fenech lived in Kondea village and that the Maltese farmers had written to friends in the homeland to come to Cyprus.

Medical officers, he went on, could not seem to find true malaria.

"Rather it is an ague. There is no malarious cachexis, no enlargement of the abdomen and no real reports of shivering and fever except when patients are closely questioned." A partial list of patients included Michael Grech and his wife Anna, fever and bronchitis, and Philipo Magra and his wife, Eleanor, four boys and one girl, the wife weak with fever and a boy with dyspepsia.

At this point, the Maltese government suspended further aid to Mr Fenech pending final reports of the enterprise. There had been other accounts reaching Malta that some of the emigrants were ill, impoverished and wanted to return home.

Finally, on August 17, 1880, the Cyprus High Commissioner wrote to the Governor of Malta: "... I regret to say that they (the colonists) were suffering from fever and were removed to Larnaca. I regret that this colony was placed in such a spot which, though fertile, is one of the unhealthiest in the island. The colonists lived on a very spare diet and weakened." The Larnaca Commissioner, Mr C.D. Cobham, "had found them in a most pitiable state," he added.

Reported Cobham: "Everyone was stricken with fever and they lay on the floor. Eleven were carried to Larnaca hospital. I sent for Mr Fenech because they knew only Maltese. One person died and three others, including two children, were still very ill. All were weak and helpless.

"They refuse to work anywhere in Cyprus and want to go home. They have been paid up to last Saturday. Fenech is paying their hospital stay but he expects them back to work. The emigrants refuse."

Thirty seven people were ill, he continues. "I found Carmen Abela dying while still in her village. She died before she left. Her husband is also very ill.

"Part of the land was a snipe marsh which the Maltese were turning up for cotton. There was an excess use of fruit and a low diet. Their systems weakened....

"Fenech had told them that to go to Larnaca meant breaking their contract and that he would not be responsible for them... The colonists at Kouklia were horribly dirty. I told Fenech that he should have bought them clothes and made them keep themselves clean.

"He had furnished them with mutton, he says, but they dislike it and preferred fat pork from Larnaca in which they delighted. Some also drank too much." In another letter to the governor of Malta, the High Commissioner to Cyprus writes "It was a private enterprise, which neither asked nor received advice from the (Cyprus) government."

Eventually, the government of Malta paid the costs of bringing what was left of the emigrants back home, less then seven months after the little colony had arrived. It was the beginning, and the end, of what official records refer to as "the Maltese Colonisation of Cyprus."

SAINTS & DUKOBORTZI

Cyprus may well be the island of towering saints, of pious hermits and holy warriors who slew dragons and built churches while empires clashed and enemies rattled the gates.

But there were also ghosts a-plenty here, even in recent history – mean-spirited trolls and ghastly goblins who leapt and gibbered at travellers as they made their unsuspecting way along inter-village routes.

Things seemed especially lively last century at Akheritou village between Larnaca and Famagusta, where persistent complaints finally brought priests and even the local bishop to the scene for a showdown with the shades, according to one account.

The worst trouble spot was a stony pass between two small hills outside the village which passersby claimed was haunted with violent and aggressive ghosts "who sallied forth at night with uncanny shouts and leapings to the great disturbance of peaceable travellers on the highway."

There, the clergy "cursed and exorcised the ghosts by all lawful means, stamping them morally flat and abolishing them." Much to everybody's relief, they have not been seen or heard since that day. Moreover, says well-known author (Henry) Rider Haggard, the rude crosses that the clergy had scored upon every rock in the vicinity meant that no troll of dubious origin could stop there even for an instant.

Author Haggard had told some very imaginative tales himself to the delight of three generations of schoolboys, including the classic "King Solomon's Mines" and a jungle shocker called "She".

The latter was the story of a white African queen, "she-who-must-be-obeyed" who finally disintegrates horribly and irrevocably before (later) cinema-goers eyes because of her sins and other reasons connected with longevity.

Haggard visited Cyprus at the turn of the century and his book, "A Winter Pilgrimage in Palestine, Italy and Cyprus", was published by Longman's in 1901. In it, he writes that Cyprus was one of the few countries in the world that he had felt sorry to leave, despite the surfeit of trolls and goblins that villagers had told him about.

Moreover, if asked to state "the loveliest prospect of all the thousands I have studied in different parts of the world, I would answer the aspect from that little window of the refectory of the Abbey of Bella Pais in Cyprus" (now under occupation).

He described the view: "The thousands of colours of the eastern day drawing down to night ... the slow flash of heaving oceans, the bending of the cypress tops... woods and mountains and olive groves ... the dizzy fall of the precipice and the birds of prey soaring above."

He also describes another, less congenial area in the island, a grey and desolate tract where 2,000 "Dukobortzi", a sect of vegetarian Quakers from the Caucasus, had sought refuge after conflicts with the Russian government. The group had a horror of killing, relates Haggard, and refused to serve in the army there.

They had been persecuted "mercilessly," Haggard said, and finally the English Society of Friends had settled about 2,000 of them in Cyprus at the village of Pergamos, near Famagusta. But the heat was too much for them and "so the poor people sickened rapidly and a considerable number died."

A place less suited to their purpose could scarcely have been found in the whole island, he goes on. Although the Dukobortzi were vegetarians, the land in the area was not irrigated and there was rainfall only half the year. Moreover, they were distinguished from their country men, the Friends, and indeed the rest of mankind by "various peculiarities," he relates. They had no marriage ceremony, all their earnings went into a common fund, and whole families slept in a single room.

The climate at Pergamos was very hot, not at all congenial

to emigrants from the Caucasus "with a perfect passion for over-crowding at night." Although they could not bear the sun, some went to labour at the new irrigation works, others tried working at night and resting during the heat. But still the area did not agree with them.

In the end, they were helped to join another group of Dukobortzi which had earlier settled in Canada. The only trace of their unhappy stay here was a group of deserted huts at Pergamos, out of one of which ran a large, rough-haired Russian dog "which must feel very lonely," Haggard writes. "That dog is all that is left of the Dukobortzi," a villager had told him. Clearly, "although they were an estimable people, gentle and kindly, Cyprus was no Promised Land for them."

Haggard believed that Cyprus should become a half-way house for troops enroute to India. Despite the Dukobortzi's miserable experience, the island was comparatively healthy and troops could grow accustomed to warm climates. "What a training ground for a mounted infantry who could shoot, think for themselves and ride over rough country!" he wrote.

There were horses, he pointed out, and perhaps the best mules in the world in plentiful supply here. The country was wild and mountainous, and there was every conceivable physical difficulty to be found for training purposes. There was also heat, cold, droughts, rains, flooded torrents, precipices, forests to take cover in and plains to scout over. "Why didn't government keep a garrison of 5,000 to 10,000 men here, invaluable in wartime and the place was so cheap besides?"

He also had something to say about other friends from home, this time feathered ones which the climate had also affected.

The chaffinches and sparrows looked "exactly as they do at home, only they are somewhat paler, as in the case with almost every other bird I saw. I suppose that the sun bleaches them," he commented. "One sparrow was almost pure white, and the larks were almost dust-coloured."

Haggard also tells of a strange grove of trees near the tomb of St. Catherine. It was forbidden to touch or chop them down because a terrible disaster would strike the perpetrators. He had never seen another tree of this kind, "spectral looking," with no new leaves. It did not die or rot, being saved from actual decay by a faint new growth on its stems.

He had found the whole of Famagusta "a ruin... the gaunt skeletons of churches, the vast circle of fortifications... foundation walls of long-fallen houses....

"What buildings are here! Millions of square yards of them, almost every stone, except where Turks have cobbled, bearing still its Venetian mason's mark."

Because of the heat, he said, most of the population lived about a mile outside the walls in a new town called Varosha. At nearby Engomi, a British Museum excavation had uncovered Mycenian gold ornaments now in its Gold-room in London, and a splendid ivory casket worth thousands of pounds.

The ancients must have been curiously unselfish, he thought, because they buried all the most valuable possessions with the deceased.

"Few heirs of today would consent to objects of enormous value, such as pictures by Titian or gold cups by Cellini, being interred with the bones of the person who had cherished them in life." Even the tomb-breakers seemed more sensitive than us moderns — "they generally didn't take everything."

From Kyrenia, the writer could see the coasts of Karamania about 30 miles across the water, he relates. They were not often visited by travellers, however, "whose throats the inhabitants are apt to cut."

It was a paradise for sportsmen, as ibex and other large game lived upon the mountain ranges there. For three shillings he had purchased an enormous pair of horns of an animal that had found its way across the straits. Ibex, he had been told, hurled themselves off precipices when alarmed and landed unharmed upon their horns.

A major form of festivity which had just reached the ancient home of Cyprus was The Book Tea, the author continued. "I could have spared it, since of all varieties of intellectual exercise this is the hardest that I know." Another new past-time, especially at Nicosia, was golf which was played on nine holes. It was odd, he writes, to do the round with a gentleman in a fez acting as your caddie and to observe upon the greens (or yellows for they are made of sand, he writes) Turkish ladies veiled in yashmaks doing the brushing and weeding.

Beyond lay the wide plains across whose spaces from time to time wended strings of solemn camels, the head of each tied to the tail of its brother in front.

Earlier, the author had seen a similar string at a half-way house at Chirokitia, off the Nicosia-Limassol road. The inn itself, actually a hotel, he recalls, was prettily situated over a green and fertile depression through which a torrent "brawled".

The guest room was stone-paved and furnished with a table, bench, a bed and some rush-bottomed chairs. The resthouse keeper, a woman whose husband was currently in prison following "false evidence" against him, was about 26 years old but looked 60, the result of childbirth on a regular, yearly basis.

Several pretty little girls stood about in the mud outside, says Haggard, bootless and ragged.

"You shouldn't have so many children," one of the visitors had told her.

"God sends them," she had answered with a sad little smile.

The scene from the veranda, at least while it rained, was not much more cheerful. There was a little patch of garden with nothing particular growing in it, surrounded by an untidy fence of dead thorns. Behind were filthy sheds and stables in one of which knelt half-a-dozen angry looking camels, great brown heaps with legs doubled under them, showing their ugly hock-joints, Haggard goes on.

The saddles were on their backs, the loads beside them. Resting against these were their drivers, smoking; motley-garbed men with coloured head dresses, half-cap, half-turban, who stared at the wretched weather in silence, he writes.

In front of the house, a pair of geese waddled in the mud and a thin cat mewed incessantly. Later, amongst the grasses near a stream, he had found several beautiful flowers,– ranunculi, anemones, and others. Soaring overhead, bleached by the sun, were the familiar sparrows and chaffinches. But the dust-coloured larks didn't soar like their English cousins.

THOMSON

He saw the clear mountain springs and the tight, walled conservatism of Nicosia's frugal houses, the muscled strength of the hill villagers and the bloodied outdoor slaughter ring near the capital's main gate.

Cypriot women at the wells reminded him of those on ancient vases — "the beauty of the Greek race" — and even the poorest loved to wear their ornaments.

He captured the rude jetties and wooden piles at Larnaca's waterfront and commented that the town itself seemed to be "groping its way seawards in search of purer air or social reform."

John Thomson, F.R.G.S. was a master photographer, an Englishman who visited Cyprus in the days when the camera was a hobby rather than a profession and people brought home "views" or "snaps" to show their friends.

Thomson had arrived at Larnaca only a few weeks after the British in 1878 "to explore Cyprus with a camera" and take "views of whatever might prove interesting on the journey." Earlier, he had taken stunning photographs of life in China, Indo-China, the straits of Malacca and the streets of London.

Thomson's first impressions after landing here were gloomy ones and he almost "set my face homeward," so dreary was the sight of newly arrived merchants and speculators at Larnaca. They were bemoaning their ill-luck in coming to an "exhausted" island filled with pestilence, poverty and no buying - power. Rents had also soared from £40 to £300 pounds per year.

But Thomson stayed on, and for the next several weeks, well into the autumn, roamed the country with a camera, a note-book and a 12 shilling-a-day dragoman to guide him through "impartial" pictorial confrontations with the island's people, their daily lives, their houses, their animals, their priests, their landscapes and their soaring monuments.

The expedition was not without some toil and discomfort, he says later, along with "some dangers, some real, some imaginary." The real included a near-fatal fall when his mule slipped on a cliffside, and his devastating bout with "Famagusta fever" or malaria on the eve of his departure.

The result, nevertheless, was a superb and sensitive collection of 60 photographs showing life at the time, warts and all, along with the hefty and informative whole-page texts he had written to accompany them. The album was published a year later in London, in 1879, under the title, "Through Cyprus with the Camera, in the Autumn of 1878".

The photographs had been printed in permanent pigments, according to the photographer, and the work had been dedicated "by permission" to Sir Garnet Wolseley, the first British administrator and High Commissioner to Cyprus. Wolseley's photo, bareheaded but be-medalled,was taken by Thomson himself and appears under the dedication.

Although "a picture is worth a thousand words", according to the old adage, Thomson's text certainly fleshes out some of his otherwise mute subjects.

We would not know, for example, that local lepers begged for their living and lived in tombs; or that Cyprus camels shifted and bellowed hideously when suspecting that their owners were overloading them; or that it was nice to offer a gift to the children after accepting hospitality in a poor man's house.

Nor would we know that young and pretty women filling water jars at the "Jacob's Wells" across the island often happened to be there just at the moment when a group of young males were to happen by.

Over the past century, Thomson's book had become so scarce that in 1978, the "Collector's Centre" in Nicosia published 400 numbered copies of the rare first edition and made them available to "those who love books, especially the Cypriots. Thomson has saved a whole world, the world of Cyprus at a certain time of its history," said the editor of the Cyprus re-print.

The album was not merely a record, for the photographer captured time after time the vulnerability and quiet endurance of a country that had known many conquerors.

His photographer's eye also picked up bleak, rocky seasides and the vast empty spaces of remote mountain valleys. He showed the everlasting poverty, sometimes hunger, of generations of its people, the toil of the plains farmer and his wife, the bronzed, work-worn peasants with their shabby clothes and shapeless women, caught in a cycle of endless labour.

Thomson was aware that the island had once been a renowned commercial centre in the Levant, and the fate of this seemingly exhausted place saddened him. He hoped that under the new British rule it would regain some of its old renown.

While writing of various places here, he sometimes muddled or mis-spelt names, we are told, either because they were wrongly heard or pronounced, or were incorrectly given at the time. Most are decipherable, however.

At St. "Pantalemoni" monastery at Kyrenia, he pictures a group of monks learning over a balcony under carved arches and tells us that the Greek and Latin monasteries are "the best resting places for travellers" in the absence of inns.

They are the recognised rest houses of the island, where a warm welcome awaits the wayfarer, he says. A small financial contribution was hoped for. As a rule, the monks were wealthy and independent, he writes, and their abodes were furnished with at least the "simple and indispensable adjuncts of civilised life."

He described animated scenes in the monastery each morning, where at the first streak of light the chapel doors were thrown open for worship and for votive offerings from caravan owners who had sought shelter during the night.

"All is bustle and confusion until camels, donkeys and mules receive their loads of inland produce and move towards the coast."

Of the "Cyprian" mules and donkeys, he remarks that they are "most leisurely" in their habits and have a "wonderful aptitude" for patiently awaiting their masters. The animals could stand for hours without stirring from the same yard or two of shade, their heads turned toward the sun to follow the shadow.

Mules had a peculiar charm for a photographer, he says, citing the perfect immobility of their repose when once at a halting place. They were invaluable in Cyprus especially in the mountains where there were no roads. "But they are timid creatures and take fright easily."

The sudden tinkle of a goat's bell had caused his own mule to fall as they rounded the edge of a precipice. Fortunately he and his mount were saved by a tree growing from the rocks.

Donkeys were used for carrying brushwood and other loads, with the owner of a troop carrying the usual stick armed at one end with a short iron spike.

Generally, the "mere shadow of the weapon has a marvellous effect in quickening a quadruped's pace." But on a long journey, the driver must tickle their ears and the tender parts of the spine to produce an involuntary and perpetual motion in the beasts limbs, he comments.

The Cyprus camels were the chief beasts of burden here, with climate and pasturage well suited to them. Their use was restricted to the lower plains and seaboard and their pliant foot was admirably adapted to rough paths and soft, sandy tracks. Because distances were comparatively short, their powers of travelling for days without food or water were never put severely to the test, he remarks.

Camels were long-suffering creatures, but that last bale could provoke loud lamentations. A wise master would reason calmly with them as the burdens were secured, then coax them with soothing words until they rose and took the load.

The life expectancy of mountain villagers was about 60 years, he writes, quoting a local priest during a visit to "Kalopanagiotissa village (Kalopanayiotis). "The work was so unremitting and severe that the strongest died rather early, prematurely worn-out men and women." The priest's home had been built partly burrowed from the hillside, as had been many others.

Walls were of stone, with pine rafters and brushwood roof which had been wattled into thatch and coated with clay. While the rustic abode was charming to the eye, he goes on, it was unhealthy because of lack of ventilation and the simplest sanitary devices.

Although rainproof, the roof absorbed moisture which "moulders the bones of the stoutest peasant and racks his limbs with ague." The few who suffered from fever seemed to throw it off as mysteriously as it was contracted, and were rarely compelled to miss work.

There were 15 chapels at the village and a population of 500 whose production included olives, silk and cotton. Bread was baked only once a fortnight in an outside, household oven "to save time." When stale and "hard as flint" the bread was soaked in water before use. Thomson experimented with it but found it very detrimental to the teeth.

During a climb to the Mt. Olympus summit with a volunteer guide from Prodromos village, they were caught in a violent storm with thunder shaking the mountainside and lighting flashing at every side, he writes. Later, drenched with rain and enveloped in gloom and mist, the scene at the top seemed weird and foreboding to the photographer, with clouds in grey masses pierced with dark pine tops.

They found the remains of an old well, and all round cairns of stone that did not correspond with the local rock formations. They had possibly been brought from elsewhere as part of some local tradition, he thought.

He deplored the destruction of the fast-thinning Troodos forests, logged out by half-naked hillmen who used teams of oxen to drag the logs from the mountainside. Massive trunks were strewn about and some of the finest pines had been destroyed merely to supply resin or pitch. Even women took part in the logging, climbing to the highest branches and lopping off parts as they ascended. Finally only the bare trunk remained, ready to be fired near its foot and toppled.

He sympathised with Cypriot farmers and peasants who toiled in the fields or laboured elsewhere for 1½ shillings a day. Their women, often working as ordinary labourers, received half the amount for the same work. Amongst the lower orders, he commented, the women were little more than domestic servants, taking their full share of outdoor labour as well as doing the drudgery of the household.

But surviving amongst them, he says, was an aptitude for the arts that belonged to a bygone civilisation, and in chests and ancient cupboards in their rude houses were stores of fine linen and holiday attire woven, spun and decorated with tasteful designs created by themselves.

He also noted the solicitude for the elderly in some Cyprian homes. Their toilets were carefully attended to, an armchair set out for them in the shadiest nooks in the courtyard, and there they would rest or wander about at will, staff in hand. There were daughters in Cyprus, he goes on, unblessed by parental endowments, who spent their days in sedentary toil in order to make life pleasant for these aged relations.

The modern Cypriot man was strong and nimble, affable and courteous, "with a frame whose power and development would adorn the ranks of the finest regiments." Their earnings varied, depending upon "the labour to be got out of them."

The male peasant often wore a fez bound round by a coloured cotton kerchief and a jacket of striped cotton. Girdle and trousers were of the same material. The boots were the most costly part of his attire and protected the feet from snakes. The women dressed modestly, in general, and many kept the greater portion of their face covered "in Turkish fashion." They had regular features and light brown to black hair.

The native beauty was best seen in children, for many women "lacked much of that grace that comes of gentle nurture." Before reaching maturity, many were sent out to field work and trained early in a life of toil, he added. Women from the wealthier classes were better -dressed, he tells us, and some would look creditable walking down a Parisian boulevard. Other comments from Thomson:

* The word, "baksheesh" was unknown here and begging was not widespread.

* A Nicosia-Larnaca omnibus operated daily between the two towns but most transport was by mule or bullock cart.

* Only small vessels could anchor at the "pygmy port" of Kyrenia, which resembled a small fishing station in southern Europe.

* Houses there were of stone and roofed with clay, and sanitary arrangements were of a "simple order." Fires were not needed for warmth in Cyprus.

* Kyrenia verandas were in disrepair and many seemed to dip dangerously shorewards. Whole families would sit on these frail platforms, enjoying the evening breeze. Kyrenia had once been the capital of a small kingdom, and was said to have been founded by Dorian colonists under Praxander and Cepheus.

* One of the most delightful resting places for foreigners was at Lefka village with its shady orchards and abundant fruit, pomegranates and walnuts. "We had breakfast spread for us in a garden, beneath trees which shed down ripe peaches onto our table."

* At Paphos he purchased from a "native" a Roman signet engraved with the figures of Jupiter and his eagle; also a number of pre-Christian coins.

Limassol was without doubt the finest town in the island, with pleasant courtyards and fruit gardens. Houses were built of honest brick and stone and during the day busy traders bargained through their barred windows or open doors in oriental fashion. Their back alleys, though recently cleaned, "must still at times be tainted with all the odours of decay peculiar to Eastern towns."

In the evening, well-dressed Greek ladies and their fashionably-attired lords paraded up and down before the stores.

At Famagusta, in front of St. Catherine's church, now a mosque, was a cafe propped upon an old Gothic porch. Here, worshippers met and sat for hours, smoking their hookahs and drinking coffee in silence. "They have long ago exhausted all the subjects of conversation that so lonely a spot can supply."

One forlorn individual had made his funeral arrangements many years before, and his chief wish was to mingle with the surrounding dust as speedily as possible, wrote Thomson.

At Avgorou village in the Famagusta district, the local priest provided his own subsistence from offerings from parishioners in return for various services. These included benedictions, exorcisms, the granting of divorces, marriages and services for the dead. He was highly respected.

With a good dragoman, the tourist was sure of spending a pleasant holiday in Cyprus. Good, plain food was obtained without difficulty everywhere, and after a hard days journey in the hot sun even rough lodging with a hearty welcome will seem luxurious.

"The traveller may have to make his bed in a sleeping room common to some of the family's males, but the linen will be spotless and hospitality of the highest."

The richest farms in the Levant may soon lie in the plains near Nicosia, he thought, but currently vast tracts lay fallow, filled with thistles, shrubs and stunted herbage over which sheep and goats roam.

COSTABELLE AND THE TITANS

On an island where the water shortage is as old as the Byzantine era, there are some years when gardening in Cyprus is like a clash with the Titans.

It's all rout, rally and rout — the stunning droughts, the long rainless summers, the time the lemon trees got sick – when the best laid plots in field and glen oft go awry.

It is a situation that no gentlewoman should be made to face, yet for more than three decades Emily Alice Murphy, better known as Lady Murphy, gardened in Cyprus at the Kyrenia home she called Costabelle. She planted and potted and hoed through war and peace, rebellion and riots, and some of the worst droughts in living memory here.

While it was challenging, healthy and good for the waistline, she also fought long waterless summers and the vagaries of the local climate when the snow either banked on the Kyrenia mountain foothills or winter never really came at all. Finally, she was to create one of the most colourful and admired gardens in the island.

Lady Murphy wrote a book about her methods, sometimes experimental, and the story of her own garden. It was aimed at helping newcomers to the island, amateur gardeners or otherwise , eager to establish a first garden yet unaware of the traps inherent in unfamiliar local conditions.

She called it the "A.B.C. of Flower Gardening in Cyprus" and dedicated it to her husband. The manual was first published in 1956 by the "Times of Cyprus" and six years later in a second, enlarged edition. Some of her articles had already appeared in the government's "Cyprus Review" at the behest of its then-editor, Lawrence Durrell.

Forty one years after the book's first appearance, it is still in demand as a simple, step-by-step guide to the unwary who enthusiastically plan a sumptious garden but may forget that the gardening season is upside down here. The book also contains a planting and monthly gardening calendar, along with hints tailored to the realities of local conditions and how best to plan economically. She also lists her failures.

Lady Murphy had written it for her time, when many "gadgets" as she called them were unavailable to make a gardener's lot easier. Life has since moved on in the gardening world, but the essentials are there as she set them down. (Other books on Cyprus gardening have since been written.)

She had arrived when the island was still a British colony — the snow was so deep one December that friends could not reach Kyrenia for a Christmas party! she writes, and one of her oldest friends, Mrs Bolton, had just put together the only "really succesful" wild garden in Cyprus.

Few gardens were properly laid out and lawns were almost unheard of here. There were few hedges and only a limited variety of trees and shrubs. "Eventually a few brave souls imported some bulbs, but it took some time before experimenting came into fashion."

Although she always considered herself an amateur, after decades of garden work Lady Murphy probably knew more than most professionals about how each precious plant would behave, or misbehave, which were best suited to which soil conditions and how much water was actually needed for a decent garden to survive.

The reader also learns of the hard work necessary to "share in the glories of the garden," the difficulties of finding knowledgeable help or useful tools — she made her own "dibber" for lifting out seedlings — and her distress when forced to "starve" some of her plants of water in order that others would survive.

There was other practical advice, such as how to build a handsome Italian pergola economically with local materials, how to lay out paths and beds — don't forget to "ram" the paths down as hard as possible — and which bulbs and flowers seemed to thrive better in Cyprus. (For the pergola she used terracotta drain pipes cemented round an iron pipe.)

Through it all, she writes, she felt "thankfulness for the beauty of the earth" and the tranquil shield that her much-loved garden provided against the "changes and chances of this mortal life." She was thrifty, clear and realistic, and time after time her pages are well seeded with the basic rule of Cyprus gardening — "always verify your water supply."

Never plan an extensive garden unless you are sure of plenty of water, she cautions readers, not only in winter but more particularly in hot weather. The success of a year round garden hinges on this certainty, she warns, and of being able to keep all your plants growing during the long rainless seasons.

During droughts, it is a "perpetual struggle" to get good results in local gardens. "Not so many years ago, one could count on 18 to 20 inches of rainfall, cold weather and deep snow on Troodos, sometimes even in Nicosia or on the Kyrenia foothills. The mountain springs never ran dry, nor did the wells and it was possible to water one's garden the whole of summer. But in 1961, hundreds of wells ran dry."

Therefore, "cut your coat according to your cloth," she advises. If the water supply is poor, she suggests planning your display of flowers chiefly for winter and spring. "For this, bulbs are invaluable. They flower in autumn, winter and spring, and go to sleep in summer so they are off your mind... trees, shrubs and climbers then take over, and any water to spare can be given to them."

Important also, find out what kind of soil you have. If it's sandy loam, as in many parts of the island, there will probably be a good deal of lime in it already. This soil is very easy to enrich with organic manure - farmyard, sheep, pig, vegetable matter or poultry (the last becomes very hot, however).

Another, less desirable soil type is clay, which is liable to clog in wet weather and crack in dry. It must be lightened with builders' mortar rubble, well broken up and with lime in it. This type of soil needs far more digging than sandy loam, and the usual manure and humus must also be added.

Through years of drought, she had learned that many established shrubs will live through the hot weather without any water, or very little, and even perennials will survive on a reduced ration. "But this applies only to shrubs that have been in place for years," she stresses. "Anything newly–planted must be watered."

Aside from various successes or failures in Cyprus gardening, she still maintains that in a normal year the island can be called a "gardener's paradise."

In Lady Murphy's gardening days here, there were comparatively few garden shops or commercial green houses, but new varieties could be ordered through the existing ones. Government nurseries also supplied limited types of flowers, seedlings and saplings for sale to keen gardeners, although at the time most of their experimental work was on cereal varieties.

Gardening seasons in Cyprus are totally different from Western ones, she stresses; while it may seem very unorthodox to start a garden in September and October instead of early spring these are the months in which real garden work can begin and the sowing season is very short.

By October, cooler weather and the welcome rain will soon be on the way, and there will be seven months in which garden work can continue in one form or another. But no two years are the same, and it means pitting ones wits against the vagaries of the climate. But a lot of gardening, she maintains, is just common sense.

During the five rainless months from May to September, even the most enthusiastic can do little active work except weeding and watering. September means getting out plans and making the necessary preparations for the new season so that no time is lost.

In laying out a new garden, measure your land beforehand,

make a rough drawing and a list of what you want to grow. Don't forget some trees, shrubs and climbers. It is a great advantage to have even one tree for shade, Lady Murphy writes, which could also be a focal point for sitting out. Also have a look at other people's gardens and learn what they have successfully grown.

Personally, she preferred a rather formal layout, with straight paths and beds and trim hedges. Winding paths, unless one wishes to hide something, often make a garden appear smaller as there is no vista.

With flowers difficult to grow in summer, the value of trees, shrubs and hedges are enhanced, she thought. Most are evergreen and can look after themselves fairly well once established.

(Note: Today, as in Lady Murphy's gardening era, many varieties of pines and cypresses can be had economically at forest nurseries and other government gardens, including Athalassa near Nicosia.)

Quick-growing flowering trees were also available, such as the evergreen sophora with its white flowers, the robina with pink blooms and the yellow acacia. They should be planted when autumn rains begin, then staked.

The flowering shrubs she recommended generally included hibiscus, poinsettias, oleander, buddleia and duranta, geranium, rosemary, lavender and plumbago. Planting time is October onwards, the earlier the better. Besides hedges, there are also easy-to-grow climbers such as roses, bougainvillea, wisteria and jasmine, to be planted from October to December. Bougainvillea is best planted in April or May, however. A real grass lawn should only be attempted when there is shade and a plentiful water supply.

Lady Murphy also devotes space to the care and pruning of roses, seeds and seedlings, bulbs, potting, roof and veranda gardens ; she also lists over 40 kinds of flowers that can thrive in Cyprus .

Bush roses, she writes, have a very long flowering period and, if watered, will flower nearly all year round. But this weakens the plant, she says, and may cause diseases. These roses should be forced to rest by withholding water in hot weather (but only if they are established plants). Young ones should never be allowed to dry out. When resting, older plants need water every two weeks only, but mulch first to keep the roots cool, she says.

Lady Murphy was very fond of her own miniature gardens which she created in low gypsum sinks and prepared for planting with a solution of permanganate of potash and water (this turned wine-coloured). Since gypsum is porous, water and more crystals could be added daily if needed.

The sinks were left to soak for five days, then emptied and refilled with plain water for a few more days. When the sinks have dried, "distribute drainage more evenly by making a few more holes and small grooves from them to the sink's sides." To save an aching back, place the sinks on pedestals before filling them with earth (too heavy to lift afterwards, and awkward to care for) and use good soil sprinkled with peat moss and with drainage crocks or stones scattered over the bottom. She suggests several types of miniature gardens — cactus, dwarf perennials, miniature tea roses or dwarf bulbs. Sink gardens need regular watering.

When water is very restricted, a pot garden may be a good idea, she writes; it is very little trouble and can have great charm and colour.

Her affection for pot plants, she writes, dates back from "the time in India when I saw, at Ajmer, Rajputana, a whole flower show of them. It was desert country and impossible to keep a garden going there. Yet people wanted flowers and it was amazing to see what a splendid display could be made with plants and annuals grown in large pots."

Undoubtedly they are very economical, for every drop of water is used, she said. For her own pot garden, she used such plants as asparagus ferns, dahlias, geraniums and white begonias.

Further, "I don't think we appreciate sufficiently the shades in green which can be used in a new Cyprus garden... the difference in colour and form of trees, the two acacia wattles, the dark green of Cypress sempervirin, the blue green of the Aleppo pine." Then, what a contrast in hedges, she writes, between dodonea, rosemary and lavender, not to mention the silvery varieties.

Cut flowers should be kept in the coolest part of a room, but not in draughts. "Don't shut them up all night in a room full of tobacco smoke. In hot weather put them into a hall or veranda, and to freshen plunge them into a basin of water or up to their necks in a jug of water.

"Remember that violets drink through their faces and last longer if kept tied in a bunch. They also like a daily bath in a basin or under a tap."

Roses, chrysanthemums and shrubs should have their stalks split or crushed for a couple of inches before being placed in water, and a pinch of salt helps to keep them fresh.

She also found that a brass or copper container seemed to keep flowers fresh longer in the semi-tropical Cyprus climate.

During her gardening epoch, Lady Murphy pointed out, wild bulbs from the foothills often transplanted succesfully, but she cautioned moderation in their removal from their natural surroundings. (Today, ecologists and environmentalists strongly discourage their removal under any circumstances, fearing that they may disappear altogether from their habitat.)

There are several indigenous bulbs in Cyprus, she continues, including the iris cypriana, tulipa cypria (known locally as the Myrtou tulip) and the cyclamen cyprium. The Kykko tulip is also found in Palestine, but its home is in north Persia, where it is indigenous.

From earliest ages, monasteries were known to have gardens, she writes, and it was customary for travellers from other lands to offer plants or bulbs in return for hospitality. "Did some wandering friar come to Kykko monastery and leave some of the scarlet bulbs?" she asks.

Lady Murphy also advises keeping a garden diary, for memory can be treacherous and one can forget what has been planted months before. "I remember all the difficulties I encountered when I first came to the island... but surely few of us, even in the midst of hard work, can fail to realise the wonder of the pageantry of the seasons as they unfold."

THE SPINY MOUSE AND OTHERS

There were wild ducks and skylarks and eagles and grebes. There were bats and bustards and a wood-brown creature called the Cyprus spiny mouse with "spines over the hinder part" and a tail so brittle that it often dropped off.

Tiny warblers called "beccaficos" were carried to Cyprus on the backs of giant cranes every autumn from Asia Minor, according to popular belief. Mallards flew into the marshes along the Cyprus coast, there were scorpions and centipedes in abundance, and a certain female ant was dreaded because it was thought to carry the anthrax bacillus.

These are only a few of the 15 species of wild mammals and over 230 kinds of birds which flourished in the island in the early 1900's along with the rodents and insects.

There were no squirrels or woodpeckers then — there still aren't; But there were hares, thousands of blue-grey Cyprus hares with beige tummies which were trapped legally year round. They lived in the hills and mountains and were considered vermin because they ate their way through vineyards and young crops.

(Note: Although it is not generally known, Cyprus today is the main centre of "endemism" in Europe and the Mediterranean. It has the largest number of endemic species of birds and reptiles in comparison, and more endemic vegetation also. The birds specially cited are the Cyprus warbler, the wheatear, the jay and the coaltit.)

The island's close connection with animal and bird life goes far back into antiquity, with ancient vases frequently depicting wildlife and hunting scenes. The hunters are sometimes shown stalking their prey to a point only feet away, the target often remarkably unperturbed as it grazes or stares into space.

Strabo and Pliny had talked of deer swimming across to Cyprus from Cilicia long ago (there are also theories that they were rafted over) and in 1902 the bones and teeth of dwarf elephants and hippos were discovered in the Kyrenia range by a renowned woman paleontologist.

She was Ms. Dorothy A.A. Bates, a member of the British Museum staff, who dated her finds from the Pleistocene Age and said that both were akin to dwarf species whose traces had also been found in Malta and Sicily. She called them "Hippopotamus Minutus", and the pigmy elephant "Elepas Cypriotes".

There were also hunting scenes on Ptolemaic vases found at Salamis in 1890, one inscribed with the word "archikinigos" or "chief hunter".

During the lengthy Lusignan rule in Cyprus, which pre-dated the Venetian takeover, a favourite sport of kings and courtiers was hunting when bird and beast were pursued across the island by trained falcons and cheetahs. One count of Jaffa kept over 500 hounds, it was reported, with every two dogs equipped with their own servant "to bathe and guard them for so must dogs be tended here."

Another sovereign, Jacques I, kept 24 leopards and 300 hawks for hunting purposes. The leopards, possibly mis-identified, may have actually been cheetahs or a type of lynx. He also possessed a "carable" which was possibly a weasel, polecat or ferret. It was described as a "little beast, no bigger than a fox which caught partridge, hare and wild sheep."

The official "Handbook of Cyprus" for 1909, which records all of this and more under the heading "Wild Animals and Sport", goes on to say that although deer and pheasants had been officially listed late last century as living here, actually they did not. Perhaps some official, according to the Handbook, had entered the listing with the intention of importing them, but never did.

Compiled annually for some years by Claude D. Cobham, a highly respected Commissioner of Larnaca, and Sir J.T.Hutchinson, a Chief Justice of Ceylon, the Handbook also mentions that some pheasants had been imported by a Lord John Kennedy and turned loose. "But nothing more was heard of them."

The red-legged partridge was indigenous to Cyprus, the Handbook claims. They were generally found in the hills "but they are not increasing in number." This may be because "fair sport may be had by an active man with a good dog," according to the writers.

Five pairs of another variety had been brought from England and "turned down at Colossi chiftlik in standing barley, but they were believed annihilated shortly after by local sportsmen." It was illegal to kill game without a license to carry a gun.

The tiny warblers or "beccaficos" referred to earlier were also known as vineyard or "fig" birds and were captured, says the Handbook, "by placing sticks covered with bird lime in places frequented by these little members of the warbler class." They were considered a great delicacy, either fresh or pickled in vinegar or wine.

Today they are called ampelopoulia and there is a law on the books against liming or netting birds in general.

The original list of Cyprus birds appearing in the 1909 Handbook was taken from a publication called "The Ibis," of 1889, but it had been updated and enlarged by Ms. Bates, the paleontologist, after her 1902 visit here.

Also listed was the black-tailed godwit, the sandpiper, several types of owl including the barn and scops, the peregrine falcon and the Cyprus crow.

(The Cyprus hooded-crow is very intelligent, according to Nicholas Symons, biologist and scientist, who heads the Environmental Studies Centre at Kritou Terra, Paphos district. But there is no trace here, he said, of the exceptionally smart type of crow found in South Pacific rain forests recently which makes its own toolkit including a lock-pick type of probe used to extract worms and bugs.)

Scientists who discovered the tool-making crow say that all members of the crow genus have innate problem-solving abilities. Although it may be cleverer than the Cyprus crow, the local variety here is handsomer in appearance.

Say the Bannermans, writers and experts on birds, in a publication called "Birds of Cyprus": "Anatomists say that the Cyprus crow has the most highly developed type of wing and foot. Every quill and wing covert is perfectly formed. It is very intelligent."

In the meantime, the Handbook also mentions the rat-tailed worm, and the mosquitos, sandflies and leeches that could make life uncomfortable in 1909.

There were silverfish too, which attacked clothes, pictures and book-buildings and could only be kept at bay by oil paint.

A few moufflon or wild sheep were still surviving in Troodos and Paphos then, and a law was passed for their protection with a special permit needed to hunt them. There were also many varieties of snakes on the island, but only one type was poisonous.

A Cyprus branch of the RSPCA had been founded in 1902, says the Handbook, noting that "Cypriots as a rule are by no means unkind to animals but here, as in other countries, there is always room for improvement."

FROM A GENTLE EMPIRE

Were Cypriot women so enchanting that certain sea-going travellers over the centuries dared not weigh anchor in Cyprus lest they fall under their spell?

Did they have such power to bewitch that men were transfixed in their presence and very soon "knew the rapture or the bitterness of love?"

It seems they were and they did, to hear a leading 19th century travel writer tell it. At one point he appeared almost smitten himself.

Alexander Kinglake, who set out on a Grand Tour of the Near East in 1834 and included Cyprus briefly in his itinerary, called the product of his journey, "Eothen — Traces of Travel Brought Home from the East". Also included were his impressions of Serbia, Bosnia and the Levant.

"Eothen," which means "from the East", is the only "hard" word in the book, according to an introduction to a reprint published in 1991 by the Oxford University Press.

The chapter on Cyprus tells of dining with local families whose children had immortal names like Socrates, Aspasia, Alcibiades, his impressions of local girlhood and women, and random conversations.

Part of the young Cypriot girl's attraction, wrote Kinglake, seemed to be her grace and diffidence on public occasions, a kind of self-contained and deferential style which was almost ritualised.

This was apparent to Kinglake at a birthday celebration when he went to congratulate a "noble old Greek" in his Limassol home.

"During all the morning, there was a constant influx of visitors... a few of these were men... but most of them were young, graceful girls." Their visit seemed part of a ritual. "Almost all of them went through the ceremony with the utmost precision and formality: each in succession spoke her blessing in the tone of a person repeating a set formula -- then deferentially accepted the invitation to sit.

"The girls partook of the proffered sweetmeats, and the cold glittering water. They remained for a few minutes either in silence or engaged in very thin conversation then arose, delivered a second benediction followed by an elaborate farewell, and departed." The bewitching power attributed to the women of Cyprus was somehow connected with the worship of the sweet goddess who called their isle her own, he thought.

They were not so beautiful in face as the Ionian Queens of Ismir, he goes on, but the Cypriot lady was tall and slightly formed; there is a "high-souled meaning and expression -- a seeming consciousness of gentle empire that speaks in the wavy lines of shoulder and winds itself... around the slender waist."

He praised their richly abounding hair (not enviously gathered together under the head-dress) which descends the neck and passes the waist in sumptious braids, he writes. Their dress was graciously beautiful, especially that worn by the Limassolians which fell in soft, luxurious folds.

It was generally thought that, although the Cypriot women were less beautiful than their majestic sisters of Smyrna, they were no less devastating for it. It was the Cypriot lady who ensnared the traveller or broke his heart.

The Greek, the author was told, may trust himself to one and all the cities of the Aegean, and may still weigh anchor with a heart entire.

"But so surely as he ventures upon the enchanted isle of Cyprus, so surely will he know the rapture or the bitterness of love." The reason for this overpowering charm, we are told, derived from what people call the astonishing "politics" or "politiki" of the women, meaning, he thought, their "tact and their witching ways."

But even the Greek, with all the wealth of his generous language to draw upon, could barely describe the strength of the spell which Cypriot women held over men, Kinglake goes on.

Later, the author took what he called his "pagan soul" to Paphos to see the source of all this enchantment. There lay the ruins of the temple of Aphrodite (the fragments of one or two prostrate pillars on a bare promontory). He describes his pilgrimage, and his thoughts as he anticipates the encounter.

"I take no antiquarian interest in ruins, and care little about them unless they are either striking in themselves, or else serve to mark some spot very dear to my fancy."

He admits that while he was aware of the sparseness of Paphian ruins, there "was a will and a longing more imperious than mere curiosity that drove me thither."

Kinglake was waiting for Aphrodite.

Although he had no intention of forfeiting his inheritance for the life to come, he wished to live, however briefly, "as a favoured mortal under the old Olympian dispensation -- to speak out my resolves to the listening Jove, to hear him answer with approving thunder."

But most of all he wanted to believe "for one rapturous moment" that in the gloomy depths of the grove by the (Paphian) mountainside, "there was some leafy pathway that crisped beneath the glowing sandal of Aphrodite... not coldly disdainful of even a mortal's love!" This vain, heathenish longing, he said, had been the reason for his visit to the scene of ancient worship.

He described the island as beautiful, with its flowery fields and a thousand bright-leaved shrubs that "twined their arms together in lovesome tangles." The very air was warm and fragrant as the ambrosial breath of the goddess. Although he was not "infected" with a faith in the old religion, he had a sense and apprehension of its mystic power — "a power that was still to be obeyed, by me."

Just before his arrival at the site, he was to pass a "sadly disenchanting night in the cabin of a Greek priest -- not a priest of the goddess but of the Greek church.

"There was but one humble room, or rather shed, for man, and priest, and beast," he tells us. It was a charmless reality which abruptly ended such notions as "golden sandals" and the "hundred altars glowing with Arabian incense," awaiting him at Aphrodite's sanctuary next day.

Finally reaching Paphos, Kinglake encountered a Greek husbandman who acted as a kind of "deputy-provisionary-sub-vice-pro-acting-consul of the British Sovereign," and who promptly changed his Greek headgear for the cap of the consular dignity and accompanied him to the ruins.

There, bereft of the enthusiasm for the mystical which had originally propelled him, Kinglake said that he felt "not the slightest gleam of his previous pagan piety."

He had ceased to dream, he said sadly. The entire sentimental pilgrimage now seemed pointless.

Having no taste for research or any intention of searching for inscriptions, he took refuge in provoking a discussion about possible hidden treasure. This would cover his lack of interest in the site after such a long and anticipatory journey, and also cause others to think him perfectly sane, he wrote. Forcing the dark Earth to show you its hoards of gold was always a reassuring topic.

If there were any mystical vibrations that remained from the ruins, they were quickly annihilated. "When we returned to Baffa (Paphos), the vice-consul seized a club, with a quietly determined air of a brave men resolved to do some deed of note.

"He went into the yard adjoining his cottage where there were some thin, thoughtful, canting cocks, and serious, low-church-looking hens, respectfully listening, and chickens of tender years so well brought up as scarcely to betray in their conduct the careless levity of youth.

"The vice-consul stood for a moment quite calm – collecting

his strength; then suddenly, he rushed into the midst of the congregation and began to deal death and destruction on all sides.

"He spared neither sex nor age; the dead and dying were immediately removed from the field of slaughter, and in less than an hour, I think, they were brought to the table, deeply buried in mounds of snowy rice."

Later, the auther gave the vice-consul his handsome clasp-dagger brought from Vienna, hoping in some way to contribute toward his stay; he felt that he could not offer money.

It was part of his last farewell to Cyprus, for soon he was to sail over the water at last to Beyrout (Beirut) and another legend, this time of the Levant – a strong willed Englishwoman called Lady Hester Stanhope who had once "reigned in sovereignty over the wandering tribes of western Asia," the Arabs.

She lived in a convent on the Lebanon range, according to Kinglake, and her refusal to see Europeans only added to her mystery. At one point it had even been hinted "with horror" that she had claimed to be more than a prophet.

ARCHAEOLOGY--LIFE IN THE TRENCHES

To what extent is archeology one part science and one part stunning, visceral connection with a "living place" that seemingly died thousands of years ago?

What causes archeologists and their teams to excavate for weeks in blistering heat after a breakfast of coarse bread and black olives and then return next year for another season at the site?

Does the sudden glimpse of an almost intact statue far older than Christ compensate for the long, draining hours sifting through dirt "sector by sector, inch by inch," before the curve of an artifact made by long-dead hands suddenly springs into sight, or oftentimes doesn't?

And finally, do archeologists form emotional ties to the cultures they uncover, or does the scientist over-ride the man?

Two archeologists who have excavated in Cyprus years apart, and who came from very different cultures, may help provide some of the answers from their own experiences here. Many of their views are surprisingly similar.

They are former Swedish-Cyprus expedition leader, Einar Gjerstad, who spent four years in Cyprus excavating ancient sites between 1927 to 1931, and Famagusta-born Michael Toumazou, a Greek Cypriot associate professor of Classical Studies at Davidson College, North Carolina.

For the past six summers, Dr. Toumazou has been heading a rapidly growing team of professors, ex-students, undergraduates and local assistants working to unearth a site spanning 2,500 years of the island's history near inland Athienou village. The dig is in a fertile valley called Malloura and falls in a demilitarised zone patrolled by U.N. peace-keeping troops.

Both Toumazou and the late Dr Gjerstad tell us in separate accounts of the important role often played by local villagers in pinpointing possible hidden sites (such as that peculiar looking stone artifact that surfaced after spring plowing, or old looters' tales still fresh in village memory).

Local inhabitants can also unwittingly provide insights into prehistoric events, thought processes and lifestyles, especially in the absence of any written records.

Dr. Gjerstad develops this and other themes in his book "Ages and Days in Cyprus", an account of his excavations here over 60 years ago during which "the ancient and the modern became so intertwined that they were almost inextricable." An archeological expedition is not all excavation, he pointed out, but also conversations with people living near the sites.

He also believed that through long and constant association with village people the archeologist could attain "a psychological understanding of the results of the excavation. When everybody returns to the kafenion (coffee-shop) then the real talking begins. The talk is of money and plots of land, of poverty and oxen, of local taxes and of saints, of love and lies, of death and eternal life."

He found many similarities between classical antiquity and the cultural heritage of Cypriots only 60 years ago - in houses and tools, in habits and customs.

How much difference was there 60 years ago between a village house of mudbrick with one room and an earth floor, and a Bronze Age dwelling with its utilitarian "furniture" and basic utensils? he asks; a half-century ago, Cyprus farmers were still clinging to their wooden ploughshares tipped with iron as in classical antiquity.

His lengthy excavations in the island included sites at Lapithos, Karavostassi (Soli) and neaby Vouni, a mountain which seemed to "grow out of the sea." All are currently under Turkish occupation.

Wherever Gjerstad and his team worked, permission to dig was needed from both government and the scores of peasant-landowners who owned the fields. Many stalled, thinking that the foreign group were in reality treasure-hunters who should somehow be made to share the profits. Sometimes days were needed, along with the good-will of village leaders, to convince local peasants of the mission's purely scientific scope.

Along with other Swedes in the expedition, Gjerstad had included his wife and two young sons with whom he shared living conditions almost as primitive as those he sometimes uncovered. He jokingly divided the Vouni expedition into two periods - "the first when we lived in tents and the second when we occupied a stone hut" built for the purpose.

Gjerstad's wife was also to cook many meals huddled amongst rocks over an open fire. Her sons called her "Ulla the Brave", not because of her culinary hardships but because she protected them against wild sheep.

It was a local shepherd boy called Prodromos who had first informed the team of Vouni's significance after spotting an Archaic head built into a stone wall.

After a few disappointing weeks of fruitless excavations, a Greek Cypriot workman suddenly unearthed a crowned head of a woman - "the most beautiful head in Cyprus" - which was part of a life-sized statue. In his elation, the author's malaria was forgotten.

"I knelt on the ground. The earth was fragrant wtih Archaic art. The scratch of a knife brough forth a fragment of a robe, the rounding of the hips, the breasts and the braided hair.

"There were two sculptures, three sculptures, many of them. Statues, heads, statuettes...almost all of them ranking as works of art...young women dressed in gracefully-draped robes, kore figures similar to those found on the Acropolis in Athens...

"Look at her, this flawless specimen of a girl who moments ago was a secret hidden in the ground...she is adorned for a celebration, there are stars round her hair, her face radiates both serenity and anticipation, happiness and assurance." Pretty heady stuff in a scientific world.

Gjerstad dated the finds from the end of the Archaic and beginning of the Classical epoch - from the end of the 6th century BC to the middle of the 5th BC.

The ecstasy infected the workmen as well, the author says - the expedition was heavily dependent on local labour. "Kristos led the dance. He roared with delight as he performed the dance of the Archaic lions, while the full moon rose in a clear sky."

The group then uncovered a majestic staircase leading to a private temple of Athena and finally a vast palace with a large open courtyard, official reception rooms, kitchen and storage areas. In one, the team found wine jugs leaning against the wall just as they had been left 2,300 years ago. The dig also yielded fine bronze sculptures, gold and silver jewellery and bowls, coins and scores of statues and other artifacts.

When it ended he seemed desolate. "Gone were the great and beautiful moments, the supreme joy of creation but a memory.

"But one does not say farewell to Vouni...it is eternal and shall live eternally in our hearts...I see a flash of fire in the cool space of Athena's temple. The mountain rises quietly like blue smoke towards the stars."

For Dr. Michael Toumazou, whose team has just completed the season's dig, the reaction is perhaps less lyrical but no less ardent.

"I love being in the field. I love the outdoors. I love Cyprus, and of course I love the study of cultures," he says.

For him, the archeological breakthrough came in 1986 when local informers at the village told of "pieces of statues and pottery strewn all over their barley fields," wrote J. S. Stockdale in an account of those early days published in the college journal. Dr. Toumazou then cobbled together a small team of six, including Davidson students anxious to participate in a dig.

After permission from the Cyprus Department of Antiquities, the "Athienou Archeological Project" was on with the support of Davidson College. In just five years, more than 120 outside participants joined the expedition, including two new co-directors for surveys who eventually found 30 other sites dating from 7,000 BC through modern times in the 20 square mile area.

Malloura itself dates from the 2nd century BC, and survived up to 1878 with intermittent interruptions. It contains the three major components of an archeological site - tombs, a settlement and a sanctuary, the last flourishing for almost a thousand years.

Since the beginning, Toumazou has been the force that makes the project go, say colleagues and students. "He cares passionately about his work... he just livens things up... brilliant... he really cares about us... makes me work harder... a perfectionist in archeology... loves his native country... motivates students though his own zeal for classics... shares this with them..." are some of the comments.

Each year, in reports to the Archeological Symposia held annually in Nicosia by the Cyprus-American Archeological Research Institute here, Dr. Toumazou tells of the dig's progress.

Uncovered until now is statuary representing an array of deities -Apollo, Herakles, Melqart, Pan, Zeus-Serapis, and Artemis. But there is also evidence of severe looting of the sanctuary in years past.

Other finds included thousands of pieces of pottery, stone vessels, tombs, lamps and jewellery. Recently, the team uncovered a helmeted Herakles, jewellery, metal artifacts, and terracotta figurines of warriors and animals. One tomb yielded the remains of a young women with well-preserve fragments of a hairnet and cloth.

Yields generally have been impressive, Toumazou agrees, but the significance of Malloura, he stresses, lies less in the wonderful sculptures and artifacts found there than in its "newly-recognised importance as an inland site."

What of the students who sign on for the summer excavation? For some, it is a "profound fascination with digging in the dirt, although life in the trenches is ardurous." One student reports: "It combines history and anthropology and mythology, making it all very tangible...when you find a statue of Hercules, you think about the people who made it...how they lived. You wonder what they believed in and how that kept them going. It's a powerful experience."

A typical day in the trenches begins at 6 a.m. to avoid the heat; by early afternoon temperatures have soared. The group have lunch, clean and mark their samples, write in their daily journal, nap or later visit the village.

They are closely tied to village life through wedding invitations and other events or parties. Then there are field trips to other sites in Cyprus, and visits to local coffee shops.

"We do archeology here in the midst of a living place. We do archeology on somebody's farm lands, we live in a gymnasium, we sometimes eat in people's houses or in restaurants. We're very connected," another ex-student says.

The team are very grateful to Athienou residents, including municipal authorities, police, military, school board and clergy, for their support to the excavation. Along with other special favours, they provide free housing at the local gymnasium, buses for weekend trips and free supplies of cheese and bread.

Dr. Toumazou sees a long excavatory life for the team at Malloura, with nothing foreseeable going "hog-wire." This is a special English expression used by Toumazou, a "Michaelism" which combines the American idioms "haywire" and "hog-wild", and which he never gets quite right.

One day, when the sanctuary is completely excavated, Toumazou hopes to see an official archeological park on the site, owned and maintained by the Department of Antiquities.

Perhaps one day he may even retire there - Athienou is his mother's village. Then, unlike Gjerstad, "the great and beautiful moments" would not be gone for him. He might even see an occasional flash of fire in the cool space of the sanctuary.

THE COFFEESHOP

There's a lot to be said for the village coffeeshop in Cyprus, that great national equaliser and hub of village life.

Land is bought and sold within its walls, work discussed, and there is a captive audience for grassroots political orations. When card games are initiated the loser usually buys the refreshments.

This male-bonder and busy social centre is often a modest structure, furnished with worn wooden tables and rush-bottomed chairs — functional, noisy and cheap. Sometimes there is a faded print on a whitewashed wall, usually of the September Morn variety or a mountain scene. A single cup of coffee can last a pensioner an entire afternoon and eventually the whole world will pass by. This is one reason why regulars hate having the road outside re-routed by busybodies attempting to improve the village traffic flow.

Eventually, most of the male population, including the teacher, mukhtar, labourer and priest, gather there at some point in the day where each cup of coffee is brewed to the individual's taste ("not too much froth and boil it up twice"). It is served with purpose on a clanging metal tray and always with a glass of water standing in its own slight overspill. Here, the senile can sit for hours looking on or staring into his own thoughts and nobody minds or hustles him out or tells him it's bedtime now.

Sometimes there are great coffeeshops, such as one belonging to Michael Demetriades, the mukhtar (headman) in the Solea Valley village of Evrikhou.

It is a wide, white room with thick, cream-coloured arches supporting the roof, and was opened 90 years ago by his father, Xenophon, a real "meraklis" (a person with discriminating taste), it is said. He was known to serve partridge, hare and other treats on special occasions.

Evrikhou is a lively, semi-farming village that hangs

between town and countryside off a main highway to the Troodos mountains. Many of its men commute to work in the towns, but it has not become a mere dormitory village. Sited in a spectacularly scenic valley halfway between Nicosia and Troodos, it is still nailed to the land through weekend farming and other local enterprises. There are hopes that along with other unspoilt villages in the valley, it may become part of an agro-tourism venture in the near future. The area's fire service and police force are based there and a local hospital serves surrounding villages. It is also the seat of the Morphou Mitropoli (Bishopric of Morphou).

Even their coffeeshop is rather important, the regulars point out. For over 40 years it was open round-the-clock during the decades when many Evrikhou villagers were part of the crews pulling copper ore from mines as old as antiquity a few miles down the valley.

The men worked in shifts, and with its wood-burning stove driving off the chill in the dreary winter dawns, the coffee shop was a convivial meeting place. Sometimes 200 miners piled into the room when their shifts overlapped.

They had all been part of the Cyprus Mines Corporation (CMC) operations dotted round the valley toward the sea, where thousands of men from villages all over the mountainside worked in galleries that rarely closed. Labourers often descended 300 feet below the surface, pumping, drilling and loading up the ore for transport to coastal Xeros and waiting boats. In the early days, mules pulled the ore cars to the sea whenever the little wood-fired locomotive broke down, which was frequently.

The crews recall corporation bosses such as Charles Godfrey Gunther, who had first prowled across Egypt by camel caravan in the 1920's looking for telltale slag heaps and other signs of mineralisation before setting off, discouraged, for Cyprus. It was Gunther, a New Yorker with a degree from the Columbia University School of Mines, who was to rediscover the ancient copper mines here. (He also had a deep interest in archaeology.)

The CMC mines closed over 20 years ago, but the coffeeshop regulars at Evrikhou still recall the era when bicycles, trucks or buses bounced them over the country roads to work.

Solon Riris, who spent 40 years as a foreman at Mavrovouni mine remembers that there was good copper there, "first class stuff," he says. Like other miners, he speaks easily of places like Foucassa Hill and Skouriotissa, Mavrovouni, Katydhata and Apliki, where CMC had launched its early operations within a few miles of each other. Ancient slag heaps there had tipped off Gunther that if there wasn't gold in the hills, there must at least be copper. (In fact some gold was mined in the area, and at Mathiati village, but quantities were small, it was thought).

Men worked in eight-hour, round-the-clock shifts. There were three tiers of galleries (tunnels) eight feet high with air continually pumped in and out for ventilation.

Most men became accustomed to working underground, Riris says, forgetting that they were far below the earth's surface or that other men were working in other galleries above or below. They wore short pants when the heat built up, Riris says, and pumps worked continually to carry off the water leaking into the tunnels from walls and ceilings. In the early days, candles or torches guided the men as they worked through the darkness; later they used headlamps powered by acetylene and eventually batteries. Smoking was prohibited, but some men smoked anyway, secretly.

There was sulphur in the water seeping through the ore, highly corrosive when touching tools or human skin. Fire was an ever-present hazard because of sulphur dioxide being released. Moreover, the traces of gold or silver found in what miners called "devils mud" looked dry in the ore band where it occured; but it contained free sulphuric acid and when squeezed ate away tools, clothing and caused sores on workers' bare feet.

Riris insists that the mines were safe as long as miners followed the rules. Others believe that there are always hazards inherent in certain types of mining. By the 1930's the men were paid four shillings a day, reaching seven the further underground they went. Both Greek and Turkish Cypriot women worked above-ground cleaning or screening copper ore, and some young boys started training on simple jobs at age 14.

Another former employee, Andreas Constantinou, pointed out that accidents did occur sometimes, however strict the pre-cautions or tough the regulations.

One Evrikhou resident, 85-year-old George C. Kotrofos, worked for seven years in the Number 6 mine, he says, where he "didn't know very much in the beginning" but later became a CMC foreman.

"We were six people using pickaxes and we worked 40 feet down for 4 shillings a day. We used a winch to take the ore out, and a bell to communicate with the surface.

"I was so strong then," he said, somewhat wistfully. He left the company in 1953 to became a farmer.

Evrikhou's mukhtar, Demetriades, worked only six months as a miner — "I didn't like it down there" — and another 15 years as a steward at the CMC club. We were all children, he recalls, in the days when his father had first opened the village coffeeshop. "As soon as we were old enough, we all helped my father. We lived upstairs above the coffeeshop, girls in one room and boys in another. We all sat round the dinner table together."

When still a young boy in 1931, he remembers British soldiers hurrying down from Troodos to arrest co-villagers suspected of pulling down the British flag and hoisting the Greek. There were about 20 boys from Evrikhou who all attended Newham's school (The English School) in Nicosia, he said. Although the troops suspected them, they weren't arrested. "I think that it's because they spoke English so well."

According to "The Story of the Cyprus Mines Corporation," a book by David Lavender published in 1962 by the Huntington

Library in California, the mines in the area were already well developed by the time of Solon's visit to Cyprus in 575 B.C., as mentioned by Plutarch. (It is believed that the Solea Valley is named after the famous poet and lawgiver from Athens.)

Slave labour, Lavender says, did gruelling work in those mines some 2,000 years ago, no doubt developing a keen nose for ore deposits while searching very much at random. The slaves made exploratory openings as small as possible, some only four feet high and two feet wide, and the sides bowed out to accommodate the shoulders of a man carrying an ore basket on his back.

When sufficient ore was found, tunnel sizes increased. Although attempts were made to aid ventilation, Lavender writes, the sulphur dioxide must have been dreadful under any condition. Only a few tools have survived from antiquity because of the highly corrosive nature of water draining through pyrites, he says.

Ancient tunnels were inclined, rather than level, with pitches as steep as 30 to 35 degrees from the horizontal. Timbering to hold up the gallery ceilings was skillfully done, and some pieces more than 2,000 years old have survived in a well-preserved state.

Working conditions were generally abominable. Space was cramped and the pyrites caved in readily. Temperatures were intolerable when the ore oxidized, and the resulting stench unbearable. The only light came from small olive-oil lamps set in niches carved in tunnel walls; other, waist-high niches acted as handholds for slaves as they struggled with their burdens, he writes.

A few miles from Soli, Gunther had identified an ancient mine mentioned by the first century physician, Galen, where slaves worked 600 feet under the earth stripped to their loin cloths and gasping in the noxious air. They brought up thick green water in clay amphorae which, after evaporation, became "chalcanthos", later identified as ferrous sulphate or green vitriol.

Almost 2,000 years later, when CMC's Gunther climbed Foucassa Hill and walked about collecting ore samples into a sack for later testing, he was certain that copper lay underneath.

The hill was glowing red, Lavender writes, and there was a great Arizona-like ridge of black slag across the road from an abandoned monastery nearby called Panayia Skouriotissa — Our Lady of the Slags.

Moreover, pottery shards lay near the entrance to a nearby mine at Mavrovouni (Black Mountain) and had probably been used by slaves to bail out water. Copper had been mined there as early as 3,000 B.C., he had been told, and by 1500 B.C. the puppet kings of Cyprus were using it to pay tribute to the Egyptian pharoahs. Gradually, Gunther restored the monastery for use as living quarters for himself and his drill foreman.

Gunther had been reluctant to hire women workers in the early days, but physical labour was no novelty to peasant women in Cyprus, he was told. For older women, the job meant extra food at home; for the younger it meant dowries. He never permitted women to work underground.

CMC had its share of disputes, walkouts and illnesses and there was always danger of fire. Pyrites are inflammable and men smoked secretly in the galleries. The company had a rattletrap railroad, malaria was a menace, and shepherds had to be trained as sailors on the loading barges.

Gradually, permanent housing was built for employees from remote districts, along with a hospital at Pendayia. Next came canteens, hot showers, shops, recreational facilities, bakeries and welfare programmes.

In the meantime, Lavender says, CMC had acquired a small colony of White Russians, part of an army chased to the Black Sea by the Bolsheviks in 1920. They arrived at Famagusta aboard two ships, about 1,700 destitute refugees who were immediately quarantined at Famagusta by British authorities here because of typhoid on board. A few eventually made their way to Skouriotissa, including a former chemistry instructor at a Leningrad University called Nicola Matoff, according to the author. Later he became part of the CMC team and a key official there. He also brought over his wife and two children.

Payday was twice a month at the mines and swarms of vendors with donkeys gathered at the sites and at Pendayia, selling their wares to veiled Turkish Cypriot women and their Greek Cypriot counterparts in long black robes.

Meanwhile, ventilation problems still plagued the mines. Wheelbarrow handles sometimes grew too hot to handle, ore crumbled and timbers loosened in the heat. There were fears of a cave-in and fires from blasting, candles or igniting dust. In 1925 the worst happened. Eight men died in an underground cave-in and the entire work force walked out. Mining eventually re-commenced, but from then on safety along with pay became key issues. Eventually, fire stations, concrete tunnels, alarm systems and patrols were amongst the precautions introduced.

The following year, lightning struck an ore crushing mill at Skouriotissa and destroyed the structure completely, the ore in the bins turning into "a vast incandescent mass". Six days later the hospital burned down. There were no casualties in either accident, and patients were moved to a shelter nearby.

Inside the hospital, Lavender goes on, the Reverend Canon F.D. Newham, "over from Nicosia to visit this part of the parish," had been taking a bath. "He calmly finished, walked outside with his clothing over his arm just before the roof collapsed, and stepped behind a bush to dress."

Over 2,500 CMC workers lost their jobs after mining cutbacks during World War II. Company managers feared bombing attacks by German aircraft either against the mines or at loading jetties at Xeros, and only small quantities of gold or copper were being brought up. As Axis forces drove toward Suez, the company braced for an invasion. Welfare programmes were introduced for remaining workers and their families, clothing was distributed and first aid training began. Skouriotissa and Xeros were flooded with refugees from abroad.

One Sunday morning in 1940, Axis aircraft dropped 14 bombs

from a great height onto Xeros harbour and later made several machinegun runs. The only casualties were several baskets of fish. At war's end, mining resumed, quickly reached its pre-war scale and continued for another few decades when production finally ceased altogether.

Coffeeshop regulars at Evrikhou say that a new group of companies has re-opened the mines recently, hoping in their turn to bring up what the ancients and the Evrikhou coffee shop crowd had left behind, perhaps even the gold.

LEFKARA

She was almost as old as the century and her hands had held a thousand needles in her lifetime. "When I was a girl, we embroidered everything that we could lay our hands on. It took me all day to make a 'corner'. We embroidered our dresses and slips and night-gowns. We wore transparent dresses over our undergarments so that people could see the embroidery underneath. We should have been ashamed, I suppose, but we wore the see-through dresses anyway, because we wanted our work to show."

This was Mrs Evanthea Lyssarides, (no kin to the Cyprus Socialist party leader). Her family home in the busy centre of Lefkara village has been silent and shuttered since her death in 1993. Its turn-of-the-century rooms above a tourist restaurant have gradually become an unofficial museum of "lefkaritika", the highly prized embroidery and lace for which the village is well-known locally and abroad.

She had made all of them herself through the decades, and in her nineties she was still one of the great needle-women in Lefkara. Like many other women of her time in the village, she had lived much of her life through the eye of a needle, and much of it often alone. She was the product of an era of oil lamps and charcoal braziers, trained in the day when female hands were never idle, and needlework was an art form to be sold abroad from cardboard suitcases by travelling lace-merchants, often their own husbands.

All of the work began with a blank, unhemmed piece of linen, in the case of embroidery the design to be picked out by the needle-woman herself who could spend months working on a large tablecloth. This was the time, still in living memory, when Lefkara village men changed their "vrakas" or baggy trousers at Larnaca port for European suits, bid their wives and children goodbye and sailed away, sometimes for years, to sell abroad the work for which their women had become noted. In those days, it was one of the few options open. Land was poor, water was scarce, and only olive and carob trees seemed to survive on the rocky hillsides that had once been the summer playground of Venetian rulers here.

Entire generations grew up in a matriarchy, with occasional exciting visits from Papa who brought home lavish gifts in his suitcase and tales of life abroad to break the calm momentum of village life. The gifts could be clothing, toys or the first wind-up gramaphones to reach the Cyprus countryside, or records of "that new Italian singer, Caruso."

They also returned with new ideas, the rudiments of foreign languages and the knowledge of another world beyond the confines of their plateau village where their families waited.

Lefkara men still play bridge in the coffeeshops.

Most of the women stayed at home to raise the children and produce the work to fill yet more suitcases, sitting in circles in the Lefkara sunshine along the cobbled streets. Twice each year the women whitewashed their stone-built homes and courtyards and finally, everything else in sight including the flower pots. As the decades passed "we produced beautiful, careful work," Mrs Lyssarides had told me, talking of embroidery and how the charcoal brazier glowed in the winter parlour as the neighbour women gathered for company while they worked.

"I can remember packing tablecloths large enough for tables seating 24 people, complete with napkins, to send abroad. The entire set cost £20 then -- this was in the late 1930's. "Each 1½ inches took me three hours to embroider and the cost was an estimated 3 piasters for each part.

"Personally, I worked day and night. Finally I went with my husband to Sweden in 1955 to help him sell lace. He died there — he was a wonderful man — and my sons, Georghios and Polyvios, have settled in Stockholm," she said. "I didn't continue the business after he died — I'm not a businesswoman — but before that there were several women in Lefkara who embroidered for us and sent the work to Sweden for us to sell.

"It takes a lot of patience and care to produce really good lefkaritika," she said. "My eyes bothered me when I became older, but then I got glasses with a bigger number and now I can see better." Her home was packed with richly-worked "shamays" displayed on the walls behind glass, lace coverlets on the beds, and curtains so finely cut and embroidered that when the Lefkara sun shone through, they glowed like cut crystal.

"I keep the shutters closed in this room," she had explained, moving slowly amongst a stack of her embroidered tablecloths. "Do you know that sun and air will eventually cause the linen to disintegrate? These were made with that good linen from Zodhia, and it's not available anymore (Zodhia is under Turkish occupation). Now we have to use a substitute." She had unrolled yet more examples of her work, pieces so stiff with embroidery and so closely stitched that the cloth held shape without starch.

"I work on my embroidery almost every day, after I finish my housework. I don't have many of my old women friends left anymore, so I sit with a neighbour lady to work." She had travelled annually to Stockholm to visit her sons and their families, and later they paid frequent visits to her in Cyprus. "Otherwise my life is embroidering."

Her conversation had been rich with the vocabulary of her art. There are many kinds of "rivers" that can be designed on a piece of linen, including the "arvalatos" and the "arachnatos" which may look much the same to the uninitiated, but are instantly recognised by the expert.

Then there are "caroullas" and "carres" and "koftes" and "tsimbis" as well as the popular "phinikoto" or margarita design. Sometimes the women create their own designs and usually they recognise each others work at first glance.

How does one look after and preserve these works of art which many have taken months to create? "Never put your "lefkaritika" into a washing machine," she warned. "If you do, it will surely lose its colour. Soak the piece instead in medium warm water and a mild soap powder. Remember that sun and air will spoil it, so dry it in the shade. I don't put starch in my lefkaritika, I prefer to iron it when still damp. That way the wrinkles are smoothed out and it becomes fresh and new."

What to do about wine stains? "I use a little white spirit on the stain, then rub it with water. Sometimes this will take it out. You have to be very careful about wine."

Much has changed in Lefkara since Evanthea Lyssarides' epoch, especially after an exodus during recent decades when lace merchants began to emigrate permanently and took their wives with them. Later, as local work opportunities declined even further, they were joined in New York, London or other European cities by other tradesmen and job-hunting youth, who set up Lefkara social clubs abroad and wrote homesick letters back to the village.

The population drain that had skimmed off much of the younger generation has finally ended, however, thinks the mayor of Lefkara, Sophoclis Sophocleous, and its present population has stabilised at about 2.000 in Pano(upper) Lefkara. Less than a mile down the mountainside, in Kato (lower) Lefkara, the latest head count indicated about 200 inhabitants.

But a new life and rhythm has returned to Upper Lefkara, with a half-million tourists annually, restaurants, coffeeshops, two new hotels, a museum, silversmiths and embroidery and lace shops. "Actually, all Lefkara is a museum," Sophocleous said of the colourful, stone-built village, once the summer resort of the Venetians almost five centuries ago. Whatever the future of Lefkara, nobody can take away its past — the days when Lefkara people were shocked if foreigners hadn't heard of their village.

An old, but well-known joke illustrates their certainty of a place on the map. It goes like this:

Some years ago, a Lefkara lace merchant temporarily in Paris asked a local travel agent there for a ticket to Peking. The agent, asking the whereabouts of Peking, was told that it was the capital of China. "Where's China?" the agent had asked. After pinpointing it on the map, the Lefkara man was finally given a ticket. On his return to Paris, he visited the same travel agent, this time announcing that he wanted to go to Lefkara.

"Pano or Kato?" inquired the agent.

HORNED MEN AND HENNA

An 18th century scholar sent to the eastern Mediterranean on a scientific mission by his French king thought that Cyprus may have been inhabited at one time by horned men.

This could account for its earlier name of Cerastis, or Horn Island, the scholar pondered, unless it was because of the narrow capes or points along its coast which resembled horns projecting into the sea.

It was the spring of 1777, and C.S. Sonnini was gathering information for his book to be called "Travels in Greece and Turkey" written on orders of Louis XVI. He was also to rely on information from seamen, geographers and other "most modern and esteemed men," he says. The island's more common Greek name, Kypros, could refer to a mythical hero, its copper wealth, or to the henna-producing leaves of the Kypros shrub, he added.

"The women still delight to adorn themselves with the Kypros flower ... the powder of its leaves, dried, also serves them to dye, with a durable bright orange colour, all their nails ... palms of their hands and the soles of their feet."

When the Greeks of Cyprus have a newborn child, he says, they bury wine in large, Ali Baba-type demi-johns which are taken from the ground only for the marriage of that same child. Local men were noble, agreeable and hospitable, he found, but lacking in moral character. The women lived up to all reports of their charms but were not as oppressed as thought, unlike their ancestors who had paid homage to Persian queens. The duties of these women had included flinging themselves between cart wheels or presenting their backs for use as footstools.

Excerpts from historical works such as Sonnini's were frequently included in a monthly pictorial magazine published here in the 1950's called the "Cyprus Review", which was edited for a time by writer Lawrence Durrell. This was a hopeful, colonial government-backed publication in Greek and English aimed at explaining the administration's role here, as well as the benefits in general of continued British rule in the island.

The reader was reminded that malaria had been completely wiped out, 85 percent of children now went to school, elementary education was free though voluntary, and large sums had been spent to improve agricultural methods and irrigation (the latter despite a hounded Water Department official's querulous remark reported at the time, "Madame, I cannot make water"). There was also a 10-year development plan costing £7 million which would help the economy considerably.

Enosis was not to be discussed, naturally, as was any notion of sovereignty, but there was a new constitution in the pipeline which would give a healthy and well-deserved measure of autonomy to the local population within the existing structure, readers were told. This was the era in the 1950's when the "Review" was also advertising a Cyprus Airways "creative" return fare from Nicosia to Athens for £31.50 in association with BEA and BOAC.There were always abundant photos of such highlights as the annual Queen's Birthday Parade in the moat when RAF Vampire jets flew over the gawking crowd as the governor took the salute; the first 20 boy-graduates of a Turkish technical school at Lefka; and the story of a young Cypriot film director called Michael Cacoyiannis. The "Review" cost 8 shillings (although often given away), its text could be freely re-printed, and blocks for photo reproduction were available on loan.

It articles usually avoided direct politics and reflected the government's sanguine "life goes on" attitude despite growing tensions and political alarm bells which finally culminated in the exile of the Ethnarch and national leader, Archbishop Makarios, and the launching of the EOKA-led rebellion; the latter was euphemistically referred to as "The Troubles".

The contents may have varied in quality or depth of research, but one regular column always appeared. Called the "Spy-glass," it featured news and photos of reassuring visits from foreign and colonial office officials, gatherings at Government House with photo line-ups of Greek and Turkish Cypriot guests, the latest CBE awards, and prominent figures from both communities and their accomplishments.

There was the Mufti, M.Dana Effendi and his clerk at a Government House reception for the vice admiral, a Gordon Highlanders piper entertaining Xeros village children, a dancing party at the Dolphin Kermia, and an exhibition of costumes and handicrafts by the Cyprus Turkish Women's Association at the Chettin Kaya Sports Club.

Contributors sent in original drawings or sketches, short stories and poems, and Franklin Lushington wrote a three-piece series about the Cyprus Regiment. There were special articles on rug-making, tanning, day-old chicks and a report on a play staged by the girls at Nicosia's Phaneromeni School called "Her Son Became Rich". A skilled gardener called Lady Murphy also wrote a charming monthly page which greatly encouraged newcomers and others struggling to maintain a garden in a country with long, rainless summers (plenty of shrubs and hard work, she advised).

Passers-through or local residents with a flair for writing or other talents were also pressed or shanghaied into offering the occasional "Review" piece or sketch. They included Gerald Durrell, Sir Harry Luke, Steward Perowne, Osbert Lancaster, David Bannerman of ornithological fame, Victor Canning, Freya Stark, Elektra Megaw and Patrick Leigh Fermor.

An Englishman called Adrian Seligman, researching a book on the Turkish Cypriots at the time, writes that the agrarian community were more interested in land than money, and that a well-brought up Turk would never cross his legs in the presence of his father. In another "Review" issue, four special colour pages were devoted to the work of a former barrister-turned-painter called G.Pol Georghiou, whom it termed the "Cyprus Gauguin" and whose work had found its way into all great collections. "Those who know him best adore him when he throws off all reserve and becomes a delightful, witty and child-like companion," the "Review" remarked.

The magazine was often fattened considerably by advertising. The Loucoudi cinema offered "the best films in town", Antonaki's Bar was a regular with its "house of 5,000 bottles", and the Acropole Hotel in Kyrenia reminded the potential guest of "hot and cold water running in the rooms".

You could also buy a knitting machine so impressive that "tomorrow you will recommend it to your best friends".

The Ledra Palace advertised itself as the hotel "par excellence", the most-up-to-date in the Middle East with "CENTRAL HEATING and running hot and cold water in all rooms".

Its bar in Nicosia was the rendezvous of "the most distinguished society", and a first-class orchestra played in its magnificent ballroom and summer garden. It was under Swiss management and the telephone number was 3101 — five lines. (The hotel is now occupied by the U.N. and marks the only official crossing point between the government-held south and the Turkish-occupied north.)

Sir Harry Luke, writer and traveller, also had something to say about the military ambience and its reliance on body heat. He was recalling his days back in 1911 as an ADC to a former governor here. Life was pleasant in those days, he says, despite "the then Government House being an austere, mid-Victorian, prefabricated, MILITARY wooden bungalow," where there was of course no central heating.

His duties were manifold, he goes on, and apparently included keeping the fires banked up. He would also make sure, he tells us, that there were always two bottles of ink beside the visitor's book in the hall. One was red for the Archbishop in case he called, one blue for other visitors. During tours of the hill villages in summer months at Troodos (it could be chilly there, too), there would be hot hip baths in the bedroom tents and a hot dinner in the more elaborate dining-sitting tent.

In those early days, the island was not yet prey to domestic difficulties, and servants were good, cheap and plentiful, he says.

The only problem he could recall occured during a schism in the Cyprus church between 1900 and 1910 when the kitchen boy at the home of the King's Advocate (later called the Attorney-General) attempted to slit the throat of the cook who lay bleeding on the kitchen table just before dinner guests were to arrive.

There were two candidates at the time for the Archbishop's throne and the domestic staff were often fiercely divided in their support. The planned dinner was hastily called off.

He also mentions the unexpected appearance in the island in May, 1913 of the ex-Grand Vizier of Turkey, Mehmet Kiamil Pasha, and his large family. The ministry of this eminent, Cyprus-born figure of 80 years old had just been overthrown by Enver and the Young Turk leaders in a bloody coup, and it was Sir Harry's task to find them accommodation.

He offered his own house on the Roccas bastion in Nicosia, as he was enroute to Troodos anyway. (Five weeks later, the Young Turk successor was assassinated.) Sir Harry writes that the old pasha's family included a son of 60 and another aged 5 or 6.

Also featured in the "Review" were accounts of two other visitors to the island — the French poet Arthur Rimbaud who arrived just after the British takeover in 1878 to work as a foreman at an Oroklini village stone quarry in the Larnaca district, and a writer called William Lithgow.

The latter had arrived in 1611 following a hasty departure from his hometown in Scotland. There he was known as "Lugless Will" after four brothers allegedly cut off his ears for tampering with a certain Miss Lockhart.

Rimbaud, who is described as an "enfant terrible" who revolutionised poetical conception in the early 1890's, was regarded as a loner who was lost in Cyprus "among countryfolk whose mentality was so different from his own... and who believed in the evil eye." They also nailed horse or sheep skulls to their garden gates. He was to become increasingly introspective and withdrawn, according to "Review" writer Legangneux. One reason could be the habit of curious villagers who, unaccustomed to foreigners, stared at him through his cabin windows as he cooked his meals. Others, hoping to catch sight of him, sometimes squatted hopefully a short distance away.

In letters to his mother he complained of the intense heat — "one must sleep near the seaside, in the desert — nothing but a chaos of rocks ... not a single tree," he told her.

He seemed to take a childish pleasure in exaggerating, comments the writer; at the foot of the quarry now is an ancient olive tree, he says, under which Rimbaud slept many times or ate watermelons with his workmen. After recovering in France from typhoid fever contracted in the quarries, he returned to work at Troodos where he helped to build what he called the "palace of the Governor", otherwise referred to as a "cottage".

Rimbaud died at Marseilles at the age of 37, and there is a commemorative plaque to him now on the walls of the Troodos summer residence.

Lithgow's book, which appeared in 1632, was described as a "Total Discourse of the Rare Adventures and Paineful Peregrinations of long 19 years Travayles, from Scotland to the most famous kingdomes in Europe, Asia and Affrica". This included Cyprus and his journey to Nicosia "in the midst of the kingdom" (the Ottomans had taken over Cyprus 40 years before his original visit), and he suffered extreme heat and thirst, he said, due to lack of water. He was carrying sufficient wine for the journey, "yet durst I drink none there of being so strong and withall had a taste of pitch."

The Cypriots kept their wine in great earthen jars interlarded with pitch to keep the vessels unbroken, but "the taste there of was unpleasant to liqurous lips." The island was also producing sugar cane, oil, cotton wool, honey, corn and fruit.

"But the greatest imperfection of this Ile," he wrote, "is the scarcity of water, and too much scorching heat and sabulous grounds. While the inhabitants were civil and affable, robust and good warriors, they were also much subject to melancholy." Lithgow's last book was published in 1645, and he was never heard of again.

The "Cyprus Review", for all its attempts at readability and brightness — no easy task for a government publication with a lot of convincing to do — was itself to disappear eventually, eclipsed by the armed rebellion of some of the very readers it had hoped to persuade and finally by the island's independence.

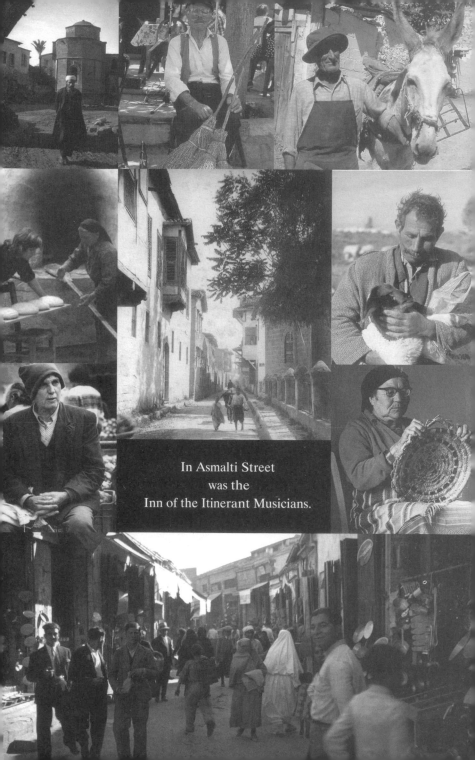

In Asmalti Street
was the
Inn of the Itinerant Musicians.

...walking between
the mountains and the sea
talking by chance with men
in perfect armour ...

G. Seferis

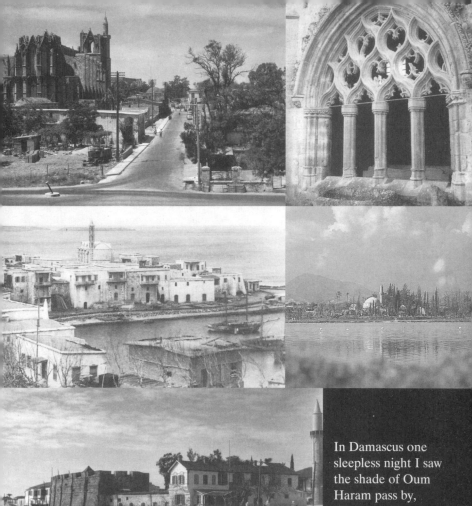

In Damascus one
sleepless night I saw
the shade of Oum
Haram pass by,
the venerable
kinwoman
of the Prophet.
I heard the clatter
of hooves like silver
dinars,then I saw
her, seemingly crossing
hills of salt towards
Larnaca, astride
her mule.

-- G. Seferis

In a country
Where those who lived below the castles
were forgotten like last year's earth.

G. Seferis

DANCES IN ARMOUR

The dead kings of Cyprus were carried to their tombs in ancient times by fully armed soldiers who led the funeral procession dancing at the head of the line.

These spectacular dances in armour, called "pyrriches", are thought to have originated in Homeric times and were amongst customs brought to the island by early Achaean colonisers after the Trojan wars. It is known that the Lacedaimonians, also amongst colonisers here, danced the "pyrriches" or "pyrrichii" to music before going into battle. It was a rite also practiced by the Pontii.

Augmenting the funeral dances in Cyprus were great athletic events and games organised to further honour the dead monarchs of Cypriot city-kingdoms of the time, including the great Evagoras of Salamis and other rulers of Soli, Paphos and Marion-Arsinoe.

It was a practice that persisted here for more than a thousand years, according to one report, at a time when athletics played a far greater cultural, religious and social role in the island than previously assumed, and from a much earlier period. The funeral events would have included chariot races, boxing and wrestling, foot races and sea games. These were costly celebrations which in one case provoked criticism from a 4th century BC sourpuss from Athens who believed in mind over muscle anyway.

These intriguing revelations and propositions concerning the island's athletic and cultural past were made by a young Greek Cypriot woman scholar and expert in Physical Education called Dr. Clea Constantinou Hadjistephanou.

She cites Aristotle, other ancient figures such as Isocrates, and considerable archaeological evidence to support her contentions about Cypriot funeral rites and the key role of games and sports in character-building.

So important was the "sound mind in a sound body" principle to become that "gymnasiarcheis", the men who headed the sports complexes or "gymnasia", would be on par in community importance with today's Ministers of Education, she says. Until now, this aspect of the island's history is little known, one reason being that in-depth research is still thin on the ground.

Another is that researchers and others generally assumed that sport played only a minor role here until about four centuries before the Christian era — ie. from the Hellenistic-Ptolemaic period from 325 BC to 30 BC. Not so! thinks Dr. Hadjistephanou. Go back at least another thousand years and the dating could be just about right.

This would be from the end of the Late Bronze Age, through the rise of the Ancient Kingdoms when massive immigration from the Aegean into Cyprus sparked thriving new settlements, and down through the Classical period too.

Along with their language and religion, earlier Greek colonisers such as the Myceneans also brought their beloved athletics with them, she believes, in about 1,500 BC. This meant that bull-jumping, acrobatics, four-horse chariot racing, wrestling, boxing and hunting from chariots were well-established here comparatively early.

(Note: At one period dancing was considered part of athletics too, and included round or "ring" dances in which participants danced in a circle with joined hands, with the musician in the centre. This is shown on amphorae and as sculpture, and may have been part of religious rites also.)

And those spectacular funeral dances by the army in full armour?

It was Aristotle himself, she points out, who named the "pyrriche" as the invention of Achilles during the Trojan wars when he caused it to be danced at the funeral pyre of his dead warrior-friend, Patroclos.

Aristotle also claimed that it was known in the Cypriot dialect as the "prylis" and that "when a local king here was buried the army advanced in front of the line dancing." It was the Achaeans who had brought the custom to the island, he added.

Dr. Hadjistephanou is the author of a probing history of athletics in Cyprus — physical education, games and sport from 1500 BC through the Roman era ending in 330 AD. Her own research was carrried out early in the decade as a partial requirement for a Master's degree in Physical Education from a California university and is contained in a lengthy thesis called "Athletics in Cyprus and the Greek Tradition". It is available in book form. The author also holds a doctorate and is now at the University of Cyprus.

To help unlock these aspects of the past, she cites not only written sources and archaeological finds both here and in Greece, but also refers to over 40 publications by well-known archaeologists and historians, Cypriot and foreign, to help support her contentions.

She names as a particularly important source the "monumental" work of Hadjioannou in "Cyprus in Ancient Greek Sources", where he collected and categorised numerous inscriptions found on ancient statues, "steles" (plaques) or other monuments, mostly praising certain athletes or others from Cyprus during the Hellenistic and Roman periods. Unfortunately, there are still many gaps concerning earlier blocks of time and much ground to be covered in original, painstaking research with few written sources yet apparent.

However there are glimpses -- provocative, intriguing glimpses into pre-Trojan war sport in Cyprus, such as the 14th and 13th century BC clay models, vases and amphorae depicting such hefty pastimes as chariot racing, boxing and sailboating. One ships model is shown with a socket at its centre to receive a mast, and with small holes in the gunwale for fastening sails. "This type of ship was used until recently in villages and towns near the sea for boat races using sails."

Mycenean objects uncovered here, including kraters from the 14th century BC, also depict boxers, hunting scenes and bull jumping. One amphora fragment from this period found at Hala Sultan Tekke in Larnaca, near ancient Kition, shows an acrobat in a bent position on a bull's back. At the same time he is holding the animal with his hands, head downwards .... "he is probably trying to raise his feet and stand on his hands."

The acrobat had exceptionally long legs, and with the jumper's face "reserved, with a rounded chin and thick neck reminiscent of the ivory bull jumper at Knossos...." Further, "his head hangs down, brushing the bull's back; his long arms are spread on the full to propel his flight. ..."

If that were not daring enough, yet another amphora depicts a single rider placed between the backs of two horses.... "It probably recalls a kind of warfare in which archers used two horses, the second one being mounted by a follower or sometimes the cavalryman himself holding the bridle of his reserve horse (Dikaios, 1947)." Another artifact from Chrysochou in the Paphos district which shows chariots, also depicts riders clinging to a horse's neck (850-750 BC).

Further, according to Plutarch, "there can be no serious doubt that all Cypriot kings, especially those of ancient Salamis and Soli, not only had expert knowledge of athletics but were actively involved themselves in organising competitions and events here."

How did all this happen in ancient Cyprus, and especially that apparent upsurge in sport after the 4th century BC?

Finally freed from the Persian yoke, says the writer, and "incorporated in a Greek kingdom as that of the Ptolemies was," the island could develop its athletic potential and strengthen ties with the mainland. For the first time, Cypriot athletes were beginning to win Panhellenic games, with their names inscribed in stone along with that of certain "gymnasiarcheis." And in Cyprus, where gymnasia existed in at least five city-kingdoms at the beginning of the Hellenistic era, inscriptions were honouring not only the athletes but those who sponsored, trained or organised the events.

The "gymnasiarcheis had names like "Aristagoros of Salamis," 2nd century BC; Diagoros of Salamis, son of Teucros, 2nd century BC; Diocles of Citium, 2nd century BC; Potomon of Paphos, 2nd century BC. (The 'Union of Cypriots' honoured Potomon with a statue in the sanctuary of Aphrodite at Palaipaphos.) Another, at Marion-Arsinoe, was identified as the "son of Stessagoros".

Who were some of the local Cypriot athletes participating in Greek mainland games? Down through time some of the names have survived, or at least their origins.

They include Heracleides the Salaminian, who won the short foot race in the 144th Olympiad in 204 BC. Another Cypriot from Karpasia, name not preserved, rode the winner of a race for "young riding horses" at the beginning of the 2nd century BC.

Another Karpassian called Ariston, son of Nicon, was the champion rider in the "mature riding horses" class. A contest for heralds and trumpeters held in honour of Apollon at Euboea in Greece was won by the trumpeter Aristonax, from Paphos, in the 1st century BC.

Even the kings of Cyprus were not left out. Nicocreon, the last king of Salamis (332-331 BC) took part in dances and tragedies organised by Alexander in Phoenicia just after the beginning of the Salaminian's reign. He was honoured for contributing bronze for the prizes. The next century, nine Cyprus cities contributed to the Argos gymnasium which organised the "Heraia" there — local games honouring the goddess, Hera.

Salamis and Citium sent the largest sum with 208 drachmas and two obols each, while Paphos sent 100 drachmas . Smaller amounts came from the Carpasians, Amathusians, Golgians, Tamassians and probably the Lapithians, according to Dr. Hadjistephanou.

At Paphos, mercenaries from the Ptolemaic army posted there

also contributed to the local gymnasium. The men were drawn from eight different cities and their donations were used to provide oil for anointing the athletes' bodies, according to records. They had promised from 100 drachmas to two months salary, and one mercenary even pledged five months pay.

(Note: to remove excess oil or perspiration from their bodies, athletes used a curved iron or bronze scraper, hand-held, called a "strygil." They have been discovered in Cypriot-Hellenistic tombs. At one necropolis excavated by archaeologist, Pavlos Florentzos, in a suburb of Nicosia called Ayioi Omologitae, seven strygils were unearthed in a family tomb that had been in use for 1 1/2 centuries.)

Here are some special terms for those of us not necessarily conversant with sporting and other terminology, especially of the 2,000-year old variety (courtesy of author Hadjistephanou).

Amphora: Jar with narrow neck and with two handles, used especially for storing wine.

Athletics: Used in the broad sense it includes physical education, games, events, sport, recreation, festivals, or "simply any activities that have to do with the physical - dance, music, etc."

Arete: Basic Greek ethical term meaning "virtue" in the broad sense. Includes concepts of excellence, manliness, valour, nobility, justice and goodness ... a noble goal and ideal to be pursued and reached by any Greek with high standards.

Boxing: One of the oldest contests in ancient Greece. Competitors were not classified by weight. It lasted until one of the contestants was unable or unwilling to continue.

Frigidarium: A Latin term for the bathing chamber with cold water in the bathing complex.

Gymnasium: The place where boys and men performed their gymnastic exercises, an essential part of Greek education. It had a running track, a boys' wrestling enclosure, rooms for ball games and punch-ball practice, dressing rooms and bathrooms, an oil stove and a room for the athletes to "powder themselves before training". Some gymnasiums were large enough for riding lessons and parades, for jumping-pits and for discus and javelin practice.

Olympia or Olympic Games: The most famous Panhellenic festival, held at Olympia at midsummer in every fourth year in honour of Zeus. It drew great athletes and others from many Greek states, along with poets, historians and orators. The victor won a crown of olive.

Trireme: An undecked warship with three banks of oars, and with three rowers sitting in a bench, each man rowing one oar. In battle it was propelled by the oarsmen but on a journey it could go under sail.

Stadium: A running track, about 200 yards long and 30 yards wide. It was also a sprint race.

* * *

The reign of a man thought to be the greatest king of Cyprus. Evagoros, who united many of the island's city-states, perhaps best underlines the importance of athletics here in the 4th century BC.

Not only did his son, Nicocles, organise a "pyrriches" for his dead father, but also a costly but glamourous chain of contests and other celebrations in his honour in 374/3 BC. This provoked strong criticism from Evagoros' friend, the famous orator and erstwhile kill-joy from Athens called Isocrates, who thought athletic's and athletes in general were highly over-rated. Besides, the celebrations cost too much. In an era when the gymnasia and nearby theatres were the basis of cultural life, this broadside could not have been too welcome.

Grumbled Isocrates: "...many times have I wondered at those who first convoked national assemblys and established athletic games...amazed that they should have thought the prowess of men's bodies to be deserving of so great bounties.

"...Those who toiled for the public good in private, or trained their minds, are apportioned no reward whatsover.

"...if all the athletes should acquire twice the strength which they now possess, the rest of the world would be no better off. But let a single man attain wisdom and all men reap the benefit...."

Rather than honouring the dead, the contests brought honour to the winners instead, he argued. Undaunted, it seems, Nicocles pressed on with the games in honour of his father, and Isocrates duly recorded the spectacle, including the "races with triremes."

And when the Romans took over Cyprus, games and sport became even more popular, according to the author, with a variety of events at Salamis, Lapithos, Citium, Chrytri, and Curium. Ceremonies honouring Julius Caesar were also organised.

Particularly colourful must have been the gladiatorial contests and races-in-armour for men at Citium.

But opinion about Cypriot wrestling matches was not very complimentary. Hesychius, the author of a Greek lexicon in the 3rd century tells us: "...by some it is called fighting by all means or with all ones resources; others call it rustic and clumsy, on account of fact that Cypriots wrestle unskillfully i.e. without due regard to the rules."

KARAGHIOZIS

The beloved little shadow puppet with the big feet and leering grin who made generations laugh wherever Greek is spoken, is still alive and well in Cyprus and may even be ready for a gleeful comeback after years in virtual retirement.

The popular folk hero of the shadow theatre, known as Karaghiozis in the Greek world, has been called hilarious, cunning, bawdy, endearing, knavish, heroic and a rogue by his admirers.

For over a hundred years here, until upstaged by radio and TV, he was all of that and more to the thousands of delighted villagers and townsmen who at one time paid one "bakheera", a piastre each, to sit before the illuminated, transparent screen of a makeshift stage and watch the absurdities of his life unfold through the art of the puppeteers.

As the oil-lamps flickered, the master puppeteers who sometimes became as famous as the characters they snatched on and off stage as plots thickened, told their familiar stories and myths, or probed the fate of the have-nots through the adventures of Karaghiozis and others in the colourful cardboard cast. To his fans who howled with delight at the puns, antics, fights and preposterous impersonations of the misshapen little upstart as he schemed to outfox the establishment, Karaghiozis was an endearing figure, a lumpen loser with motives as transparent as the screen he played behind.

He was the joy and mirror of the masses, an expression of a culture at a time when entertainment, any entertainment, was rare and highly appreciated in a largely impoverished and isolated countryside. For the townsmen, too, he was the supreme defier of authority and a welcome tonic in a provincial setting.

The touring puppeteers, preceded by vivid posters announcing their imminent arrival, moved their paper characters from festival to festival and village to village for weddings and other events, very often "doing" all of the voices of the cast, human and animal (including dragons). The voices ranged from high-pitched squeaks, trebles for the ladies, to an authoritative bass. The Karaghiozis puppet usually spoke in a running staccato to emphasise his underlying anxiety and the necessity for haste in realising his plans before authority struck.

Often the puppet-masters designed and cut out their own two-dimensional puppets, sometimes from patterns if available; when necessary they sought the help of other folk artists. These also assisted in designing or painting the sets and outsize props when needed.

Early puppet-masters could be as illiterate as their audiences, but that was no obstacle. "Karaghiozis is not written, it is told," puppeteer Antonis Mollas once explained. From Dexameni in Athens, he was one of the earlier, brilliant puppet-masters who eventually taught others.

Another great, Evgenios Spatharis, once commented, "neither myself nor any Karaghiozi puppeteer reads the lines. We know the plays by heart, just as the story-tellers know their fairy tales by heart. Two performances of the same play may have different words and different jokes, but the meaning stays the same." Many great Cypriot puppet-masters had originally learned their art in the past from performers in mainland Greece where the Karaghiozis theatre was known since the early 18th century. Others were taught from an early age while assisting puppeteer-relatives at work here.

The Karaghiozis tradition itself dates from 1799 in Greece, but has its origins in the Ottoman Empire, according to two professors at West Chester University in England called Linda and Kostas Myrsiades. Their book, "Karagiozis, Culture and Comedy in Greek Puppet Theatre", was published in 1992 by the University Press of Kentucky.

The type of language used in the plays depended upon the

character and his social status, or the impact of various periods, they write. At one point characters also included the Arab, the Jew, the Vlach, the Albanian, the Persian and Armenian. "The roots of the Karaghiozis phenomenon lie in folklore and classical mime, which was the dominant form of entertainment from the 4th century BC to 1400 AD."

This particular shadow puppet theatre performance was born out of an Ottoman "subterfuge," they point out, "responding to an Islamic prescription that only permitted artistic representation of human figures when they appeared as shades cut with holes to allow the spirits to escape."

In both Turkish and Greek forms, "the performance capitalised on its association with the mime grotesque, the carnival fool, the divine madman and psychological shadow figures. Karaghiozis is the humpbacked fool-hero who wears the rags of the poor Greek and turns the world of the rich and powerful upside down."

As urban folklore, scholars sometimes compare it favourably with the old "rebetika" in Greece, a musical style of the fringes which reflected a singer or composer's bitter alienation, despair and rejection of and by the establishment.

While the old "rebetes," sometimes refugees, were macho shadow figures who exhibited a deep distaste for life and often chose to live in a shadow world, the comic Karaghiozis figure was a positive force who was never to give up. In the larger Greek towns, the creators of both folkloric forms often became firm friends, although their art reflected widely different reactions to similar problems. Both had reached their zenith at approximately the same period.

Cypriot performers occasionally created their own plays built round village happenings, legends or folk stories — "The Father's Curse", "The Prince Who Turned Into a Snake", "Kucuk Mehmet". But audiences also enjoyed many of the cherished stock plays based on heroic deeds, battles, fairy tales and encounters with their betters. Liberties were also taken in changing the story line, and nobody seemed to mind. In one popular play, Alexander the Great marries the Sultan's daughter.

If blessed with a passable voice, the puppeteer himself sang the songs that the audiences came to expect with each play, and also mimicked the regional accents in each district. On some occasions, itinerant musicians were hired to play violin and lute accompaniment.

During the Ottoman period, the local dialects contained many Turkish words, and pashas and other Turkish officials figured prominently in plays of the time.

Karaghiozis had many faces and disguises, and like the rest of the cast behind the illuminated screen, did everything in profile. Although the stationery props, usually outsize, were designed full-front, the puppets were almost always drawn in profile for flexibility and easier movement. They were painted on both sides to facilitate a choice of direction behind the screen. Mainland Greek puppets were of leather or cloth, and painted in rich solid colours, but the Cypriot counterparts were usually in black and white and fashioned of cardboard and wood.

All were two-dimensional and manipulated by the puppeteer and his assistants, if he had any, by means of a stick fixed onto the puppet's body by a metal device. Sometimes the hands were pierced to hold objects such as a sword or flowers.

Standing behind the illuminated screen, the puppeteer could move the characters from beyond the range of the lighting, snapping them on and off stage as needed or bringing them in from the "wings" with little hops. So skilled were the masters that their puppets could engage in massive fistfights and other confrontations, all the while rolling out dialogue to fit the action.

Recently historians and folklorists have begun to take a closer look at the world of Karaghiozis and the social, moral and political conditions built round him and other paper characters.

According to a 1994 edition of a government review called "Cyprus Today", the hero's main friend was called Hadjivatis, who wore Turkish attire and a fez. This character vacillated between cunningness and honesty but usually ended up in trouble "because of the mess he creates round himself."

Then there was Barbayiorgos, the hero's uncle — "probably the only good-looking puppet", who was tall, fearless and elegant and wore the typical, swirling white skirt of the Greeks called the "foustanella". He was portrayed as miserly and a dedicated rival of a local police officer called Velingekas.

Velingekas was an Albanian Turk, a "tool of the pasha," a typical gendarme who spoke atrocious Greek. Others in the cast included Dionyssios or Nionios, an impoverished aristocrat in a top hat from the Ionian islands.

Karaghiozis lived in a ramshackle hut with a bossy wife called Karaghiozina, rarely seen but often heard, who nagged her husband and regarded him as a "shameless home-wrecker" and a lazy spendthrift. Their son, Kollitiris, was a "miniature of his father, always hungry and up to mischief to get hold of something to eat."

Hunger, in fact, was supposedly a main motivation for knavery on the part of Karaghiozis himself, who yearned for more and better food along with a higher social status.

There were colourful animals and serpents in his life, too -- wild boars, cows, bulls with splayed feet, an ostrich, gorillas, mice and horses, and all appeared either in Greece or Cyprus in fairy tales or stories of village life.

Karaghiozis appeared in many skits while impersonating someone else to achieve his own ends, sometimes grotesque or sly, sometimes endearing or pitiful. He could be Karaghiozis the soldier, the detective, the bridegroom (once he even played the bride), the baker, a Macedonian fighter, the pasha, the monk, the doctor, the prophet.

Although the main plots concerned Karaghiozis and his antics, there could also be other, separate stories on the same theatrical bill and which could star such puppet favourites as Kolokotronis, the Turkopalikari, Rigas Feraios, the Emperor Justinian or Empress Theodora, and Greek and Roman officers.

Mainland Greek puppet masters frequently had several hundred figures and story lines in their repertoire, but their Cypriot counterparts kept things simpler. Whatever the presentation, and however hilarious was the comedy in disguise, "Karaghiozis is in fact the sad story of the outsider trying to be assimilated in a world he cannot understand," according to the review. Yet "this unglamorous figure so unfairly treated by nature and life.... does not preach to the spectator, but simply presents the reality with lots of humour and liveliness."

"Cyprus Today", a quarterly cultural publication from the Ministry of Education and Culture, drew for its story on a book by Dr. Costas Yiangoullis called "The Art of the Karaghiozi Shadow Theatre in Cyprus", and another prepared by Yiannis Kissonerghis called "Memoirs of a Puppeteer".

The folk artist was a constant observer of people and events, according to Dr. Yiangoullis, and "gave vent to remarks which nobody would dare utter in public in scathing satire that was perfectly acceptable during Karaghiozis' public performance. This Greek version of Mr. Punch in shadow play, he goes on, was brought here from Greece at the turn of the century, but the local hero, although an extension of the Greek, was often re-shaped to reflect local problems, conventions or events.

Immediately before and after the Balkan wars, Greek puppeteers had surged out to all parts of the world where Greeks lived, he says, and they taught their art to Cypriots who in turn spread it to towns and villages. Some came regularly, and some finally settled in the island. Amongst the first from Greece was Yerasimos the Keffalonian, considered the father of the Cypriot Karaghiosis theatre along with another great called Charilaos Petropoulos.

The list of great puppeteers is long, both in Greece and Cyprus, with the latter including Idhalias, Pais, Paphios, Tsillarias, Karaviotis, Tselingas, Themistocleous, Hadjittofis, Kokonas, Charalambous, Nicolaou, Paplomatas, Nearchos.

Sometimes Turkish artists came to perform at Nicosia's seraglio or elsewhere in the island, but in general their audiences seemed to prefer the Greek Cypriot stories and being familiar with the language, attended those performances too. Other Turkish Cypriot artists often appeared professionally in Greek at Greek Cypriot villages.

For decades women and children were discouraged from attending the performances, not only because women were barred from the all-male coffeeshops were many of the shows took place, but because of the ribald nature of some of the lines. Later, they began to join husband and family whenever Karaghiozis and his friends came to town or village. Puppet-masters took care to clean up the dialogue.

According to the review, shadow plays reached their zenith between 1925-1940, when thousands of workmen and their families gathered close to mines such as Amiandos, Mavrovouni and Mitsero to watch the shows. Karaghiozis and his troupe were also very popular at such holiday resorts as Pedoulas, Kakopetria, Platres and Lefkara.

Cypriot audiences could be demanding, and puppeteers would lengthen or shorten plays accordingly. There was never a compromise on songs. Audiences disliked cassette players, and the puppeteers were obliged to either possess a good voice or hire professionals to accompany the performances. Especially loved were the songs of the Mesaoria, Paphos, Akanthou, Leopetri and Morphou.

Karaghiozi puppeteers still play in villages occasionally, or at government or municipality-sponsored events and festivals, including the well-known puppeteer, Georghios Idhalias. But most have died or retired, and there are many Cypriot children and teenagers who have never sat before the makeshift screen to watch an art form that reaches far back in time.

One enthusiast may change all that, a 47-year-old teacher called Christodoulos Antoniou, whose grandfather, Chr. Paphios, was one of the greats. Before he died he taught Antoniou many of the old plays, and left him his puppet collection and old transparent screens.

Antoniou says that he is determined to muster support for even a modest revival of the art "before the technique dies out completely" and the stories of surviving puppeteers are lost to modern times. Hopefully, before the flickering light goes out forever on Karaghiozis and his friends.

WHEN OXEN KEPT THE FAMILY WARM

Entire families lived, ate and slept in the same large room even into the 1930's in many Cyprus village households because they were too poor to build better accommodation. In over 50% of the cases, their oxen lived there too, tethered in a far corner where they were mute witnesses to round-the-clock peasant life in the island.

Many families could not afford separate stabling and had often found it convenient to keep the animals nearby anyway, according to colonial reports of the time.

During hard-working periods, oxen were fed throughout the night, and in cold winters they generated welcome warmth for the sleeping family. Only the richer Moslem and Christian villagers could build additional sleeping rooms or provide glass windows for their homes. (This was also a period of considerable Cypriot emigration to Africa, Australia, Britain and the US.)

According to colonial reports dated 1935, the layout of villages in the island was a reminder of ancient times "when men crowded together on account of fear". Houses were built close together, streets were narrow and there were open spaces only in front of churches and mosques. Hill and mountain homes were constructed mostly of stone, while plainsmen preferred mud-brick (plithari) on a stone plinth or base. Roofs were of beaten clay or tiles if available. Floors were of beaten earth or paving stones.

Each house was usually surrounded by a courtyard entered by a double door, and normally consisted of one long, low room with one or two small openings which served as windows and were closed with wooden shutters. The houses proved warm in winter and cool in summer, and a limited number of the more prosperous villagers lived in two-storey dwellings. Damp-proof courses were not used, however, and sanitary arrangements were often non-existent. Drainpipe openings high up on the wall allowed smoke from household fires to drift out, and in hill villages old petroleum tins acted as chimney pots for the rough fireplaces.

Although there was an acute shortage of better-class housing in Cyprus towns during the 1930's, the reports continue, there was considerably activity in general home building.

Stone was gradually replacing mudbrick, but town housing still had many of the same defects as village construction — no damp-proof courses and a tendency to build cellars for washing rooms which were small, unventilated and dark.

Water closets were being installed increasingly but there was little uniformity of type and no real system for disposal of affluent. New municipal by-laws in 1935 would make it obligatory to provide proper sanitary conveniences in all premises within the municipal limits, and sanitary authorities would be appointed to inspect all premises. New provisions were also being drawn up to widen the old narrow streets so typical of towns in Eastern countries, reports added.

The island's population had doubled in the 57 years since the British arrival in Cyprus, when it stood at 186.173. By 1935 it had reached 365.372. The majority were Orthodox Greek Cypriots, with somewhat over 1/5 being "Mohammedans." The majority of Cypriot villages were inhabited by members of both communities. The Armenian community tended steadily to increase and there was also a Latin community in the island.

Cyprus is a land of many creeds, one report states, adding that "race in the Near East is inseparably linked up with religion." The main language was a "local dialect of Modern Greek, often very corrupt, but retaining a number of archaisms and showing traces of the island's history in a large proportion of words borrowed from French, Latin and Turkish sources."

Somewhat archaic Osmanli Turkish was spoken by the Moslems and (in the villages) was free from Persian and Arabic forms. The "Mohammedans" were also familiar with Greek.

The new Turkish alphabet had become obligatory for all official purposes in 1932 and was in general use, while knowledge of the English language was becoming more widely diffused. Except in the most remote villages, someone could usually be found who could speak, read or write it. To a lesser degree, French was spoken by the more educated classes.

ARCHBISHOP

The Archbishop of Cyprus was so powerful by the end of the 18th century that both Greeks and Turks here regarded him as the real governor of the Ottoman-held island rather than the appointed "muhassil", some historians claim.

From his palace in Nicosia, the head of the Cyprus church administered the entire island indirectly, filled district posts and sent off to the Grand Vizier in Istanbul the annual taxes due the Ottoman Porte from the Greek Christian community here.

No Turkish government had ever learned the exact number of Greek Cypriots living in the island to double-check the assessments, however, and figures varied from 32,000 to 100,000 Orthodox souls. When the Porte finally sent a commissioner here from Istanbul in 1805 to make a head count, he was "got at", loaded with gold, and "went away somewhere".

The gradual ascent to power by the Cypriot archbishops, who represented the Porte's Christian subjects, had begun about a century after the Turkish occupation of the island in 1571, according to Archimandrite Kyprianos, whose "Chronological History of the Island of Cyprus" was published in Venice in 1788.

Until then, he wrote, they had remained politically in the background but had the Sultan's permission to exercise their ecclesiastical duties. Their power, once established, was to remain unshaken for over 150 years here, reaching its peak during the reigns of the Ottoman Sultan Selim III, finally deposed in 1807 after a long reign, and of Mustapha IV, also de-throned a short time after.

Back in Cyprus, the archbishop had by then annexed so much administrative authority that he was virtually independent of Istanbul-appointed governors. According to Mr. Louis Lacroix, a 19th century writer, the archbishop very often determined their appointment and even recall. (Mr. Lacroix had published his "Iles de la Grece" in 1853.)

Portions of Mr. Lacroix's work on Cyprus were translated and included in Mr. Claude Cobham's "Excerpta Cypria", a compilation of historical and other writings on the island's past by selected writers and visitors covering much of the Ottoman and earlier periods here.

By 1804 the archbishop's power had begun to erode, he tells us quoting earlier sources, especially after the Cyprus Turks began to rebel at "seeing themselves fall under the rule of men whom they had of old conquered." It was to be the prelude to bloody catastrophe later, in 1821.

Stirred by rumours of pending food shortages, Nicosia Turks and others from surrounding villages rose in revolt against both the Archbishop and other officials, Greek and Turk, whom they believed were colluding with the former over financial and other privileges. For a time the rebels were masters in Nicosia, but the revolt ended after the arrival of two pashas from Asia Minor and the intervention of the consuls of England, France and Russia here, he reports.

But the intrigues of the chief Turks against Greek headmen continued, Mr. Lacroix writes, and in 1821 the authority of the Greek clergy was finally overturned and the government restored to the pashas. The previous year insurrections had already begun against the Ottoman empire in Moldavia and Peloponnesus, he relates, and fearful of other uprising, the Porte had sanctioned "every measure" to keep its Christian subjects in check elsewhere.

Although the Archbishop at the time, Kyprianou, had repeatedly assured the Porte of his love of peace and his submission to the Grand Signor, the Ottoman government was convinced of a Cyprus plot to shake off its rule, the writer continues.

In the meantime, the Greek Cypriots had remained entirely aloof from national movements which stirred other islands and the mainland, he insisted. "It was not they who were crying out against tyranny and thought of taking up arms." Rather it was the Turks, he writes, who were impatient of the bondage in which the bishops had kept them for the past 50 years, and wished to "snatch back the reins of power".

The Turks then brought bands of Arabs, bedouins and Ansariya brigands into Cyprus and scattered them round the island. Terror-stricken, the Greeks allowed themselves to be disarmed.

In July, 1821, wishing to make an example of the alleged trouble-makers, the Grand Vizier petitioned the new administrator here, Kuchuk Mehmed, to hand over Archbishop Kyprianou and three bishops to the janissaries who murdered them at the Serai (palace) in Nicosia.

(Note: Other sources tell us that the Archbishop was hanged in the Serai square, while the three bishops were beheaded. Local tradition also says that earlier, Kuchuk Mehmed had solemnly assured the Archbishop that he would never shed his blood; therefore he hanged rather than beheaded him.)

That same day, when Greek notables assembled at the palace unaware of the previous deaths, they were also killed. It was the signal for a general massacre which continued for six months, according to Lacroix. The local population either ran to the hills or mountains, or fled to Larnaca and the protection of the foreign consuls there; some sailed for Venice or Marseilles.

How could Cyprus archbishops have assumed so much administrative power in an Ottoman province in the first place, and for which they were to pay so dearly later?

According to Archbishop Kyprianos, quoted in "Cyprus Under the Turks" by Sir Harry Luke, the Cyprus church had taken no part in general government or politics for at least a century after the Ottoman takeover. Instead, they had been content with the sultan's "berat" or commission to exercise their episcopal duties. Further, they never failed to meet imperial officers, ...call on them ceremoniously...or to offer the usual "baksheesh" or gifts to the pashas, governors or mollas.

By about 1660 however, when the population had been seriously thinned by plague, overwhelmed by taxes or had escaped abroad from debts, the Porte "probably thought it politic to recognise the archbishops as guardians and representatives of the rayahs (slaves)."

In addition, the Porte had also wished to "curb to some degree the rapacity of the Turkish authorities, the rayah perishing under the exactions and tyranny".

Eventually the archbishops began to appear "boldly" in person before the Grand Vizier, travelling to Istanbul and stating their complaints or asking for tax cuts. They also begged help for other necessities. Sometimes they were heeded and assisted, he continues, sometimes imprisoned or banished after accusations of wrong-doing or through the "malevolence of the Cypriots" and other intrigues.

In other cases, the very clergy whom the Porte had permitted to grow powerful, gradually formed alliances with those same officials they were intended to check, according to German historian Michael de Vezin, whose allegation is included in "Excerpta Cypria".

Eventually, the temporal task of tax collection was to be allocated to the Dragoman to the Serai, who was actually appointed by the bishops as the agent between the government and the Christian community. He also carried out other important duties. "The Dragoman...holds one of the principal posts assigned to a Christian," according to Giovanni Mariti, whose book "Voyage to the Island of Cyprus" was translated into English in 1791.

His title means "interpreter," the writer says, but in reality he was the agent who treated between the Christian population and the governor. "He must be a man of tact and sense, for his position is a very important one."

The ascendency of the dragoman did not, it seems, affect the importance or respect shown to the archbishop, whose power remained intact. One visitor to the island in 1806, who called himself Ali Bey Al Abbassi but who was actually a Spaniard, has this to say about his visit to the head of the Cyprus church.

"The Greeks are very submissive and respectful to the Archbishop. In saluting him they bow low, take off their cap and hold it before them upside down. They scarcely dare speak in his presence." There were 30 servants and an archimandrite waiting to greet the author when he arrived for the meeting, he said. The bishops, too, were highly respected, and were carried up and down the stairs by their servants.

The writer calls the Greeks "a community of slaves, with their bishops as a rallying point. Through them the community exists... it suits the people to give them political power."

SHADOW ON THE SEA

Goats were to blame, he thought. They had been everywhere — Cyprus, Syria, Palestine, the Dalmatian coast.

Goats, with their great big grabby teeth that crunched their way through dense woods right up to the brushwood on the water's edge.

It hadn't been like that in classical times, but things change and there were no more great forests now. Goats with soft noses and long floppy ears had seen to that, pawing and snaffling until the best had gone. But "Cyprus looked exquisite" anyway as the author stood gazing at her over the ship's rail that dawn in the early 1930's.

He had just survived his last night on board the cargo boat by sleeping on deck, having retired earlier that evening to his cabin, hoping for a restful sleep. As soon as head touched pillow, however, "three glistening cockroaches" ran from under it and disappeared beneath his bunk, he writes. He disliked particularly "their revolting bent legs," their speed, and the distinct impression that they would suddenly fly. Once cockroaches invaded a ship, he said, they can never be driven out unless the ship is torn almost to pieces.

From the deck, he had been one of the first to see a shadow on the sea in the early half-light... and knew that it was "the long, eastward thrust of Cyprus... the land where once the copper breastplate of Agamemnon had been beaten into shape."

Travel writer H.V. Morton had been following "in the steps of St. Paul" and was gathering material for a book of the same name eventually published in 1935. Taking the Acts of the Apostles as his guide, he traced St Paul's journeys from his birthplace at Tarsus to the scene of his martyrdom at Rome.

This meant a journey through Syria, Palestine, Cyprus, Turkey, Greece, Rhodes, Malta and Italy. This part of the world, he says, once enjoyed the unity of the Roman Empire, but was now divided amongst many nations, with national frontiers, different flags and different languages. St Paul had moved over a Roman road, speaking Greek all the time, he pointed out.

Travel had been easier for the saint than for those who followed him, for the once famous ports and highways that he used were often no longer there, or difficult of access. Rather, it was an exploration off the beaten track.

The harbour at Antioch is desolate, he says, and Ephesus a nesting place for storks. But for anyone wanting to make the same journey "there is nothing that cannot be done given time and patience. ...Only in very remote places will the visitor feel compelled to make the Aristophanic inquiry: which inn is the least interesting entomologically?"

Antioch and Aleppo were more familiar to the French traveller than to the English, and apart from Istanbul and Ankara, Turkey offered neither freedom of movement nor the comfort which the general traveller demands. "But to the students of St Paul, no country promises a richer reward."

Greece also was one of the few countries in the world which does not disappoint the most ardent admirer, he goes on, with a good road system and excellent hotel accommodation. It was one of the cheapest countries for those travelling with the pound sterling. The distant British colony of Cyprus would attract far more British travellers if communications were improved. It is an "exquisite island", with excellent roads, small but admirable hotels and a superb winter climate.

His book, he went on, would describe the actions of St Paul the Traveller, and would not deal with the theological aspects.

"Every word written by the saint has become a battleground on which European and American scholars had for generations matched learning against learning, theory against theory.

..."To the respectful eye of a non-combatant, it seems at times that the battlefield itself has become obscured in the conflict."

Enroute to Cyprus, he had shared the ship with several human passengers, 200 goats driven on board at Alexandria, a number of Syrian cows, hens and turkeys, and 12 Arab horses who thrust nervous heads from their boxes. The goats had sprung nimbly from derrick to companionway, he wrote, and had driven all the third class passengers forward to the first class deck. One animal, a malign old red goat, nipped silently into the tiny saloon and stole a lettuce.

The ship, as he describes it, was "an inferno of heat, throbbing engines and oil smells." There were 12 cabins, "and all opened onto the ships's domestic life." From one there was a view of the Scottish engineer descending a steel ladder to his rhythmic engines. From another there was an excellent view of a Greek cook bent over a greasy stew, and from the third a pantry "in which the cook's dusky assistant prowled, grasping a dead chicken."

After the goats departed, bleating, at Haifa, the third class passenger returned to their own quarters aft, "where they lay in distressed attitudes as the ship rose and fell.

"A veiled woman would now and then totter to the side and shamelessly uncover her features to the heaving deep." The only English passenger, a large, middle-aged man who had settled in Palestine, had told him: "I came out and stayed out. No, I never get homesick, I like the climate. Dash it all, man, we've a short enough life. Why should we spend half of it in fog and rain?"

He was enroute to Cyprus to enquire about orange-growing, and called an orange 'a citrus fruit' - a term that "grated on me as if I had bitten a lemon." Later, the author warmed to him, for he knew all about St Paul.

Although Cyprus had been a British holding for over a century, Morton found upon arrival that the English language had not made much progress. One inhabitant, however, did speak American. He was the driver of a saloon car for hire and had replied. "Sure, step in boss," when told that the author wished to be taken to Salamis.

Later he had confided: "I'm the best driver in Cyprus." He had spent six years in the States where he had "saved up enough dough to come here, get married and buy this car."

They drove past fields where oxen yoked to ploughs turned rich earth, and flat-roofed houses huddled in mud-coloured villages surrounded by pomegranate and orange groves. Reaching Salamis, the author left the car and plunged into dense wood growing on sand hills near the sea. He found the stump of a marble pillar, he said, then another.

There was a flight of marble steps half-covered with grass, and the remains of three market places once paved with marble and surrounded by marble temples. St Paul had probably trod on the steps of one large forum in the main square, Morton thought.

But a ruined city in a wood is terrifying, he writes. There were only sand dunes where once was a splendid harbour. "An earthquake had wrecked both city and port and brought down proud Salamis," he wrote. Scattered over the island there were relics of two civilisations - Greek and Medieval. Little was left of the Greek, he found, but several castles had survived from Crusader and Venetian days. Later excavations turned up ample Greek remains.

The day that England signed the convention with Turkey and assumed Cyprus' administration, he goes on, the British vice-admiral, Lord John Hay, received a telegram telling him to take over Cyprus in the name of the Queen. The admiral then drove to Nicosia in a wagonette, accompanied by two mules loaded with English sixpences to pay off the Sultan's arrears to his officials. (The inhabitants remained technically Ottoman subjects until Britain annexed Cyprus when Turkey entered World War I on the side of Germany.)

In 1915, he continues, when Bulgaria had invaded Servia, "we offered the island to Greece if she would march to the aid of Servia, but she declined." (Note: Venizelos had urged the then Greek king to accept Britain's proposal. The king declined.)

Cyprus became a British colony in 1925, over a decade before the author's visit. In the meantime, "one of the most beautiful islands in the world remains unknown to all but the few discriminating people."

Morton praised British rule for many improvements, he said, including roads, health and agriculture. Under Ottoman Turkey, it had become a wasteland in which neither life nor property was safe, he says, referring to accounts of foreign travellers during Ottoman rule. "The Christian Greeks were oppressed by the ruling Moslems and the Moslems oppressed by their own tax-gatherers." One of the most fertile islands of classical times had degenerated into an unproductive waste, he says.

When one traveller, John Carne, arrived here in the 1820's, the writer continues, large domains could be bought for a trifle and included a chateau with garden, a small village and a large tract of land, all for a few hundred pounds.

In 1935, Cyprus was the last place in the world where an old Turk could still be seen unaffected by European reform, now that Kemal Ataturk had abolished the fez, Turkish dress and habits. In Cyprus, the Turk still wore his fez, pleated trousers, and smoked his hookah outside a Turkish cafe.

Morton describes being given a room in an "admirable hotel in Famagusta which contained an enormous bed whose hearse-like proportions were contradicted by an immense bridal mosquito net whose rents even the least experienced mosquito would have treated as a jest."

There was a rich, tropical look about Famagusta, he thought, a haven of rest that women friends "instantly declare as a perfect spot for a writer to settle in and produce a book." He could still hear those decisive, ringing tone... "what a lovely place... so quiet, so peaceful, nothing to distract you... those tones that have plagued many a poor man's soul."

It has been proved time and again, he says, that the perfect place for a writer is the "hideous roar of a city, with men making a new road under his window... a barrel organ... a man waiting on the mat for the rent." He found the peace of Famagusta distracting. In the boundless silence, "the mind swoops and dips and refuses to come down to earth... There is nothing to concentrate Against... there was only exquisite procrastinations."

He called Famagusta a "Mediaeval Pompeii," except that the ancient churches and walls had not been destroyed but permitted to fall down instead by the Turks. "It is a lack of energy for which scholarship should be eternally grateful." The Turks had sworn that no Christian would ever live there again, he continues.

He thought the town one of the most remarkable in the world, and that Britain should prohibit building within the walls, reconstruct churches, preserve frescoes and establish an archaeological centre there. He had explored about 12 churches, all built within a few hundred years of each other — "any one of them would have been the treasured possession of a European city." Outside the cathedral he had noticed a stone which was used as a mounting block. It was the base of a statue and bore the words in ancient Greek, "the city of Salamis offers this statue to the Emperor Trajan".

One of the churches had been a Turkish stable, he was told, until an angry St George, according to the story, had come down from the mountains and thrown a camel from one of the rose windows. The saint's icon was festooned with votive offerings - wax legs, hands, arms, ears, feet, fingers. "The most remarkable was a complete little man made of wax, two feet high and bearing the word, Mehmet." Even the Turks venerated the icon, he was told, because St George was a great healer.

He thought that the models looked much like the terracotta votives dug up at ancient temples in Cyprus.

Nearby, one fine old Gothic church was being used as a storehouse for oranges. There was also a bastion where Venetian blacksmiths had repaired the armour of the knights. The ground was blue with ancient cinders, he writes, which in time had been beaten into the earth.

Another bastion, called the Djamboulat, was named after a brave Turkish general of the 1571 siege of Famagusta, who had ridden his horse into a Venetian wheel of knives. Both were cut to pieces, but Djamboulat's ghost, sometimes observed by his compatriots,was seen waving his scimitar in encouragement and holding his head beneath his arm.

At St Barnabas monastery, the author could almost hear the crops growing, he said, so still was the building in the afternoon heat. A monk was seated at an easel, using a bamboo guiding rod and intensely painting touches of red, blue and gold on an icon. He was using a technique from the Byzantine age, handed down from monk to monk. The Greek Orthodox Church forbids statues in its buildings, he said, "a ban dating from remote times when sculpture was associated with pagan worship... But it delights in icons, no matter how small the church. Country people sometimes attached to them all manner of miraculous qualities."

Tiny birds called beccaficos were caught in Cyprus as early as the Crusader period, he said, and later were pickled in vinegar and salt and sent to Venice. By the 18th century, 400 little barrels of the birds were exported annually to Europe and Turkey.

Nicosia was the first round town that Morton had ever seen, "as round as King Arthur's table." About 20,000 Christians had been killed in the street fighting there when the Turks conquered the Venetian-held town in the 16th century. "The last, thin flickering flame of the (earlier) Lusignans had been finally extinguished in the person of a poor, little, shrunken lady in the 19th century." She had been called Eliza de Lusignan, lived in a London suburb and had been a governess in Ceylon.

At the museum, Morton saw a blue, cone-shaped stone reputed to be the Aphrodite of Paphos, which had been found in a cowshed. He was curious that the pagan goddess associated with physical beauty should in her original home bear no resemblance to human form.

The olive trees in Paphos, according to local belief, had grown from the stones which Paul and Barnabas had thrown away after eating their food at the wayside. "Does an olive tree ever die?" Morton had pondered. New ones grew from the old when decayed.

Later, during a visit to Kykko monastery, the abbot had asked if the author believed that St Paul had been whipped at Paphos. When the author answered "no," the abbot had said, "I don't either."

THE MISSION

They were determined to save the East from itself, or at least a small corner of it, and they had names like Josiah and Lorenzo and Eli.

With Christian zeal and a steamer trunk full of Bibles, they came from across the sea to confront the citadels of entrenched eastern creeds. It was the early 19th century and they were the first Protestant American missionaries to the Eastern Mediterranean, including Cyprus.

The region's total strangeness must have been somewhat mitigated by their familiarity with the Testaments, along with earlier reports from merchant-visitors to the region.

Righteous, committed and upright, they came from the U.S. Eastern seaboard armed with a sound theological education and often with degrees as well in Law or the Classics from some of the best universities in America — Harvard, Yale, Princeton.

They were to confront Islam in action in the Ottoman Empire's heaving polyethnic provinces and finally, in Greece and Cyprus, come face to face with the flaming cross of the Eastern Christian church with its ancient liturgy and political savvy.

It wasn't going to be easy, but they already knew that. With bonneted wives and their children too, they sailed from familiar harbours for the East, their high, winged collars and wide cravats framing fresh, hopeful faces. Their mission could not begin soon enough for them. Some had only just received degrees from theological seminaries when they were on the first available steamer out of Boston or New York.

Later, scattered graves in foreign lands far from home would testify to their committment and sacrifices, and that of their families, as well as to the deadliness of Eastern plagues and the misery they caused. One Yale graduate, missionary Eli Smith, lost his first wife in 1836 after she died of exposure when shipwrecked off the Cyprus coast. His second wife died of dysentery in Beirut six years later.

Another missionary, Elnathan Gridley, plagued by ill-health and an unhappy love affair, moved to central Turkey where he climbed Mt. Argaeus near Kayseri in a heavy rainfall.He had been testing Strabo's statement that "on a clear day you could see from the summit both the Pontus and the Mediterranean." He sickened and died, fulfilling a premonition that his "sorrows might give me a grave in savage Cappadocia." It was 1827.

It was still the era of slavery in the U.S. and elsewhere, the Alamo had yet to happen, and European colonialism was insisting that with its help meaningful African history was just beginning on that continent. Only a few decades before, Napoleon had marched up the Nile and defeated the Mamluke army at the Battle of the Pyramids — "the first non-Moslem invasion of the heartland of Islam since the Crusades," one historian had commented.

British trade was picking up in the Mediterranean after an advantageous taxation treaty with Ottoman Turkey, and the first Christian schools were opening in Syria as part of a modernisation policy under Mohammed Ali's son, Ibrahim. Meanwhile, with God's grace, fervent prayer and a good example, perhaps there was a chance to help the semi-saved in Smyrna, Constantinople, Cairo and finally Cyprus.

The fact that most Moslems seemed quite contented with their own faith meant that much effort would be needed by Protestant Christian missions to carve out a small niche alongside Islam, however tolerant its adherents appeared.

Moreover, Greek and Cypriot Orthodox Christians were still recovering from a mainland Greek rebellion against the Ottomans, with massacres there and in Cyprus where church leaders had been hanged and hundreds of civilians massacred. The Cyprus church had already survived the Lusignans, Venetians and the Ottoman Turks, and it was doubtful if they were prepared to embrace western Protestantism, however powerful its ecclesiastical armoury or likeable its exponents.

The missionaries were not the only U.S. pioneers in the Mediterranean, nor were they the first. A century before, there had been traders, merchants and gentlemen archaeologists.

In a publication called "Beyond the Shores of Tripoli," written by Andrew Oliver, Jr. in 1979 to celebrate the centenary of the Archaeological Institute of America, we learn of the earliest Americans to venture here.

Many had shown a genuine interest in antiquity, he writes, but he also cites the amateur nature of their haphazard excavations. Nevertheless they managed to send scores of valuable artifacts, sarcophagi, ancient tablets and statuettes back home, now displayed in U.S. museums, institutes, or academies.

A cuneiform tablet from Nineveh is now at Bryn Mawr College, shipped over by a missionary who acquired it, he said "from an Arab while riding through the mounds opposite Mosul." A massive gold ring with garnet was discovered in an ancient marble tomb on Melos in 1825, purchased for 500 pounds later in Smyrna by a U.S. merchant and eventually donated to New York's Metropolitan Museum.

Some businessmen wore Turkish costume during their Mediterranean travels, including John Lowell who collected Egyptian antiquities on the Nile and later died in India, and Mendes Israel Cohen who visited Cyprus during his long tour of the Mediterranean. Cohen flew the American flag from his Nile boat, according to Mr. Oliver, and wore his Turkish dress with a turban, later replacing it with a tarbouche (fez).

Cohen's collection of antiquities from Karnak, Thebes and elsewhere is now at John Hopkins University. He also kept a diary.

Other American visitors kept records of their visit, often sketched the antiquities they found, or published learned papers or reports about their travels. Many are now in archives attached to universities or historical bodies.

In 1842, the American Oriental Society began publishing a "Journal" with contributions by many eastern travellers, Mr. Oliver goes on. One of the most dramatic acquisitions, perhaps, was a giant granite obelisk from Aswan known later as "Cleopatra's Needle". It was a gift from the Khedive of Egypt to America in 1879. It had been lowered, crated and shipped to New York by a U.S. naval officer on leave, and now stands in the Metropolitan Museum.

Another traveller to Egypt was Philip Rhinelander, Jr. one of the growing number of American tourists there. He travelled with four fellow New Yorkers and finally sent home "all the curiosities I have collected during my stay." He also dressed as a Turk... "my vest is of rich silk and over this is worn a large jacket with sleeves open to the elbow.

"Round my waist is wound a sash of crimson silk which passes round and round in many folds... in this I bear my arms... on my head I wear the tarbouche....

"I might almost pass for a real Turk were it not for my specs." He died in Vienna enroute home. He was 24.

One American marine lieutenant, according to author Oliver, resigned his commission with the Mediterranean squadron, converted to Islam and changed his name to Mohammed Effendi (George Bethune English, Harvard class of 1807). In Cairo he was appointed general of the artillery in Ismael Pasha's army on its way to conquer Nubia and was "the first American to record a journey up the Nile."

Two other Americans, one called Khalil Aga and the other Achmed Aga, accompanied him. A narrative of the expedition was published in Boston in 1823 under English' U.S. name.

Perhaps the earliest Americans in the Mediterranean were New England merchants hoping for a share of the Levant trade in the 17th century, but their ships were often being seized enroute by Barbary pirates from Algiers, Tunis and Tripoli.

This eventually provoked the deployment of the first U.S. Mediterranean naval squadron to protect American interests and also prevent the imprisonment of U.S. seamen. The way was now open for continuing American presence in the form of diplomats, journalists and scholars. Many ships were bound for Smyrna, which had become the most important emporium of the Eastern Mediterranean. By 1910, four U.S. firms had opened business there, author Oliver tells us.

One of his most poignant accounts is the story of an American missionary to Cyprus, Lorenzo Warriner Pease, who was ordained a Presbyterian missionary in New York in 1834 and the same day married Lucinda Leonard.

From Boston they sailed for Smyrna and Constantinople, and when finally reaching Larnaca, Pease presented his papers to a Mr. Pierides.

He was not the first missionary to Cyprus — a decade before Levi Parsons had travelled overland from Paphos to Limassol distributing Bibles. But "Pease was the first American to experience Cyprus in all its richness," travelling widely during his four year stay and speaking good Greek.

He kept an eleven — volume diary and also wrote "Researches in Cyprus" and "A Grammar of the Modern Greek Language".

Something of his life here, along with excerpts from his diary, have been set down by authors Oliver Jr. and Diana Buitron, who wrote "Lorenzo Warriner Pease, American Missionary in Cyprus, 1834-1839". It was reprinted in a Cyprus Antiquities Department report for 1988.

There seemed good reasons to establish a mission in Cyprus. The Greek Cypriots had still not recovered from the terrible events of 1821; those who had escaped the general massacre had either sought refuge with the European consuls in Larnaca or left the island.

A large percentage of Christians under Moslem rule in Cyprus were, in the eyes of the missionaries, "in a state of deplorable ignorance and degradation." The missionaries, aimed to "purify" Orthodox Christianity "in order to strengthen the possibility of converting Mohammedeans who would not be impressed by the lax morality of the local Christians."

What was needed was to set a good example, Pease believed, and even chided an Orthodox priest at Stroumbi village during a tour of Paphos for not guiding the population sufficiently and failing to provide a better example. "You must reform first and then you will be able to lead them.They will hear you. Read the gospel to them, interpret it." In reply, the priest told him: "They will not hear." An elderly priest who had overheard the conversation agreed with Pease.

The missionary and his group were also told that about 300 monks, laymen, husbandmen and others were connected to Kykko monastery in churches and elsewhere at the time.

In further excerpts from his diary, he tells of his efforts to sketch ancient churches and tombs, measure ancient walls at Kouklia in Paphos, and transcribe inscriptions found at ruins. There they were politely treated by Christodoulos, the late demogeros (village elder), and Markos, the present demogeros. "He gave us bread and cheese and raisins in abundance ...Ktima has 120 Turks, 40 Christians, according to actual examination made by the demogeros in my presence, three priests and one lame man who do not pay taxes."

Pease was especially impressed by the tomb of St. Neophytos "who for many years lived in a cave, in the side of a frightful precipice."

There, the saint had dug out of the rock a small cave in which was his sarcophagus, a marble table where he mixed his colours for painting fresco, and a stone bed where he was accustomed to lie, wrote Pease. There was a second room for altar and cross, another covered with frescoes, and yet another reached only by ladder or rope where he spent the last 25 years of his life and lived on vegetables. The saint's remains were kept in the church nearby. Pease also included a pen and ink drawing of the monastery in his diary.

Four years after the missionary couple arrived in the island, their young twins died within months of each other.

Infant mortality was high — plague, cholera and typhoid fever. According to the authors, Pease wrote a "heartbreaking letter home to his parents," describing his nightly vigils at the bedside of his last son.

His wife cared for him during the day, but the child gradually weakened "until death released him from his sufferings." An infant daughter had died earlier and the tombstones are now in a courtyard adjacent to the Church of St. Lazarus in Larnaca. That of a friend's son is nearby.

Eight months later, Pease was also dead, probably of typhoid fever.

The last entry in his diary, dated August 7, 1839 reads; "Today I have been attacked with a slight fever which I am endeavoring to subdue by fasting." Lucinda Pease said that he had seemed to improve after a week and even entertained an American newspaper correspondent. But then he worsened and died. He was just over 30 years old.

He was buried next to his twins, and the epitaph on his tombstone is in Greek and English. It reads in part:

"Sacred to the memory of the Rev.
Lorenzo Warriner Pease, Native of
the United States of America.
The Righteous shall be in
Everlasting Remembrance."

A year later, his heartbroken widow and two surviving daughters returned to Boston. Pease had died before any of his works could be published. Three years later the Cyprus mission was closed.

HEROES, ECCENTRICS
AND LAWRENCE OF ARABIA

"Anyway, the stables are good," said Lady Storrs reassuringly as their car drew up to the long, barnlike building.

Actually, it was Government House itself, a wooden structure on the outskirts of Nicosia where they were to live and which would one day burn to the ground round them during her husband's tenure on the island.

Sir Ronald Storrs was to be Governor of Cyprus for almost six years and arrived just a year after the island was declared a British crown colony in 1925. He was the first administrator to forbid the use of the word "native" by government officials when referring to Greek and Turkish Cypriots.

Local politics had begun in earnest for him just after his ship, the "Cornflower", steamed cautiously through the narrow pass into Famagusta harbour. He had already donned his uniform. A cultured diplomat and Cambridge graduate, he had wide literary and musical interests and a lifelong devotion to Greek and Latin classics, he said. But his career was to be bloodied here in the frantic groundswell of the movement for union with Greece (Enosis), where even before his arrival he had already "heard much, and evil, of the prelates and politicians of the island," he later wrote.

He had already spent two decades in the Middle East where, in varying degrees, he had been an official part of an era of great and rapid changes, upheaval, wars and unabashed imperialism. He had met and worked with outstanding personalities who changed the face and boundaries of nations in the name of the Queen, and went down in British history as heroes, eccentrics or sometimes both. Some had been heartily disliked. Others were tragic figures.

That was a very special time, Storrs was to recall with great nostalgia later in his 1937 book, "Orientations". Its feeling and ambience could not be fully understood perhaps, unless one had lived as a part of it or at least in close proximity. The epoch had spawned an unusual number of colourful military and political figures, set down by the Foreign or Colonial office in far-away, romanticised places in the Near and Middle East-- Gordon, then Kitchener, T.E. Lawrence, Allenby... .

There was a "special" atmosphere then in the streets and bazaars of great capitals of the Orient, as the region was called, and its memorable figures also included explorers, sultans and pashas, Arabists and Turkophiles, and people who could discuss politics in five languages , however shaky their accents. The sun shone hot and camel bells tinkled.

Storrs had felt at home in Cairo and its antique shops and bazaars, and in Arabia in general, he recalled. He "loved" Jerusalem, where he had been governor. He was also a friend and admirer of T.E. Lawrence (the legendary Lawrence of Arabia) who often strode in and out of his life unexpectedly and brought him the manuscript of "Seven Pillars" to read. Lawrence had carried it strapped under the seat of his motorcycle.

During his long career, Storrs had also been Oriental Secretary to Lord Kitchener in Egypt for three years. Then, in 1926, posted as Governor to Cyprus, he and Lady Storrs stepped onto an island which was "in truth deadly poor," often drought-stricken, woefully underdeveloped and too impoverished to even dig up its own archaeological wealth.

Cyprus, unlike Egypt, Palestine or Assyria, Storrs goes on, was never "original or originating. Cyprus has from the first endured, received, transmitted and been the meeting place of contending empires." It was the "clearing house" of Mediterranean civilisation.

Now, a year after it had become an official Crown colony, rapid development still seemed remote especially with Britain earmarking any substantial grants for other colonies, and the few

"Cyprus capitalists," as Storrs called them, accustomed for generations to put their money to usury.

Then, there was the annual "Turkish tribute" which Britain had undertaken to pay from the island's revenue after the takeover from the Ottomans in 1878. (Actually, it went to help pay off an old Anglo-French loan going back to 1850.)

But Storrs seemed determined to nudge the economy somehow and a first project was the promotion of the hotel industry to attract visitors. He had never considered the necessity for luxury hotels. Instead, "we should attract the visitor in search of beauty, tradition, antiquity and above all quiet." But financing was poor.

Meanwhile, during the next five years, about 200 new wells and some seven million gallons of irrigation water every 24 hours was managed. It didn't seem much, but it was not easy to maintain, he wrote. "Throughout the Near and Middle East, the traveller is apt to wonder how mighty civilisations of antiquity could have arisen and flourished in regions which seem to have been for centuries past doomed to perpetual drought, Nowhere does this astonishment recur more often than in Cyprus," he said. The great forests had been destroyed and a once-fertile plain was now a dry wilderness. Forests may not attract moisture, he thought, but they certainly preserved it.

One day a local farmer pulled from the earth a large bronze hand. The rest came later, in pieces, and put together they formed a giant statue of a Roman emperor called Septimius Severus. It generated much excitement at the impoverished Cyprus museum, where a tiny grant had been considered "derisory" by experts. Gradually it was supplemented by the sale of ancient duplicates. Meanwhile, a "team of willing ladies", noting the arrival dates of luxury cruises, also helped in their promotion. This was thought undignified by some, but it brought in much- needed funds for cupboards and shelves, and for cataloguing and labelling exhibits, Storrs writes.

The law was also amended to permit the limited export of certain antiquities after permission from government and museum authorities. The immediate result was the arrival of archaeological societies to excavate here, such as that of Sweden's Crown Prince and the discovery of important sites such as Vouni palace and the Greco-Roman theatre of Soli. An immense number of new specimens were eventually brought into the museum, along with the release of many others as saleable and as revenue-producing duplications, he goes on.

Cyprus archaeology owes a great debt to Rupert Gunnis, according to Storrs, who was the Governor's ADC and private secretary in the island for six years. Every moment of his leisure and much of his other time was dedicated to museum service, Storrs writes. (Gunnis is author of "Historic Cyprus," 1936.) The governor also arranged for a free portrait from the studio of Bellini of the last queen of Cyprus, Catherine Cornaro, which he placed in the museum.

In Storr's opinion, the Greek majority on the Legislative Council were "not too interested" in the Gothic remains of Latin Catholicism here, especially as every surplus piastre was bespoke thrice for hospitals, water supplies and roads.

Storr's friend, T.E. Lawrence, was at one point offered the post of Director of Archaeology in Cyprus, but rejected it "because of what he chose to imagine were the social duties that may have gone with the job," according to the author.

Some of Storrs other observations:

The women of Lefkara still wove the lace which Leonardo da Vinci bought in panels in 1481 for the Milan cathedral, and the Governor's summer cottage in Troodos was built by Arthur Rimbaud — "a better poet than architect-entrepreneur."

Still sailing were the archaic feluccas "digging deep for Famagusta and the hidden sun that rings black Cyprus with a lake of fire." More mundanely, they came from Damietta, Joppa, Tyre and Sidon to sell hides or buy barley or pomegranates.

The island's first Chamber of Commerce might have been more successful if members had cared to use it. Rather, they concentrated on evading subscriptions and combining, if at all, in jealousy against Nicosia. "Local chauvinism runs so deep that the leaders of Limassol or Larnaca would not hesitate to vote against the extension of Famagusta harbour which would benefit the whole island, because it might not directly benefit Larnaca and Limassol."

A new public library here had become very popular "owing to its warmth in winter," and the four thousand volumes in seven or eight langauges that it contained had been augmented by another 50 good books from Queen Mary's own library. Meanwhile, Lady Storrs had founded the St. Barnabas School for blind children, and also urged her husband to build a special clinic and nurses' home for Cyprus lepers.

Storrs did not forget his friends or old associates. As a former secretary to Lord Kitchener in Cairo, he counted it his privilege to place a marble commemoration plaque on the old, walled city house in Nicosia where he had once lived, he wrote.

Kitchener had arrived in Cyprus in 1878 as a young captain, just after the British takeover from Turkey, and had been director of Survey and the Registry Office here. "His real memorial, of course, is the map he made of Cyprus," wrote Storrs for which Kitchener had travelled the island for three years.

One resident of Cyprus at the time was Husain ibn Ali, the "King of the Arabs," the self-proclaimed caliph of Islam. He was the father of both Iraq's king and the Emir of Jordan and had been driven from his Hejaz kingdom and rescued by a British warship at Aqaba. He was then given sanctuary in Cyprus "where not a single soul knew him," says Storrs.

"I found him in a small villa, tended by his youngest son, Zaid, who had led regiments in the war, spent a year at Balliol College and was now waiting on his father day and night. About the only remaining joy of his life were his two or three beautiful Arab mares, including one particularly gentle and graceful called Zahra.

"She would step delicately up the marble stairs from the garden and walk without shyness into the Salamlik" (man's reception room; the woman's is called a haramlik). He would greet her with cries of "Ahlan," or "Ma sha Alah" or "Qurrat al-Ain" - "Cooling of the eyelids."

One morning, says Storrs, the ex-king appeared at Government House, flung himself into the Governor's arms and burst into tears. "A dastardly dismissed groom had ripped Zahra and her sisters in the night to discredit his successors and their master had found them dying in agony."

Storrs had been particularly fond of T.E. Lawrence, later known as Lawrence of Arabia, whom he had met in Cairo in 1914. "Until then I had never heard of him. He was a member of the Intelligence branch of the Egyptian defence force."

Lawrence, whom he described as of medium stature but strongly built, hated fixed times and seasons save for official purposes. "I would come upon him in my flat, reading always Greek or Latin. He preferred Homer to Dante and loved music."

He always left a list of any borrowed books behind and "gulped down all I could shed for him of Arabic knowledge. He was an indefatigable bazaar-walker and mosque visitor." During the period of revolt in the desert, Storrs accompanied him to Jeddah.

Lawrence could never have passed as an Arab with an Arab, according to the writer. He spoke Arabic "with horrible mispronunciation," although he greatly improved his accent finally. "For a time he called himself the Sharif Hasan, son of a Turkish mother in Constantinople." He had learned the customs and habits of the Hejaz Arabs, and by 1917 had put aside his RAF uniform for Arab garments.

Lawrence always stayed in Storrs' home in Jerusalem when passing through, but had the trick of "vanishing and reappearing noiselessly." He could be charming to Storrs' wife and sister who "did things," but disliked those who "dressed" and "knew people."

On one occasion in Cairo, an elderly Englishwoman, quite incapable of understanding his talk but anxious to be seen conversing with the uncrowned king of Arabia, moved toward him complaining of the intense heat, Storrs relates. "Just think, Colonel Lawrence, ninety-two, ninety-two!" she exclaimed "Many happy returns of the day," he had replied with a tortured smile.

"For Lawrence, there was only one thing in the world worth being — a creative artist. He had tried to do this and failed... I know I can write a good sentence, a good paragraph, even a good chapter," he had said. "But I cannot write a good book." There were many who disagreed with him.

"But since he could not be what he would," Storrs continued, "he would be nothing... the minimum existence, work without thought, when he left the RAF... .

"He was a loyal, unchanging and affectionate friend, and we often met unexpectedly back in England, in the street, on the bus, at a railway station. He would charge down from London on the iron steed from which he met his death to visit me in a nursing home, or run up 200 miles... to say good-bye before I returned to Cyprus."

Lawrence hated society but loved company. The simplicity of his life was extreme and he neither smoked nor drank. Some said that his military operations had been on a small scale — so had Thermopylae and Agincourt, Storrs wrote

Throughout the last months of his life back in England, Lawrence was oppressed by gloomy foreboding and spoke of an utterly blank wall after leaving his beloved RAF, said Storrs.

"Up until now I've never come to the end of anything. I can admit to being quite a bit afraid for myself, which is a new feeling," Lawrence had confided. "Days seem to dawn, suns to shine, evenings to follow, then to sleep. Have you ever seen a leaf fallen... that's the feeling." But the cottage (at Cloud's Hill) was "allright" for him.

"Every day, for the last three weeks of Lawrence's life, a

bird would flutter to his window, tapping incessantly with its beak upon the panc." If he moved to another window, the bird followed and tapped again. This strange insistence frayed his nerves, writes Storrs. "One morning, when he had gone out, his friend shot the bird. At the same hour, wrenching his (motorcycle's) handlebars for the last time, Lawrence was flung over 60 feet, head-first onto granite-hard tarmac."

Later, relates Storrs, "I stood beside him lying swathed in fleecy wool and stayed until the plain oak coffin was screwed down. The injuries were at the back of his head... his countenance was not marred.

"There was nothing else in the mortuary chamber but a little altar behind his head with some lilies of the valley and red roses. His face was the face of Dante, incredibly calm. He lay in his last littlest room, very grave and strong and noble... Lawrence of Arabia."

LIKE SOLOMON'S GLORY

Local youths in Nicosia who had learned a new jazz-age dance called the Black Bottom regarded the island's other towns as hopelessly provincial.

Meanwhile, they were showing "The Tiger's Teeth" at the only cinema in the capital in 1928. In the countryside the iron plow was still an innovation.

It was an island where men wore head shawls or straw hats with mushroom brims, voluminous "Turkish" trousers or vrakas, and heavy leather boots with the tops turned down and tied under the knees.

It was also the decade when Cyprus became a British Crown Colony after almost half a century under the Empire's administration and occupation; local political parties began to appear in profusion. Sir Ronald Storrs was governor and one of the few big business ventures was asbestos mining in the Troodos mountains. In antiquity, its produce had provided the sacks in which the bodies of Roman patricians were buried.

This was "unspoiled Cyprus" in the 1920's, one of the least sophisticated of Mediterranean lands, said "National Geographic" writer, Maynard Owen Williams, almost 70 years ago after a visit here. He had taken countless photographs, and 66 of them accompanied his lengthy article on Cyprus in the July, 1928 issue of the internationally known publication.

He had photographed the white goats which lived inside the walls of Famagusta and destroyed much of the foliage outside, the famed St. Nicholas cathedral (mistakenly called St. Sophia) with its broken buttresses and ruined belfries, Cypriot bazaars with piles of oranges and nutty bread, the biblical primitiveness of the landscape, the khans and pottery sheds, and the back-breaking toil of Cypriot village women.

He had visited the island in winter and early spring when "that barren ride from Larnaca to Nicosia through a chalky wilderness was enough to repel a very Romeo amongst travellers," he wrote. But semi-oriental Cyprus veils its charms, he had pointed out, modestly masking its spectacular beauty in remote mountain valleys and along northern shores where "no steamer stops except for carob beans for Spanish cavalry horses."

From a distance, Greek Cypriot men in their wide-brimmed hats and baggy trousers sometimes resembled little boys in wide rompers going to play on the beach, he thought. The Moslems wore kerchiefs with lace floral fringes round their red tarbooshes, pink or orange shirts, blue trousers and purple stockings. Nobody wore rags or doffed their hats to strangers.

He thought the most charming parts of the island were the neighbourly valleys "with their shrunken streams cutting the northern face of the Troodos mass."

He visited the "once rich and wicked Famagusta" where there had been a church or chapel for every day of the year. Now it was a graveyard of old churches, with ruins of small Byzantine chapels and "exploded" churches with pale frescoes on roofless walls. Nearby Salamis, now silent and empty, had been a Roman capital when Paul and Barnabas landed here, he says.

In the Kyrenia district village of Lapithos, one could buy 450 lemons for a shilling and many were rotting on the ground, a vast surplus too uneconomical to collect. (In Moscow, they were selling for three shillings each.)

Geographically, William writes, Cyprus "points its tail toward fateful Issos (now Turkey), where boyish Alexander routed the hosts of Asia (the Persians) ... you look across the strait from Turkey and you can count the serrations on the Kyrenia hills 40 miles away. If you stand on the heights of Lebanon in summer, that inky blot in the waning sunset is Cyprus."

He thought that Cyprus' women "do little to keep alive the Aphrodite tradition. One of their own sex says of them — they are rarely pretty or even good-looking, heavy of feature and clumsy of form ... their voices are harsh and shrill.

"But how could any woman be beautiful who works from sunrise till dark for a few piastres a day?"

At Rizokarpasso, "where the women walk in a queenly way, like the women of Syria carrying burdens on their head," he met a 12-year-old girl called Helene. Her job was to break rocks along with her mother on the Cape Andreas road. They made "big rocks into little rocks," day after day. The child's hands were horny with labour and her feet were encased in rude shoes. But people seemed more industrious there, with houses of stone instead of mud brick, and in general "they don't work their women so hard." The girls wore a shift of soft, straw-coloured silk with bits of clinking decoration. Over this they wore a skirt and low-cut jacket.

He was impressed with Buffavento, the remains of a castle on the Kyrenia mountain chain buffeted by strong winds, and he quoted a Dutch traveller to the site in 1683. "We climbed with our hands as well as our feet, and whichever way we turned our gaze, we saw only what made our hair stand on end, it was so magnificent."

In the Troodos mountains, writer Willliams had twice attempted to cross "that ridge" between Pedhoulas and Platres. "But Cyprus roads are run on the theory of a farmer with a hole in his roof. When it rains they can't be fixed, and when it's dry why fix them?" It seems there was no intention of keeping smaller routes in Cyprus open during the rainy season, he remarked.

From Kykko to Pedhoulas was three hours "cross lots" on foot and six hours by car, he related (today an easy half-hour). One travelled village roads by trial and error. There were no public telephones in the island, and the "excellent" telephone service was available in towns only. If landslides buried a bridge under rocks, they could be left there for months. At Kalopanayiotis, another mountain village, women washed their laundry in the streams by pressing it between their bare feet, he said. They also clubbed it with a paddle. The village of Platres was a favourite summer resort for Cypriots, Egyptians and Greeks from Egypt, and outside of limited tourism there were not many big industries.

A British company was mining asbestos "which is covering a whole facade of Troodos with slag dumps," he relates. An American company was mining copper at the coast, and there were a few silk workshops and cigarette factories at Paphos. Asbestos mining goes back almost as far as that of copper, he wrote, and its raw state "was like fire opal with fuzzy white threads in it."

Until the 12th century, vessels were still anchoring at nearby Amathus ... "in the Old World, one cannot walk through a thicket or along a beach without tangling his feet in legend or history". He mentions a bishop of Curium who "jumped to self-martyrdom and was later found with a crown on his head and a palm branch in his hand."

At one point, Williams visited a "vulgar cafe" at Limassol of the "cosmopolitan type" with caricatures plastered on the wall. A three-piece orchestra was playing and bootblacks wearing apache caps strolled in and out while dogs crossed and re-crossed the tiled floor. Three dancing girls did their best to keep the place awake, and beside their table sat four, hatted peasants, iron shod, who cast furtive, fearful glances toward the entertainers, he said.

At Ktima, in Paphos, the eternal triangle of seaside calamities — silt, mosquitoes and malaria — had driven the town up the hill to its present site.

At Lefkara, famed home of delicate lace and embroidery, "there must be a larger proportion of bad eyes and spectacles there than in any other town. Women and girls sit in bright sun in winter and in shadowy courtyards in summer straining their eyes over blindingly intricate work."

Cyprus is poor in general, he writes, and "were it not for its women it would be bankrupt. By skimping, they can earn enough to have one Sunday dress, worn for a few hours a week. The men resort to coffeehouses where they can sit and curse the government without disturbing the women at their work." Lefkara is prosperous, thanks to the women and their dogged eyesight, he says. "Unfortunately, one goes through purgatory to get there on a terrible road. If Lefkara man-power were applied as persistently as Lefkara women-power, that rough road would soon be a boulevard."

(Lefkara men, in general, did not permit their wives or daughters to work in the fields except at harvest time. Meanwhile, the men often spent years abroad as lace merchants.)

At Larnaca, he saw the tombs of young merchant adventurers who had built up the English Levant Company 20 years before its more famous offspring, the East India Company, was established. Each had been obliged to belong to the Church of England and cease work on Sundays. At some point, to amuse themselves or to relieve the monotony, the men were permitted to organise masquerades. This was stopped when they began going about at night masquerading as females, Williams writes.

The circular walls of Nicosia, with its eleven bastions, formed the hub of Cyprus. Streets were narrow, with overhanging balconies, but there was a modern flavour about the town. There were attractive suburbs growing up outside the crumbling walls, and the floor of the Armenian Church there was made of medieval tombstones "which kept alive the fashion of the day when knights were bold and ladies demure."

The cathedral of the Latin primate, St.Sophia, once mellow with hangings harmonising with vestments of its priests, was now a mosque, he says, its ghostly whiteness relieved by green and gold plaques and shaggy Anatolian rugs. During his visit, a blind man entered the mosque and from a familiar shelf took down a book, groped for his place and turned almost sightless eyes to the scripture he had come to read. A fountain played outside — "Cyprus is still unspoiled for those who savour life."

Back in the 1920's, when the skirts of Rizokarpasso women

were coloured "like Solomon's glory", the writer could only marvel at the island's capacity for survival after centuries of intruding cultures or occupations. And here were the ruins to illustrate it.

He cites the Levantine pirates who raided the northern villages, sometimes settling there, and the markets at Famagusta which had survived for centuries selling ripe olives and soft pads of sour cheese. The narrow mouths of their water pitchers were stoppered with a lemon. He photographed the khans or caravanseries which had little to offer in the way of comfort or convenience either for man or animal, he said, "yet a certain picturesqueness is inherent in the very dirt and disorder. Almost every town on the island has an old khan where the native can leave his donkey or other beasts while he goes out to shop and sell."

Some modern Cypriot pottery was almost as good in design as that made in Roman times, he says, with the commonest types being wine and olive jars holding up to 50 gallons, water pitchers, and cups for water wheels. Cypriot woven silks and cottons were famous from the Middle Ages, and were still highly prized in Europe. The homemade vegetable pigments had, as elsewhere, given way to imported aniline dyes.

Bakers carried their fresh-baked wares on long narrow planks, peddling the product straight from the oven.

His publication also carried photographs of 1920's Limassol, "a tawdry town today, devoted to its wine and carob trade. Mostly it is a modern settlement round an ancient fort. Yet history lurks in its shadows in the ghosts of the Lion Heart and his French princess, and of St. Louis of France, the crusading monarch, who stopped here on his way to the Holy Land."

Although camels, oxen and the occasional motorcar were evident in the island, "the Cypriot could not get along without his donkey. These patient little Cyprus beasts, famous as far away as India, patter back and forth between villages and towns, their sturdy backs laden with the master, his goods, or both. Sometimes they carry weights from 150 to 225 pounds."

And finally, "Aphrodite's isle, given by the lovesick Antony to Cleopatra, preached to by Paul and Barnabas, seized by the Lionhearted to avenge an insult and sold within a year... fled to by Crusader refugees... conquered by the Turks... now occupied by the British... awaits the visitor in its sheltered nook of the sparkling sea."

It was a refuge, he said, for those who turn from their own crusades to pause in a brief recessional.

THE ARMENIANS

They sat on old rugs and made a new life, so the poet said, the Armenians of the diaspora who settled in Cyprus early this century and slowly realised, with stunned regret, that they weren't going home again.

Cyprus had been a safe place to wait, they had thought, a quiet island under British rule only 40 miles across the Mediterranean from Ottoman Turkey, where their stricken nation lay in ruins.

Deported, dispossessed, hounded from village to village, thousands of survivors had scrambled onto whatever boats were available and were carried, often by chance, to the safe port of Larnaca. Some stayed, most moved on. For over two decades they had come to Cyprus in waves, some by choice sensing trouble ahead, most as despairing refugees.

A number had hopefully brought along their title deeds to property left behind back home – businesses, houses, fields. Others carried whatever gold jewellery they could save. Their lives as refugees or "kaghtaganner" would be brief, they thought. Surely when things "calmed down" in Turkey they would go back home, finally to be assured of safety in a country where their roots went back to ancient times.

Now, three generations later, the Armenians of the diaspora in Cyprus are still waiting, as are others from their nation scattered throughout the world. They still share a language, a church and a history — strong links continually reinforced for a people clinging to identity, the past, and memories of a homeland that time and deaths have changed.

They also share collective 20th century memories of long, forced marches across Anatolian borders into other people's deserts, when a half-million Armenians were shot or starved to death; then more horrific slaughter as the First World War ended.

Another wave was to arrive in Cyprus in the early 1920's,

fearful, hunted and deported. Half their nation in Turkey lay dead — almost 1½ million people in a genocide for which successive Turkish governments were never to take responsibility. (Somebody else did it, officials would say... excessive over -reaction during wartime... wanted a new Armenia in Turkey... Russian spies....)

Meanwhile, those who remained in Cyprus began to build a new life and named their infants in exile after ancient Armenian kings and great saints, or relatives they would never see again.

How was life in Cyprus for the Armenian diaspora, in Nicosia generally and in Victoria Street in particular, that borderline neighbourhood between Greeks and Turks? How did they adjust and survive? Who were the "deghatsi," the old "native" Armenian Cypriots who had come to the island long before them, some from early in the 19th century? And finally, what was the background of this decimated nation of strangers who came off the boat with few belongings, no homes, no jobs and speaking mostly Turkish?

As a nation, they had shared ancestral ties to a past in Eastern Anatolia going back 2,500 years, according to writer Christopher Walker, author of "Visions of Ararat", published recently, and which traced the nation's turbulent destiny down to recent times. An ancient people, he says, they were mentioned by Herodotus and Xenophon and in an inscription by the Persian king, Darius.

By 69 B.C. there was an Armenian empire covering much of eastern and central Anatolia and the Caucasus before it was subdued by Rome. By the early 4th century Christianity was officially adopted as the state religion, and within two centuries its church had already separated itself from the main branch of Orthodoxy following a lengthy dispute over the nature of Christ.

An Armenian alphabet had been invented, and from 886 to 1064 a brilliant medieval civilisation with a capital called Ani was to flourish in the Armenian highlands, he says. Its "magnificent" ruins still stand in eastern Turkey (Note: According to reports, UNESCO has recently declared Ani a protected monument.)

Its days were numbered, however, following a Byzantine

takeover in 1045 in keeping with that empire's policy of conquering rather than allying with border provinces. Weakened, subordinated, and unable to defend itself, Ani was overrun a half century later by Seljuk Turks after they had defeated the Byzantines at the battle of Manzikert in 1071. Within two decades the Seljuks had founded a sultanate and two-thirds of Asia Minor was in their hands.

A spiritual and national successor to Ani emerged soon after in 1080 A.D., the splended Armenian barony, later monarchy, of Cilicia, across from northern Cyprus.

After declaring independence from the Byzantines, it was to seek protection from the crusaders and in following centuries maintained close ties with the Lusignan dynasty of Cyprus. One of its monarchs was a special guest at the wedding in Limassol of crusader king, Richard the Lionheart to Berengaria of Navarre, and later fought alongside Richard at the siege of Acre, according to Walker. At one point, following intermarriages, a Lusignan was even offered the Armenian throne.

When visited by Marco Polo in the 13th century, the Cilician kingdom's thriving port at Ayas was still a gateway between Europe and Central Asia. (It is not known whether Marco Polo visited Cyprus, a short distance away.) But hostile forces were closing in on Cilicia and by 1375, with the crusading spirit already dissipating, the Armenian monarchy collapsed as Egyptian Mamluks overran the region. Its last king, Levon VI, died in Paris almost 20 years later after unsuccessful attempts to raise help in regaining his throne.

For centuries after, hundreds of thousands of Armenians continued to live in both the highlands and in lowland Cilicia despite successive nomadic encroachments and the eventual establishment of Ottoman rule. Only the "tragic events" during and after the 1914-1918 war ended the Armenian presence there, says Christopher.

There had been earlier pograms at the turn of the century,

recounted by writer-professor Susan Paul Patti in her recent book, "Faith in History, Armenians Rebuilding Community". Herself half-Armenian, writer Patti spent five years doing fieldwork and research into the memories and lives of Armenian diaspora communities in Cyprus and London. She is now an honorary research associate at University College, London, and a lecturer in Anthropology at the American International University, London. Her book was published by the Smithsonian Institute and is dedicated to her husband, Levon.

Despite promised reforms by Sultan Abdul Hamid, she writes, thousands of Armenians in Anatolia (central Asia Minor) were killed, then again in 1897. This was followed by the Adana massacres in 1909 when the nation "had become scapegoats for political unrest and other problems."

The first wave of refugees from Diyarbakir, Aintab and Kilis had found other compatriots already in Cyprus who had arrived earlier not as victims but as settlers or interpreters. They had been invited to Cyprus by the new administration here shortly after the British takeover and had been received "like angels" by officials who were desperate to communicate with Turkish authorities in their own language.

Others had arrived long before, such as the Eramian family who settled here in the early 19th century, one of the first "deghatsi" or "native" Armenian Cypriots.

One of the Eramian sons married Catherine Luigi Carletti, from a Latin Cypriot family, says author Patti, and seven of their children married Armenian spouses from Constantinople or Cilicia in arranged marriages. Others followed either to seek work or avoid Turkish army conscription. One newcomer who bought a farm and mansion north of Nicosia asked for one of the Eramian daughters in marriage, and in turn one of their sons married a "beautiful girl brought from Bursa ...in a legendary wedding." It was a "fantastic spectacle" with Persian carpets laid out all along Victoria Street in Nicosia for the arrival of bride and groom, Patti relates.

At the time, Cyprus was still part of the Ottoman empire and the customs and language of new arrivals remained Turkish. Men still wore a fez and Armenian women a veil. (The Armenian language was proscribed in Ottoman Turkey, though not in Cyprus.)

As the community grew, and nationalist feelings increased toward the end of the century, local priests attempted to introduce the Armenian language into the community, which by now lived in the main towns, around the Armenian monastery in the Kyrenia mountains, and on large farms near the capital.

One landowner south of Nicosia owned a 600-donum farm where crops and livestock were raised, and partridge, quail and hare were hunted, Patti records. About 40 villagers were employed, some Turks but mostly Greeks. There were other vast farms in the Lakatamia area also, including one owned by the Yeremian family where silkworms were raised.

But what about the newcomers, the "kaghtaganner" or refugees? They survived, and as a nation. But how was it achieved? What was their reaction when driven from one country, then settling into an unknown other, with no knowledge of customs or language, no homes, no jobs and with pograms still fresh in their minds?

These were amongst questions asked over an over by researcher Patti in Cyprus. Here are some of her findings:

The early years were taken up with finding or creating jobs. Some had brought along gold jewellery or other valuables and sold them as needed. Many Armenian men, specialised craftsmen or tradesmen in the old country, eventually set up workshops in Cyprus.

They began to prosper and train others as apprentices. One set up an ice factory with a secondhand ice machine, others used their shoemaking skills — "in the early years the Cypriots were all wearing those heavy black boots, or else imported shoes if they could afford it... the Armenians came and were able to make shoes cheaper and faster," one told Patti.

There were also copper and tinsmiths, potters, bakers, carpenters, jewellers, mechanics, soap makers and leatherworkers, all skills from the homeland. Some found too much local competition, others had no skills at all.

Farming meant an expensive outlay and "too permanent for those who hoped to return." Many men began with a simple retail business, buying in quantity and then loading the goods on their backs. They were sold not only in Nicosia or Larnaca but in the villages, and wives and daughters helped in these businesses. Some women crocheted or crafted other items that were sold with their husband's goods, she goes on. Others took in laundry, cleaned houses or worked as cooks.

Few of the newcomers spoke English, so civil service jobs were not available. A number of families worked at the asbestos mines at Amiandos, travelling there on big carts pulled by mules, Patti learned. "The work was heavy and difficult, the village cold in winter and far from the Armenian communities in Nicosia and Larnaca. But the income helped the family to get started in a new country."

Some newcomers had balked at landing when they saw the minarets at Larnaca from their boats. "What's this," one had said, and refused to land where there were minarets and Turks. "It's okay," he was told, "these Turks are friendly, and there aren't many of them." The newcomer landed - he was 18 years old and went to Amiandos.

Most settled in Nicosia, Patti found, with some going directly to the courtyard of their church where they remained until able to rent quarters. Four or five families often stayed in one house, nearly all in the Turkish quarter. Rent was cheaper there, some old "deghatsi" families were nearby, language and customs of the neighbourhood were familiar, and both church and school were nearby, Patti writes. Moreover, Cypriot Turks had clearly not been involved in massacres or deportations, and people "remembered the Turkish friends they had left behind."

As refugee houses were crowded "quilts or bedrolls were rolled up each morning, stacked and covered; many homes had no electricity or water." One description: Entering from the street there was a large main hall with a white stone floor. It was owned by a Turkish hodja (cleric). Water came from a well outside. Upstairs were four bedrooms and an enclosed veranda. There was one married sister and her family in one room, her father and younger brother in another, four sisters in another, and the oldest brother in a tiny, private room. There were mandarin trees and jasmine in the courtyard.

Most houses were occupied by an extended family — three generations, aunts and uncles, sometimes a cousin. Victoria Street was the centre, with church, club and school, the Paphos Gate in one direction, the old city centre in another, and the community's new shops and workshops nearby.

Probably none were aware that 15 centuries before, another group of Armenians had also arrived in Cyprus against their will to become guards and smallholders here. They had been uprooted from their homeland by the Byzantine emperor Justinian II — 3,350 people, according to Cypriot historian Costas Kyrris. Another emperor, Maurice, brought over 10,000 more settlers and farmers, according to the Chronicles of Agrius Scholasticus. Many were noblemen-soldiers, re-settled by the Byzantines as "trouble-makers" from home.

Apparently there were Armenians in Cyprus through the centuries, including those brought in to help face Arab attacks -most were eventually absorbed into the main culture, Kyrris thinks.

In their attempts to survive as a nation, this is a possibility that current Armenian institutions such as church, schools and many families in the diaspora in general are anxious to avoid.

They are already confronted by many complex issues, such as different levels of identity, the natural instinct to "blend in", the changes continually surrounding them, and the desire of the youth to move forward into the future. Coming from various regions in the old country, there is also the question of where exactly is the homeland specifically, and does the new Republic of Armenia that emerged from its Soviet predecessor qualify as such?

For those who live there, Patti said, and increasingly for many diaspora Armenians, it IS the homeland — Hayastan.

Cyprus, she pointed out, is not considered a homeland as such, but has become a well-loved home to its Armenian community. (Both Cyprus and the Armenians are still struggling with the consequences of rule by foreign empires and peoples, Patti added.) Meanwhile, for the Armenians, the cement of their diaspora here has been the family and the close network of relations it has created.

Other significant links are Armenian history in general, the church, local elementary and secondary schools, and clubs and associations. At the core is the general feeling that the loss of so many must never be forgotten and that those who survived must try to fill the space that they left.

Does the church in the diaspora still maintain its strength as a unifying force, even in the face of other distractions or social changes? The former Vicar-General of the Armenian Church here, the Rev. Yeghishe Manjikian, certainly thinks so. "It is a main link, There are clubs and organisations and political parties," he said, "but the church takes all under its umbrella." After 14 years in Cyprus, the Rev. Manjikian has been posted to Vancouver.

The church is a main authority in the diaspora, he said, and all Armenian schools are under its control and administration through a special committee. There is a trend to "revive" and stress the question of Armenian identity, he went on, to maintain it and keep it alive even more. He thought that the younger generation are responding well. He also thought it was not the role of the church to meddle in the "business of politics," but that social and moral questions were well within its sphere.

Asked about the survival of "Armenian -ness" and the question of mixed marriages, the Vicar General said that the church had always been against the latter on principle, but we are "now living in societies of openness. There are changes and one cannot oppose life."

It was preferable to marry within the community of course, but "we are almost in the 21st century and cannot be so conservative" should other situations arise. However, it was "good to keep the tradition" when possible — "the barley of our village is better than the wheat from another, is it not?"

Most families speak Armenian at home, and most Armenians in the island are multi-lingual, speaking also Greek and English. Nicosia children attend the Nareg Elementary school on the church grounds and later either the Melkonian Institute, the English School in some cases, and sometimes Greek schools.

He estimated the Armenian community in Cyprus at about 3,000, and thought that reports of "not many Armenians being left" were much exaggerated. "The young people are facing the same job opportunities or lack of them as those in the Greek community, and there is certainly not the crisis that is sometimes painted. Many young people also work in their parent's business."

Armenians in general felt "very much at home in Cyprus," said Bedros Kaladjian, his community's representative in Parliament. "We have equal rights and a number of benefits — we couldn't ask for a better situation." There are churches and elementary school in all three towns, Nicosia, Limassol and Larnaca, which are administered by Armenian school boards. All expenses of staff and school are paid by government.

Although his community felt very "Cypriot," their own identity as Armenians was "very strong," he said, and they were fluent Armenian speakers. "We are an ethnic group but Cypriot and bi-lingual."

Do Armenians feel safe in Cyprus? On that question they felt "no different from the Greek Cypriots," very much at home and yes, safe.

There had been only a handful of families whose grandchildren were born here, and he estimated the island's current Armenian population at about 2,000, not including those with temporary work permits. There had been about 7,000 Armenians here in the early 1950's but many left after the EOKA rebellion against Britain. Some went to Soviet Armenia, a number later returned; others settled in Britain.

In a single decade, scores of Cypriot Armenians lost their homes or businesses, once during upheavals and intercommunal clashes in 1963, and again during the 1974 Turkish invasion. They also lost the old Armenian quarter round Nicosia's Victoria street, with its familiar narrow streets, its school, church and social centres — home to many Cypriot Armenians since the turn of the century.

Gone, too, were the brick and sandstone houses and the boys choirs which sang until their voices broke, and the old Armenian hotel where every year the British governor and his entourage danced the quadrille in formal dress and white gloves. A whole way of life was, once again, left behind.

"Moving, changing places, starting over — this is the real Armenian story," researcher Patti quotes one businesswoman as saying.

WHOSE SEA?

It was the smallest, scruffiest and most antiquated passenger ship that he had ever seen, but the steamer carrying the writer from Beirut to Famagusta in pre-war 1938 offered its five customers succulent food and good Greek wine thrown in.

And although the coat hooks sprang away from the panelling and cabin door handles suddenly detached themselves into one's hands, the captain was kind and there was reassurance, somehow, in the Glasgow name-plate on the steamer's obsolete, single-cylinder engine.

Its manufacture date had been scoured off, however.

As the little Greek vessel pounded heroically through rough seas, rumours spread of 200-kilometre gales blowing up ahead. Enroute, the steamer had stopped briefly off Tripoli, Lebanon, to pick up two English dancers, the "Chic Sisters", from a tiny boarding launch that had suddenly appeared in heaving seas "from out of the murk and spray." They were accompanied by an Iraqi admirer from Baghdad, a marrying man who said he had honourable intentions but was finally persuaded to stay behind as he lacked a proper entry visa into Cyprus.

"The last I saw of him was a natty figure briefly waving a scarf as it was carried away into the raging night,"says British author, George Martelli. One of the "Chic sisters" had wept quietly.

Martelli describes the voyage and his brief visit to Cyprus in a book called "Whose Sea?" published the year of his journey by Chatto and Windus as World War II loomed and nobody was quite certain which way Italy would jump.

The scope of Martelli's Mediterranean journey, in fact, had been to determine who had more moral and propaganda muscle in the Middle East — Britain or Italy — and had followed a lunch-time altercation at the Cafe Royal between himself and an Italian diplomat. The latter was "a nice, but unhappy-looking man," who presented a gloomy picture of Anglo-Italian relations and dared his lunch partner to face facts.

"Listen, my dear fellow," the diplomat had told him, "why don't you go and see for yourself?" Shortly after, the author did so, paying assessment visits to France, Tunis, Libya, Syria, Egypt, Malta, Palestine, Jordan and finally Cyprus.

Another aim of the journey, he added, was to "bring nearer to my compatriots sitting at home a number of countries likely to figure increasingly in newspapers, and the certain problems with which they are doomed in any case to be inflicted." Although the world's attention would still be centred on Czechoslovakia when his volume was published, he thought, it was a "mistake to suppose that the problems of Central Europe would be separated from those of the Mediterranean."

The journey had not always been an easy one. The author had travelled the 450 miles from Tunis to Tripoli, Libya, in a taxi which he shared with several suitcases, baskets of chickens, the driver, a bad-tempered Italian, and a cheerful Sicilian in a cloth hat with no visible luggage. With them also was an old woman who covered her head in a black knitted shawl, the author relates, and only once left her seat during the 16-hour journey and then because she was forced to by the customs official.

Reaching Cyprus was not a simple matter either. No British liners called at the Crown colony, an Italian mail vessel came weekly only and the Egyptian service operated once a fortnight. Passengers on the little Greek steamer were apprehensive, reports Martelli, and that included a Frenchman who confessed to being "tres nerveux pour la mer," as the ship pounded along for several hours, shuddering violently.

A Greek passenger, also visibly frightened, kept his eyes on the barometer. Which was the "bon" and which was the "mauvais" side, he kept asking. But the weather couldn't have been too bad, the author goes on, because he slept undisturbed. The "Chic Sisters" did not appear for meals.

By the time they sighted the "brown shores of Cyprus" only a few miles away, the sea was glassily smooth, the sky cloudless and the sun shone down on the "sleepy little place" called Famagusta. At one time one of the richest ports in the Mediterranean, there was now only a primitive breakwater, a few warehouses, and a customs shed. It was the only port suitable for large ships, and a British cruiser was at anchor outside. Mr Eden had just resigned.

After a hot bath at the town's Othello Hotel where "you simply light a bundle of sticks under a funnel-shaped boiler and there in a few minutes is your bath," he visited the Chief Collector of Customs, one George Wilson, O.B.E., where he learned that the most important current event in Cyprus was the visit of the Princess Royal and Lord Harewood.

"It was the first occasion on which a member of the Royal Family had been seen by the Cypriots in the flesh since Richard II conquered the island...." It had aroused more enthusiasm than any other occurrence during the British occupation, Martelli learned. The Customs Collector also thought that "our mistake at home is to take Mussolini seriously. Nobody else in Europe is afraid of Italy."

Was there to be a naval and air base at Cyprus? the author asked. The admiralty had carried out several inspections, but nothing had come of it yet. "I suppose if we start doing things at Cyprus, Mussolini will fortify another island," was the reply.

Did the Cypriots still want union with Greece? Public opinion was difficult to gauge, as the Government didn't allow political meetings and the press was censored.

The only traces of Famagusta's former greatness, Martelli goes on, were a few ruins, mostly roofless, including a palace of the Lusignans now used as a tennis court. There were moderately well-preserved battlements but only three out of 100 churches had survived the centuries. The most famous, St. Nicholas, was being used as a mosque and every ornament had been removed.

It had been thoroughly whitewashed inside.

What foreign vandals had left standing, the surviving inhabitants had pulled down to build cottages or sell to foreign contractors, he wrote. Some of the finest medieval buildings had provided stone for the Suez Canal, he had been told. Culprits had also included destructive Turks and the first British troops arriving in Cyprus who had used the refectory of Bellapais for target practice. The British authorities were now attempting to unearth and preserve what remained of the past.

But great damage had already been done and Cyprus, "on which the art of the greatest ages was lavished, though it may long be a happy hunting-ground for excavators, will never more than suggest that it ever had a history," remarks Martelli.

This was not the fault of a Mr. Moghabgab, Famagusta's director of Antiquities, who was determined, he says, to literally leave no stone unturned to bring to light its former glories. "There is so much, so much, if we could only get at it," he had told the author. "It is only in the last few years that we have begun to dig here seriously...." Excavations were hampered by the shortage of convict labour to help in the digging, he went on — "unhappily the Cypriots are becoming more and more law - abiding."

In Nicosia, the author later points out, there was a wholly admirable museum where "genuine objects dating from the pre-Christian era could be obtained at reasonable prices."

Enroute to the coastal village of Kyrenia, the country was flat and treeless, though fertile, he reports. Although there were various irrigation schemes, no two engineers could agree which was the most practical and least expensive. The best "irrigator" the island ever had, he learned, was a sapper major called "Kitchener," once stationed briefly in Cyprus and an infallible water diviner. (Note: There have been reports since the Byzantine era of water problems in Cyprus, and during a later period one drought lasted 40 years, according to historians.)

Kyrenia had grown up under the shadow of its medieval castle; there was a little harbour with some ancient store-houses, and one or two fishing boats. There was also a District Commissioner and a couple of hotels. The village was used by visitors as a base for visiting St. Hilarion and Bellapais, the two "show ruins" of the island.

Martelli stayed at the Coeur-de-Lion, a modest little hotel managed by a Greek. As anywhere else, he adds, it's a good rule, if possible, to avoid hotels under English managements. He did not say why.

The hotel appeared completely empty at any hour of the day except meal-times, he wrote, when a "mysterious transformation" took place at lunch and dinner.

"First, one English woman would appear with her reticule, knitting and library book; then another. In a few minutes every table had its solitary lady. Coffee served, there was a brief concentration in the drawing-room; then one by one the figures dissolved, leaving no trace but a forgotten ball of wool, no memory but the level of the wine in the bottles which was not quite so high as before.

"What did they do between meals, those solitary single ladies? I never met them walking abroad; they were never seen in the corridors; no sound came from their rooms... it was a ghostly, creepy business."

He could not have borne it, he says, "but for the cheerful company of Admiral and Mrs. Bruin." The admiral was the leanest man he had ever seen and after a 10-mile walk every afternoon would come striding home for tea, his handkerchief tied in a bundle on the end of his stick, full of wild flowers to show Mrs. Bruin.

In 1938, Nicosia was a market town with sleepy narrow streets, plain two-story houses and a cathedral now a mosque with two minarets in place of its former towers. Martelli also learned that its name, St. Sophia, was not that of a saint, but rather meant

"Holy Wisdom." The town was also the capital and government offices were situated in a pleasant stone block. There was a native quarter, he continued, where various crafts were carried on, the coppersmith's seemingly the busiest. There were also a few inferior shops, the majority being photographers', a club, two roller skating rinks which the author patronised regularly, he said, and a charming miniature 18th century theatre now a cinema.

What did the troops do? Apart from a few cafes, there was a little tea shop with a sign saying "Welcome to the Wolseley Boys", put up in honour of Britain's first High Commissioner in 1878.

Despite considerable improvements under British administration, the island still gave the impression of a poor country, Martelli writes. Cyprus had been called the "Cinderella of the Colonies", but in the end the real Cinderella had come into her own, he pointed out.

He thought that its only real value to Britain was as a strategic base, the original purpose for which it was taken over. "Cyprus is not a country where surplus population could settle, nor does it supply any scarce raw materials." Possibly its only permanent source of prosperity would be construction of a naval dockyard, seaplane base and aerodrome, he thought, with the eventual stationing of units here. Although it offered everything to the tourist in scenery, climate and history, Cyprus did not possess a single first or second class hotel.

"Imperialism should have some justification," Martelli continued, "either to confer benefits on subject people or bring some advantage to the empire." In Cyprus there have been some limited benefits, but "as for our own advantage, it is difficult to see where it lies."

There were two reasons why the island was made a colony, he goes on — the fulfillment of Disraeli's dream, "a man dazzled by his first contact with the classical world" — and finally, by outfoxing the Russians, he had secured Britain's right to occupy and administer the island in return for protecting the Sultan's possessions from Russia.

Although not all the subjects where well-disposed, the majority seemed resigned or indifferent to British rule, says Martelli. In fact he had been surprised that the Cypriots were as amenable to the British government as they were. Their attitude was best illlustrated by a story told him by the District Commissioner of Nicosia, he said.

While visiting some outlying village, the Commissioner had asked if there were any complaints. "Yes," was the answer, "the water tap leaks and we want to belong to Greece."

AYIA NAPA

A century ago there were only 50 houses in the forgotten little seaside village of Ayia Napa. A century before that, the local fishermen were still going out in tiny boats made of "a few sticks bound together" and with a makeshift hollow of twigs in which to sit while paddling.

There were long stretches of empty land and scarred pockets where ancient quarries had sometimes split down through the soft rock into the Roman burial chambers below. (At some point there had been a brisk trade in Eastern Mediterranean clay coffins, probably made in what is now Anatolia).

Above it all, facing the sea where one of the greatest sea battles of Cyprus history had once been fought, were the scattered remains of pre-Christian sancturies to Aphrodite.

This was Ayia Napa and the region round it, victim of time and gentle obscurity where looters over many lifetimes took away what the sandstorms had not buried forever.

Once a region where important strongholds and at least one major town had flourished in Hellenistic and later Pax Romana times — probably there were settlements far earlier, archaeologists believe — the area was finally abandoned after lightning Arab raids against Byzantium and the island in the 7th century A.D.

For the next 600 years, only shepherds roamed the deserted shores; it took the ruling Lusignans, a Catholic dynasty, to nudge the region back to life again. Charmed by the sea and surrounding woodlands, they built a monastery and church at Ayia Napa. New settlers and suppliers moved in and stayed, forming the nucleus of an agricultural community with fertile land and dependable water supplies. One spring was called the "Mother of Waters".

Ayia Napa is not a saint's name, neither Catholic nor Orthodox. Rather it means "Holy Forest", named for the nearby woodland in which a miracle-working icon of the Virgin was found and placed in the church.

(Some villagers say that "Ayia Napa" is an anagram for "Panayia" or "Holy Virgin", and that the name was used by Greek Cypriot villagers during the Ottoman period to confuse the Turks.)

The monastery was rebuilt by the Venetians in the 16th century and finally turned over to the Greek Cypriots by the Ottomans when most Latin churches and monasteries were confiscated here. Eventually the region again slipped into oblivion, with its basic characteristics still little changed since Strabo described it in 23 A.D. — "then to a promontory, Pedalium (today's Cape Greco south of Famagusta), above which lies a hill that is rugged, high, trapezium-shaped and sacred to Aphrodite."

After the island's independence in 1960, even the tourist rush to Famagusta up the coast, one of the most important archaeological areas in the island, failed to provoke more than a limited runoff of visitors to the Ayia Napa region and its charming little harbour and coves.

Until, that is, a stunning tourist boom followed the fall of most of the Famagusta district and Kyrenia to Turkish invaders in 1974; Ayia Napa's fragile infrastructure trembled as it took up the touristic slack within the decade. Visiting ladies sunned topless amongst bewildering chains of new hotels along the seashore, and village boys strutted and posed or went to work in tourist-related businesses with the rest of the family.

As more discos and restaurants opened and the rock bands played on, it became the preferred destination of almost 40 percent of the island's visitors.

Napa was cool.

It was also lucrative for the locals, those descendents of fishermen and farmers amazed by the unexpected popularity of their little village on the seaside.

Its swift and relentless growth was also very damaging for nearby ancient monuments and archaeological sites as hotels and other buildings encroached. Considered a "burden to development" at the time, the sites were being destroyed, run over, buried under new roads, dug up, looted or neglected. As new buildings emerged to accommodate the inflow, alarmed archaeologists stepped up their warnings of the cultural damage being wreaked.

One of the most concerned was an archaeologist called Sophocles Hadjisavvas (then curator of Ancient Monuments with the Department of Antiquities and now the Department's director). He was already well-acquainted with the region from previous work there.

His book, "Ayia Napa, Excavations at Makronisos and the Archaeology of the Region", has recently been published jointly by the Antiquities Department and the Ayia Napa Municipality which, along with its mayor, view ancient monuments as assets to tourism rather than liabilities, he says.

In it, Hadjisavva describes his long and intimate connection with the area during past surveys and digs, his strong belief in its archaeological potential, and goes on to record the results of his own painstaking work at Makronisos eight years ago. (The name means "Long Island", but it is actually a promontory where numerous ancient tombs and a makeshift sanctuary have been found until now.)

Hadjisavvas, leading a small team, has already excavated 19 Hellenistic-Roman tombs (325 B.C. to 330 A.D.) in the promontory cemetery which had "presented a sad picture" when first surveyed, and whose entrances had filled up with trash after the looters had left.

Many of the chamber tombs had been so looted out during previous centuries (and as late as 1974), that bone fragments and portions of smashed jawbones had been hurled to the floor with pottery slivers amidst piles of earth. (Later tests indicated that the ancients had tooth cavities, or caries, just like the rest of us.)

A decade before Ayia Napa was catapulted onto the tourist

map, Hadjisavvas had been part of a small team sent to the Famagusta region by the Antiquities Department with UNESCO support to survey a wide sweep of the entire district. Earmarked was the eastern part of Cyprus from Akanthou to Komi Kebir and from Ormidia to the Ayia Napa region itself; also the Famagusta area including Salamis, Enkomi and Ayios Barnabas. Their brief was to study ways to best protect antiquities there and to seek out new sites not investigated in the past.

The damage done to Famagusta and surroundings was obvious, with its frenzied construction of hotels for more than 70 percent of incoming tourists who had chosen Kyrenia or Famagusta for their holiday after Cyprus' independence in 1960, ..."all of this activity threatened a region (Famagusta) considered the richest in archaeological remains."

In less than a year, Hadjisavvas and another staffer, Andreas Kattos, an Antiquities department surveyer, had covered a phenomenal 240 sq. km. and their range also extended to 14 other significant sites to the south round Ayia Napa. (A full account of that project was published by Hadjisavvas in 1991).

But the Turkish invasion, in 1974, he writes, "put a violent end" to the ambitious scheme, and in the meantime the small archaeological team had been trapped at Ayia Napa monastery during a junta-led coup staged by mainland Greece the week before.

(The region was no stranger to upheaval. According to Cesnola, whom Hadjisavvas describes as a 19th century "scholarly looter" in Cyprus, a famous naval battle was fought in antiquity near Ayia Napa between Ptolemy and Demetrius Polioretes. The battle had been named after a neighbouring harbour town, long since gone, called Leucolla.

Yet another source mentioned by Hadjisavvas points out that some of the first Ottoman ships to invade and occupy Cyprus in the mid-16th century had landed near Ayia Napa.)

Apparently there's also much more archaeologically in the

region than meets the layman's eye. For example, what lies under the Roman site of Tornos, identified as ancient Throni and placed by geographer Ptolemaios in 140 A.D. as being somewhere between Capes Pyla and Greco? This means only 6 km. from Ayia Napa.

A victim of treasure hunters and looters, traces of this once flourishing city lay scattered over a large area, some in cultivated fields. When surveyed there was also rubble from ruined walls and the remains of an ancient lime kiln.

Then there is the "Mother of Waters", the springs which originally supplied Ayia Napa monastery in Venetian times and brought by aqueduct from source 2 km. away. Built of dressed stones, it was plastered thoughout and its joints closed to keep the water clean. Some of the springs were covered by barrel-shaped vaults; these were destroyed by road construction only a few decades ago, Hadjisavvas says.

There is also the Ayia Thekla site with its remains of what might have been an early Christian basilica, and Ayia Barbara, a medieval domain with its own chapel. Other settlement sites include Ampas (Hellenistic and Roman), and yet another only 200 metres from the monastery. Rich in underground water, its old wells are still in use.

The most important settlement, perhaps, is the Roman town of Palio Chorko, still unexcavated. And what of the pierced monolith at Ayia Mavri, where one visitor last century was told that village girls came here to break their glass jewellery either after marriage or a betrayal.

Under some threat for a period was the Makronisos promontory and its ancient cemetery, close enough to crowded Ayia Napa beaches and hotels for visitors to wander about and perhaps damage the site. But a fast rescue operation was mounted by the Department at the behest and with the financial support of village authorities anxious to protect the site in the name of cultural tourism.

Over the past 10 years, Hadjisavvas goes on, the local Improvement Board, now a Municipality, has spent a hefty sum on antiquities' conservation, including the Venetian convent and aqueduct there.

He also cited its current woman mayor for her "unfailing support and backing," along with the rest of the council. Their interest has paid off and the sites, including the ancient chamber tombs, are now a popular tourist draw.

Hadjisavvas described the tombs, noting that every one of the 19 rock-cut chambers so far excavated had been mercilessly looted, with some fragments of the clay coffins thrown into other tombs after looters cleared the chambers. All of the tombs had been hewn out of creamy white or yellow calcarenite bedrock at random, he goes on, and are reached by a descending flight of stairs leading to an underground chamber.

These are equipped with benches or niches on which the dead in their clay sarcophagi were placed (apparently only the rich could afford the carved stone variety). The general outline of the chamber tombs resembled a cross, and ceilings were high enough to stand under. Stone slabs blocked the entrances, and great quantities of sand had choked the tombs themselves. The chambers had been re-used for at least three centuries, perhaps more, and the dead seemed to range in age from infants to adults in their 30's.

Some of the finds were unusually poignant, such as a limestone pine cone, a terracotta casserole with lid, and one gold earring. Others included clay lamps, fragments of bowls and amphorae, juglets, and many samples of cream Hellenistic ware, most shattered by time and looters.

At the peninsula's highest point, Hadjisavva and his group found a low, sacred enclosure thought to be Hellenistic but possibly much older. Red paint was still visible on the hair of one find — the head and upper torso of a draped female in limestone possibly dating to 500 B.C. She wore disc earrings and the hair over her forehead and down her back was done in a ridged, "piecrust" style. The skull was flat, the eyes large and the ears big.

Another recovery, the remnant of a face made originally from a mould , retains the fingerprints of the maker, with press marks where more clay had been added to form a nose. Many other terracotta body fragments were found, some of seated humans. There are no plans for more excavations in the immediate future.

In the meantime, what happens to late 20th century family life in a small town so inundated with visitors in the high season that a thoughtful onlooker wonders whose is the sub-culture as the whooping and hollering goes on.

Nothing very serious, it seems. According to Ayia Napa mayor, Barbara Pericleos, the winter off-scason, which seems to attract a more pensive type of tourist, is a time local families can "get together again". Family life is still close, she says, despite the hectic pace of tourism and its inevitable impact on local customs and ideas.

One custom has certainly changed. Young girls no longer smash their glass beads at the local monolith.

CYPRUS — A COLONY UNKNOWN

Except for those who didn't know where it was anyway, almost everyone agreed that Cyprus for its size was one of the richest countries in the world historically and archaeologically.

It could also be difficult to reach, judging by the hair-raising account of an early 20th century visitor whose journey to Larnaca on an 800-ton steamer from Port Said in 1906 "turned out to be a perfect nightmare." It was the first, marred impression of the Eastern Mediterranean for writer Basil Stewart, whose later account of island life was to include drought, dress, disease, religion, burial customs, heat, an extraordinary daily mirage off Cape Pyla, swamps and the British administration. He also took photographs, 50 of which are included in his book, "My Experiences of Cyprus", published by George Routledge and Sons in 1908.

But first he wrote about the 56-hour sea voyage that brought him from Egypt, when the S.S. "Fortuna" heaved and rolled its way toward the Cyprus coast in the teeth of a howling gale, a "typical Levanter", as terrified passengers crouched on deck, the crew kept fouling the anchor, and swarms of wildlife infested the bunks... "and we didn't know whether we would 'turtle' or not."

Next morning, Troodos was sighted straight ahead, "but we ought not to have seen it at all," so far had the ship been blown off course.

Finally, when the passengers were off-loaded onto a rescue barque along the shoreline six miles beyond Larnaca Bay, a crew member accidentally knocked over one of the shrieking lady passengers as all scrambled for dry land and safety. Fortunately, she was saved by an alert native who raced to her rescue just before the boat turned over, says Stewart.

(We are also told of great droughts that periodically plagued

Cyprus, including the one which lasted 15 years and almost depopulated the island entirely in the 3rd Century, A.D.)

"Even after 30 years under the aegis of the Union jack, the flag of the most successful colonizing country in the world," Stewart remarks, "Cyprus is still one of the poorest and most neglected countries in the world," although efforts had lately been made to redress this. Further, although Beaconsfield (Disraeli) "endowed it with a glitter it did not possess, and the public applauded it as one of his greatest acts — the nine-day wonder — it soon relapsed into the darkness of oblivion to which it has always been plunged from the 16th century to the present."

Cyprus was much better known to the ancient Greeks than it is to the British public, he pointed out. "Otherwise educated people ask me if Cyprus is not in the West Indies." He also thought "it is difficult to say why we ever went to Cyprus, though of course... must allow for the fact that in 1878 we were not in military occupation of Egypt."

To illustrate Cyprus' obscurity and to show just how "misunderstood the island is even amongst the highest in the land," he relates the following.

On the occasion of Queen Victoria's Jubilee in 1897, a contingent of native (Cypriot) police were sent to London to take part in the ceremonies, together with various police and military contingents from the other colonies and dependencies. They were being reviewed in the Agricultural Hall, Islington, by the late Duke of Cambridge, the story goes on.

"When he came to the contingent from Cyprus, which was introduced by Lord Wolseley, the first High Commissioner of the island, the Duke exclaimed, "You don't mean to tell me these people are white!"

(Note: Although the Duke of Cambridge was the Queen's cousin and therefore respected as royalty, he and Wolseley were not the best of friends. In fact, Wolseley in his memoirs declared him a "blab", one reason why the Duke was one of the last to learn of Britain's intended occupation of Cyprus in 1878.)

As he toured the island, Stewart concluded that "although Cyprus was a battlefield on which many nations had fought and left their impress, with each new conqueror obliterating the works of the vanquished... and earthquakes, change, reconstruction... the native has been the one thing which has remained the same."

He was particularly impressed by Famagusta which, at the height of its prosperity centuries ago, had 365 churches within the town, one for each day of the week, it was said. But by 1910 only 30 remained, some being small chapels. Further, it was probably not generally known, he went on, that Alexandria is practically old Famagusta rebuilt in Egypt.

Famagusta was the quarry which supplied Alexandria with the stones of convenient shape and size, ready for building into place, he writes. "The breakwater which protects Alexandria harbour was largely built in this way. Even today (1906) Famagusta natives can be seen digging everywhere, as if for gold, unearthing foundations of its ancient churches for export at one piastre each." Stones above ground were untouched, he tells us, but it was astonishing what enormous quantities were below the surface. "What a history these stones could tell."

They were first quarried to build Salamis' palaces and temples, Stewart writes, then razed by nature and by attacking enemies, then used to build Famagusta's fortifications, churches and palaces; finally they were sent to Alexandria. He thought that the Cypriots had been good masons, with well-built churches, decorated and with carvings on the capitals of the pillars. The doors and round windows were also well made, and "inform us of curious beasts and gargoyles."

Regarding the local population, he found that "like all orientals," the people like to bargain — the owner names a price and knowing it is too much, expects a bargain. Local or "native" food, he goes on, consisted chiefly of olives, beans, onions, bread, cheese and vegetables.

"They are probably too poor to afford beef and mutton, cheap as the latter is, and of excellent quality." Lamb was delicious but beef scarce and tough — "probably old bullock."

He thought that Cypriot men were, as a rule, tall and handsome, "but the women rarely comely after the age of 16. It is impossible to tell their age. One who looks 50 can be only half. They age quickly due to hard work, very early marriage and hard lives."

The women cared little for their personal appearance, smothering themselves in several petticoats and skirts thrown on in any way. Underneath they wore baggy trousers, "like bloomers," and worn over it all a jacket generally held together by pieces of string or tape if the buttons were missing. Both sexes wore coarse, rough boots up to the knees, with soles made of several layers of leather, an inch thick and studded with huge nails.

Life and property were safe in Cyprus, protected now by an excellent police force of both Moslems and Christians with British police officers. However, the climate, along with the water problem, could be troublesome — "that and the awful heat and fever."

The climate suffered from extremes, "Either it is drenched in water which runs to waste, or burnt to a cinder in scorching sun. One day a gale of wind, with leaden sky and thick mist, the next as warm and fine as a summer's day at home." The rainy season was supposed to last from mid-October to the end of February, although March was by far the wettest month during his time on the island, with rain until the first week in June. Then, the heat was "terrific", especially in the great central plain where sea breezes were excluded by mountain barriers north and south.

Stewart thought it hotter in central Cyprus than in lower Egypt, and at Nicosia than at Cairo. The north wind was dry and hot because of the arid plateau of Asia Minor, and the south and east of Cyprus deprived of moisture and freshness because of the Syrian and African deserts.

In antiquity, vast forests and higher cultivation tempered the insufferable heat, and currently Britain was doing its best to re-afforest mountainous parts, he goes on. "But then the goats eat up any green shoots or the native cuts down any wood on which he can lay his hands. The Messaoria plain, once covered with dense forest, has hardly a dozen trees now." The goats were ingenious in getting at the lower branches of trees. Two of them, facing each other and standing on their hind legs, would often prop themselves up by their front feet placed against one another for mutual support.

Larnaca's water during Stewart's visit was supplied from springs seven miles to the west and carried by an aqueduct built in 1745 by the Pasha, Abu Bekr, who had left money for the purpose, according to the author. One of Larnaca's sights, he tells us, was an "extraordinary mirage" which appeared daily in winter until sunset, 12 miles to the east off Cape Pyla. It took the form of a very real-looking island, about a mile offshore with trees on it. He explained it as a "possible reflection" of the promontory of Cape Greco.

Stavrovouni, the mountain of the Holy Cross, was a landmark for ships attempting to get into Famagusta Harbour, protected by a natural reef in which there were only one or two openings. A large post had been erected on the shore of Famagusta Bay, and to pass through the reef safely the ship lined up this post with the Stavrovouni peak. When the peak was obscured because of heat haze, other landmarks were used.

He also describes his trip to Famagusta in a French-built carriage drawn by a mule and two rather wretched horses. It was driven by a coal-black African accompanied by a boy whose duty was to repair the harness with bits of string when needed, he relates.

To him, burial rites were equally strange. One Greek funeral procession was headed by a chanting priest, and a couple of small boys swinging censers. They were followed by a man carrying the lid of the coffin shieldwise, then came the coffin containing the corpse wrapped in a shroud. This was followed by the family and professional mourners. The procession took half an hour to go through the bazaar and all shops closed as the coffin passed.

The ploughs used by farmers in the Messaoria plain, he continued, were "nothing more than a stick with an iron shoe in it. It only scratches the surface, and doesn't root up thistles and bulbous weeds." Usually it was drawn by oxen, sometimes a donkey and an ox. Corn was cut down with a sickle and threshed with a board studded with flint drawn by oxen. The driver sat or stands on the board exactly as was carried out on "the threshing floor of Ornun the Jebusite... the old Bible injunction, thou shalt not muzzle the ox that treadeth out the corn is faithfully observed here, but results were poor.

This primitive method greatly reduced the grains value in foreign markets because it was mixed with stones and dirt on the threshing floor. Only eight kilos daily could be produced, he writes.

Winnowing must wait for the wind, with grain and straw pitched up into the air with wooden shovels. The wind then carried off the straw further than the grain and so separated them. Grinding was done between a couple of stones, and bread finally baked in an oven made of mud and clay in the shape of a gigantic beehive.

"I don't suppose Abraham or even Adam prepared his daily bread any differently than these Cypriots do at the present day."

CESNOLA

If there is one name guaranteed to raise hackles in the history and archaeology crowd round here, it is that of Cesnola — Luigi Palma di Cesnola (like the cc's in Gucci) who last century sent five shiploads of priceless Cyprus antiquities to New York, and then decamped himself.

Depending upon what light you are standing in, he is either Luigi the Louse or a very nimble amateur archaeologist who got away with some of the best antiquities ever unearthed in the island while allegedly outfoxing the Ottoman Turks here. In the meantime, one of the Napoleons almost bought his entire collection for France, he says.

During his 10-year stay in Cyprus, Cesnola's attention was not entirely on excavating. There were other encounters to be recorded, other destinies to sway.

He met the famous "Robin Hood of the Levant," a swashbuckler who had spent seven years chained to a Constantinople wall, a colony of lepers banished from their villages by friends and relatives, and scores of Greek nationals whom he saved from deportation after intervening with the Turks. Then there was the shock of finding his favourite "digger" dead in an ancient tomb, and another blow when he realised that even seemingly-respectable visitors to his collection were not above pocketing pieces of his treasure.

He also claimed to have outwitted the Ottoman governor and various pashas countless times here when their mounted zaptiehs, foiled again, always seemed to gallop up to the seashore just after a Cesnola-chartered schooner had slipped away for the New World, laden to the water's edge with priceless archaeological finds.

Today, Cesnola would be imprisoned for illegal excavations and export, but 120 years ago he was no better or worse than scores of gentlemen archaeologists and visitors, untrained but keen, who wandered the island with pickaxe and spade. Archaeology was not yet a developed science and excavating was technically legal even during the very early days into British rule before officials clamped down.

During his stay here, Cesnola was representing both America and Russia as consul. In addition, he seemed on excellent terms with the island's governor, Said Pasha, as well as the American Minister in Constantinople, who had the ear of the Porte.

Although most visitors were content with a few objects picked up on the surface, or at most a trunk full of finds to carry home (many to be later donated to museums), Cesnola excavated tens of thousands of objects for sale to the highest bidder. He stored them in his house on the Larnaca seafront and in adjoining buildings, including his massive finds from Golgoi (near Athienou village) where he had unearthed sensational pieces, some heroic in size.

He never failed to delight in, and examine, his newly discovered treasures, he said, "which every day brought to light some new cause of wonder." Napoleon had wanted to buy them all for the Louvre, he tells us (not THE Napoleon, but a descendent), but the Franco-German war broke out and the French forgot about other people's yesterdays.

Eventually, the New York Museum (soon to be called the Metropolitan) bought most of his discoveries in two installments, including bronze, terracotta and limestone statues and heads, gold and silver jewellery, sarcophagi, vessels and coins. Many were from tombs or temples unearthed by himself with a small crew of diggers, or sometimes purchased from peasants. Some were part of what he called the "Curium Treasure", many pieces of which in fact had originated elsewhere in the island.

Nevertheless, all formed the nucleus of the New York Museum's collection and caused a sensation when exhibited there. This was despite accusations by some outraged critics that certain statues, badly packed and broken in shipment, had been carelessly glued together with the wrong heads or arms. Cesnola had also allowed simple workmen to paste a few back together, they alleged.

Although his excavations in Cyprus may have been technically legal, archaeologists today wish that he hadn't undertaken them. His methods were often clumsy, his scholarship wanting, his dating and measurements doubtful, there was no real proof of origin and he kept no day-to-day diary or records. In fact, he seriously harmed or otherwise damaged many sites for future scientists.

At no time did Cesnola consider himself a tomb robber or a thief in consul's clothing, however, and the man who was known as "The Italian" during his long diplomatic tenure here was as (unscientifically) precise as he knew how. He not only left behind sketches, photographs and long lists with descriptions of his finds, but also tells us of his dealings with workmen, villagers and local authorities.

It is all set down in his own book, "Cyprus, Its Cities, Tombs and Temples", originally published by John Murray, London, in 1877. There was a second edition by Harper and Brothers in New York the next year, and eventually another by Star Graphics in Nicosia in 1991.

The last contains a foreward by Dr. Stuart Swiny, former director of the Cyprus-American Archaeological Research Institute (CAARI) in Nicosia. He tells readers that Cesnola was sometimes prone to exaggeration or yarn-spinning, especially in accounts of skirmishes with Turkish authorities. Moreover, he believes that Cesnola's "main desire was to equal, if not eclipse, the brilliant discoveries made by that other amateur archeologist, Heinrich Schliemann" who had uncovered "Priam's Treasure" at Troy a few years before.

Cesnola's life seemed to be eventful wherever he happened to be. Born in 1832, he was a soldier at the age of 15 in the

Savoyard army, later sailed for America where he married a New York er, fought for the Union side in the Civil War, spent seven months in a Virginia prison, then came to Cyprus as U.S. consul after recommendations from friends. He was also to become consul for Russia.

Here are some of Cesnola's personal reminiscences and experiences during his stay here until 1875, three years before Britain took over from Ottoman Turkey:

He personally engineered the removal of an "intriguing old Cadi" from Dhali village who had falsely accused him of desecrating Moslem tombs and carrying off the skulls, he said. After Cesnola explained the mistake to the shocked governor, Said Pasha, who had hurried to the scene — the baskets were full of skulls from ancient burial grounds — the two men had a good laugh about it.

Perhaps his finest hour occured when, according to his own account, his intervention with the Turkish governor here spared scores of Greek subjects, including Cypriot holders of Greek passports, from deportation from the island on orders from the Porte. Tensions between Greece and Turkey had flared up, and Constantinople wanted the Greeks out of their Cypriot province. According to Cesnola, "the American Minister in a private letter to me warmly approved of my using any personal influence I might possess with the Turkish authorities to diminish the distress of the Greeks." The Greek consul had already been told by his own government to lower the Greek flag and come home, with Hellenic colony affairs to be looked after by a colleague. Instead the consul, George Menardos, avoided departure by becoming Cesnola's temporary secretary in the U.S. consulate. He had just married a wealthy Cypriot lady and was reluctant to leave, Cesnola mentions.

From every part of the island, the desperate Greeks flocked to the American Consulate, he goes on. In the courtyard and consulate square were crowds of old men, young mothers and others asking for funds to leave. "I had no funds for this purpose ... heart-rending to hear of all the distress and ruin which this order if carrried out would cause to these unfortunate people. They would be obliged to leave home and lands, and to sell their few household goods and trinkets in order to reach the shores of Greece, he says, "where utter poverty would stare them in the face."

But Cesnola triumphed ... "Said Pasha was an intelligent Turk, spoke French fluently and was not devoid of all human feeling toward the Christians. His great ambition was to be a popular ruler ... to succeed with him I must touch this powerful spring."

The Great Powers would never permit a war between Greece and Turkey, he told the governor. Moreover, Greek indebtedness to the local Turks was very large — "I became aware then, for the first time, of the manner in which these poor creatures were obliged to borrow money from year to year at an interest of 20 to 25 percent, in order to live and cultivate their lands, mortgaging to the money-lender their crops in advance."

Departure now meant uncollected debts, for the harvest was not yet in. Why not stall the deportation by asking for further instructions from Constantinople? Cesnola had suggested. The governor agreed; in the meantime the war clouds passed and the deportation order was revoked. Cesnola was a hero.

He had other stories to tell, including his annoyance when floods of travellers anxious to see the "Museum of the American Consul" invaded his garden and courtyard, asking thousands of questions and fingering the objects. "Once an elderly English lady with the proverbial ringlets who belonged to one of these parties, asked me to explain to her the mysteries of the worship of Venus" in relation to the objects from Golgoi. (She had been examining the pieces of particularly Egyptian influence).

Then, it was not always possible to prevent the great numbers of visitors from handling the small objects lying on tables and shelves. "I am sorry to say that sometimes the objects did not always find their way back to their legitimate places. It is a strange truth that there are people, apparently respectable, who think nothing of pocketing antiquities not belonging to them, or of breaking off pieces of sculpture in order to carry them away as trophies to their homes."

In Nicosia, he found about 200 lepers, including some 40 Turks, roaming about outside the walls. It was just after dawn and the drawbridge to the walled town had not yet been lowered for visitor Cesnola and his party.

The lepers lived about a mile from the town, in ancient, excavated tombs and a few sheds built by themselves, he writes. They lived on charity and begging, the largess of the Archbishop who sent them food, and a loaf of bread each every day from the government (which was rarely delivered). Their average age was between 40 and 60, he goes on, although there were young boys and pretty girls amongst them. He believed that the disease only existed amongst the lowest class, and that drought years seemed to produce more lepers.

"When the faintest symptoms of leprosy appear, all relationship and friendship are at an end, all future intercourse with him ceases, and he is driven from his native place, provided with a quilt and some food, to find his way to the lepers' village. No distinction of creed exists among them, no religious consolation is given them, and no funeral obsequies are performed over them."

To escape the summer heat of Larnaca, Cesnola, his wife and daughters travelled by muleback to a small village called Ormidhia, he said, where they stayed in a pretty little white cottage on the outskirts. There was a never-failing breeze and good water, and his family played for hours on the sandy beach looking for shells. It was a Greek village, and the priests there worked in the fields like peasants and wore conical hats not unlike those represented in statues from Golgoi, he writes.

He also mentions Dhali, near Nicosia as one of the family's

resorts where they spent the days reading, writing or resting under large walnut trees. Personally, he was more interested in excavating for nearby antiquities.

The family soon adapted the peasant housekeeping system, he relates. "We hung our plate baskets and table linen amongst the trees, and had rough chairs and a dining table, with thick mats." A tent was pitched nearby as a boudoir for his wife and infant, and another as a reception tent with Turkish rugs and divans. From June until September, the villagers lived almost entirely out of doors, placing their beds under the trees and using tree branches as a larder, pantry and clothes hanger. Dhali was wonderfully free from reptiles, he said, and infants slept on a cloth spread on the ground.

Cesnola carried out archaeological surveys during holidays there, adding that Adonis had been slain while hunting in the Idalian hills.

When travelling round the island, Cesnola was always accompanied by a cook, butler, valet, dragoman and consular guard. One of the group, called Mustapha, learned to read and write modern Greek and worked for Cesnola for eight years. His mule train carried beds and bedding, dining table, camp stools, and a complete dinner service. Cesnola said that he stayed healthy by avoiding a change in diet or daily habits as much as possible. He had found it more convenient and less expensive to purchase rather than hire animals, and became the possessor of several fine well-broken mules and two strong donkeys, he goes on, as high almost as horses and of a breed peculiar to Cyprus. The donkeys were "glossy and sleek, with large eyes, and will trot as fast as a mule; they are besides very intelligent."

During a visit to Paphos he discovered several crumbling guard-houses, apparently built by the Turks near the shore as protection for neighbouring villages against pirates from Algiers. Only 60 years before, they had raided the coast and carried off wealthy inhabitants for ransom, he said. He also saw a pirate's cave.

He found the ruins of Famagusta "not grand or imposing, yet to me they are most beautiful and touching." The fortress there contained some of the worst criminals of the Turkish Empire, many condemned for life or long years in prison. All were heavily shackled. Near one wall where the prisoners were held were two casemates filled with Venetian arms. On the handles of some were the crests of their former owners inlaid with gold and the Jerusalem Cross. He succeeded in "obtaining several" for a friend, he said.

Members of his party, including his wife and other ladies, were astonished to see a short, broad-shouldered man who had remained close-by during their tour suddenly spring to the parapet "with the agility of a cat," break off some of the blossoms from trailing crimson flowers, and present them to the women. To their horror, says Cesnola, they found that he was shackled with heavy iron links from waist to ankles. He had large, sad blue eyes and prematurely grey hair, a fine, manly face and a commanding presence, he goes on.

He was no less a personage that the celebrated Kattirdji Janni, the Robin Hood of the Levant, a robber chief who allegedly never permitted a murder by his band in his presence. He had fallen in love with the daughter of a Smyrna gentleman, his master's daughter, so the story went, and their planned elopement was betrayed by a fellow servant. Escaping to the Ephesus mountains, he entered upon the wild career which brought him finally to Famagusta and imprisonment.

The bands' speciality had been robbing the rich and holding the wealthy for ransom. Kattirdji Janni often gave money to the poor, and he allegedly endowed thousands of young Greek girls with marriage dowries, Cesnola writes. Smyrna townsmen were terrified of him, and 500 Turkish soldiers had failed to capture the elusive outlaw and his band. Sometimes the band had entered private homes uninvited, to ask for food, and then rewarded their host and his family with safe travel and hunting without fear. Kattirdji Janni never forgot a kindness, it was said.

For some reason he eventually surrendered to authorities and was sent to Famagusta after seven years chained to a wall in Constantinople. Because of his floral tribute to the women in Cesnola's party, his wife's entreaties to Aziz Pasha for lighter chains for Kattirdji Janni eventually succeeded.

One of Cesnola's greatest shocks was the discovery of the body of old Hadji Jorghi, one of the pioneer diggers at Dhali, crouched in one of the excavated tombs, he said, his knees drawn up, his eyes fixed, a pipe in his mouth. His family had abandoned him following his imprisonment as guarantor of a relative's failed debt. Finally released when close to death, he made his way slowly home, Cesnola says, where he found the poor old man seated upon a stone, fatigued, hungry and broken down by grief. Next day he tottered towards his favourite tombs "to pay them a last visit." His body was found next morning.

After 10 years in Cyprus, Cesnola decided to return to New York mainly, he said, because excavations had drained his finances and his wife had become depressed and ill "after the lonely life she had led for so many years" in the island. She had been brought up in the refinements and luxuries of a great city, and although she often assisted her husband during his inland travels, life in a small arid town had been difficult for her, he said.

During their last days here, as they "surveyed the fields full of wild flowers and their own garden reclaimed from the seashore with its lovely roses such as bloom only in Cyprus, a sense of tenderness stole into our hearts for the land we are leaving on the morrow."

Back in New York, he was to become the Museum's director for life. On the ground floor, case after case of Cyprus antiquities were on display. One of the ships containing the island's antiquities had in the meantime sunk about 50 miles off the Syrian coast, never to be found or raised.

Perhaps the only objects that slipped out of his grasp while still in Cyprus were some centuries-old china dishes belonging to poor old "Simeon the Hermit," who had made his home in a deserted chapel near Kantara, north Cyprus. "No doubt a collector of such articles would be delighted to possess them," Cesnola had thought. Actually, they were embedded in the chapel wall, perhaps too difficult to winkle out.

Cesnola had visited Simeon there and heard his story. Apparently the hermit had "roamed like a wild beast among the mountains, living on herbs, olives and wild fruits after his banishment from Constantinople. He had lost his thriving business in Turkey, the hermit said, after he had rejected "dishonourable proposals" toward his wife made by a powerful Turk. Simeon's house was burnt, his property destroyed, he spent three years in prison without trial on false charges, was banished forever from Turkey, and his wife wound up in the Turk's harem.

Once a year, local Greeks visited the chapel and brought him tobacco, matches and old clothes. He was 80 years old.

Cesnola died in 1904 -- 29 years after he left Cyprus forever and almost 40 years after he opened his first ancient tomb here.

(**Note to readers**: Sealed, silent and generally unopened even by researchers until recently, the once-sensational Cesnola collection of ancient Cypriot artifacts including golden jewellery, diadems, massive heads and bronzes has remained virtually undisturbed and unheeded in Metropolitan Museum storerooms since Cesnola's death.

Recently, however, a fresh injection of Metropolitan Museum re-think has catapulted the finds into the daylight again, to be readied for a spectacular and permanent public exhibition in the great museum's projected new galleries.

About 1,200 pieces from the famed collection, cleaned, identified and catalogued, will be on show just in time to help usher in the new millennium.

At the heart of preparations for the exhibition is Dr. Vassos

Karageorghis, scholar, archaeologist, author and former head of the Cyprus' Department of Antiquities and the Archaeological Research Unit of the Cyprus University.

Now a working Board member of the A. G. Leventis Foundation with offices in Nicosia, he spends several months a year working in New York with the Metropolitan's permanent staff of curators, conservators and other specialists to pull the collection together in time for its new millenium launching.)

KITCHENER'S CYPRUS

One of the most famous men in modern British history, the legendary Lord Kitchener, was shot at twice in Cyprus for unknown reasons and won the steeplechase at a Nicosia race meeting here.

It was soon after Britain had landed in Cyprus in 1878 to take over the former Ottoman province, and Kitchener won the race on an Arab mare that he had trained himself. For years afterwards, he proudly displayed his winner's trophy at various postings throughout the Middle and Far East.

He was a young lieutenant in Cyprus then, Horatio Herbert Kitchener, soldier, amateur archeologist, linguist, and skilled cartographer who had already helped to map out Palestine. For three years in Cyprus he scrambled over plains, mountain peaks and rough, shapeless terrain to produce the island's first modern, scientifically prepared map.

He is also credited with setting up the nucleus of today's Cyprus archeological museum with fine ancient glass, "squeezing" a small sum from government for the purpose and urging contributions from the wealthier families. Later he directed the newly re-organised Land Registry Office, "a delicate duty in a country where there are few boundaries and many lawsuits," his biographer says.

He was tall, thin and wore his thick brown hair parted in the middle, was well thought of but confided in few, and began in Cyprus what was later to be a serious, off-duty preoccupation - the collection of porcelain and antiques.

In Nicosia he shared quarters with a high-spirited British police officer who kept a bear cub as a house pet. The bear was finally banished after it had climbed into Kitchener's bath, then retired to his bed to dry itself.

In 1920, his biographer writes that Kitchener's room in the Nicosia house "was kept as far as possible in the state in which it had been while he occupied it; the owner, a Greek, declared his belief that the young English officer would one day be a very great man.

Kitchener's later career, as field marshal, fighter, diplomat, negotiator and War Minister, spanned some of the most vivid and action-filled decades in the British Empire's military and political history. Amongst other places it carried him to Turkey, the Far and Middle East, including Egypt, with which he is closely identified, the Battle of Omdurman in Gordon's Sudan, Europe, British political life and the Great War.

Death came finally in 1916 aboard the "Hampshire" in a storm near Scapa Flow as he sailed for Archangel and a rendezvous with the Tsar to discuss Russia's role in the fighting. The man-of-war had possibly hit a mine. When he died, there was international shock over his loss, for he had "inspired multitudes whom he had never tried to draw to him, who had never set their eyes on him, who knew of him only by hearsay, with a sentiment much stronger than mere admiration... describable as personal devotion." He belonged to the realm of saga and legend, says his biographer, Sir George Arthur, who in three volumes entitled "The Life of Lord Kitchener", traced his career up to his death at the age of 66. All three volumes were published in 1920.

Soon after Kitchener's arrival in Cyprus, he found that he and the country's first High Commissioner and Governor-General, Sir Garnet Wolseley, did not see eye to eye on the form that the proposed survey was to take.

Sir Garnet wanted a hurry-up map, not too thorough, and ordered the completion of a number of village surveys which would then be pieced together for the composition of a major map, according to the biographer.

The meticulous subaltern disagreed "respectfully", then appealed to the Foreign Office for permission to do it his way — on orthodox lines based on the model of the trigonometrical Ordnance Survey in England. Salisbury, the British Foreign

Minister, agreed, Wolseley did not, shut down the survey on economic grounds and within a few months Kitchener found himself shunted off to the Asia Minor vilayet of Kastamuni, in Turkey.

As vice-consul there, he was to help monitor and execute local reforms prescribed under the Anglo-Turkish convention, whose terms included administrative reform in the Ottoman provinces.

Kitchener's reports were to make sorry reading, his biographer says... a tale of misrule, corruption, extortion, bribery, brigandage, petty officialdom and favouritism — "candidates for government posts compete in examinations but are selected by favour." By the following year, "nothing had been done to mitigate the sufferings of the people."

Kitchener was also back in Cyprus. By this time, there was a new High Commissioner, Major General Sir Robert Biddulph (he remained seven years). Wolseley, at his own request, had been transfered to a war zone. With a group of Royal Engineers, Kitchener finally completed the map in 1882, "some 3,000 square miles delineated, with a scale of one inch to a mile. It was pronounced a very finished speciman of the art of cartography." It had also been needed for land registry purposes.

For a skilled surveyor, the island had offered considerable facilities, the author goes on. "The central plain was an excellent base line for a satisfactory triangulation to the serrated peaks of the northern range of steep limestone mountains. ...On one side they slope away into the long and narrow peninsula of the Karpass, and on the other, connect with the huge volcanic shoulders of Mt. Machera and Mt. Troodos at 6,600 feet," he writes.

But there were obstacles. The spur from Troodos to Chrysochou and Paphos was unexplored, and was a labyrinth of excessively steep, crumbled and twisted ridges and valleys — pathless, shapeless and in outline almost identical.

Most Cypriots spoke only Greek or Turkish, roads were few, the climate difficult and some of the islanders, he says, were prejudiced or occasionally hostile. It was during this period that an unknown gunmen opened fire at Kitchener (his biographer says that there were two separate occasions). According to the newspaper, "The Cyprus Herald", of January 7, 1881, "information was received in Limassol yesterday evening to the effect that Lieutenant Kitchener, R.E. (Royal Engineers) had been shot at near the village of Pissouri.

"It appears that, seeing a man near where he was at work, Mr. Kitchener approached him to ask for some information, when the man levelled a gun at him, and kept moving about still keeping the gun in a threatening position. Mr. Kitchener then went some distance to fetch a native to interpret for him, and on returning to the spot the man again levelled his piece, and eventually fired a shot at Mr. Kitchener, but fortunately without hitting him. The native with him bolted and Mr. Kitchener was unable to capture the miscreant."

Kitchener stayed in Cyprus long enough to remodel the Land Registry system satisfactorily "notably in his determined efforts to extricate the Cypriots from the too-frequent and firm grip of money-lenders."

As a fledgling antique collector, he also acquired a richly carved old door and frame, from which he made a sideboard.

He also promoted an Arts and Crafts show, but it was a "thankless" effort. Kitchener himself was a good craftsman and in later life liked to restore and repair antique funiture, according to his biographer. In London, he was also praised for his work in leading an archaeological excavation at Curium, which was followed by a British Museum offer to excavate at Nineveh.

This was reluctantly declined on financial grounds and finally, after five years in Cyprus, Kitchener was made second-in-command of the cavalry in the new, British-run Egyptian army. He held the rank of "bimbashi" or major, and within a few months of his arrival in Cairo the country was in crisis and "the Egyptian pot was boiling over."

Under new orders he completed a geographical survey of the

Sinai Peninsula, the desert of the Exodus, and he and his assistants travelled by camelback and slept in tents. "I got over as much ground as a camel would allow," Kitchener was to write. "They are bad beasts for surveying. I used to keep mine at a good trot for a bit until he got cross, which he showed by roaring and then suddenly shutting up all four legs and coming with a thud on the ground, at the same moment springing up again and dashing off in the opposite direction. Continued correction caused him to collapse again and then roll, which was decidedly uncomfortable." Kitchener spoke good Arabic and was well-received by various desert tribes encountered by his group. "At one point they supposed me to be a relative of the great Sheikh Abdullah."

It was a risky journey, his biographer points out, and in two months he had covered 3,000 square miles.

In the worst sandstorms, he refused to wear his British spectacles, "wishing to differ as little as possible from his companions." As a result, his eyesight was slightly but permanently damaged.

Although Kitchener's next years were to prove far more interesting to him militarily or diplomatically, he looked back on his early career in Cyprus with "pride and satisfaction." His opinion of the results of English administration was particularly high.

In a memorandum two years after his departure from Cyprus he commented that the island had been handed over to Great Britain by Turkey "in a thoroughly exhausted and ruined condition." For centuries, he said, the system had been to take as much as possible out of the island, giving nothing in return. All public works and every institution in the island were in the last stage of decay. English administration laboured under the enormous difficulty that there was no foundation to work upon. Every department was in the same rotten state, and reconstruction had to be begun from the lowest steps.

Under Britain, customs duties had increased more than 350 percent, revenue was increasing constantly and the previous year there had been a surplus over expenditure "of the large sum of

£82,366."

Money was being liberally spent on much needed roads, bridges and piers, he pointed out, and justice was now impartially administered by competent magistrates.

However, he criticised "the late Liberal Administration in London for giving the Cypriots elective self-government before they were prepared for it, or remnants of Turkish maladministration thoroughly eradicated." The upshot was disastrous, he said. New public works continually met with opposition, and the well-to-do exerted much pressure to thwart reforms in land laws, despite benefits to the general community. Here the interests of usurers, lawyers and ecclesiastics were at stake, he pointed out.

Kitchener thought that few Cypriots were interested in self-government at that point anyway, citing recent elections at Kyrenia. "Although a Christian vacancy in the Legislative Council was contested by three candidates, only 123 voters out of a total of 1,103 electors came to the poll."

However, the "great strides" made by Cyprus over the past seven years of British rule did not pass unobserved in Asia Minor, he remarked, where similar reforms were being urged by British consuls. He thought it not too much to say "that the special capability shown by British administrators in the task of governing Oriental races has now been recognised in that country. The outcome of this feeling may be of vast significance in the future."

By this time Kitchener, now a major, was well-settled in Egypt, training local forces against the Mahdi and carrying out political intelligence work in the Upper Nile in preparation for an expeditionary force into the Sudan. Neither Kitchener nor a relief force reached General Gordon in time to prevent his death and that of 3,000 others in beseiged Khartoum, however.

It fell to Kitchener to write the official report of the disaster. Just under 15 years later, Kitchener was appointed Governor-General of the Sudan.

MRS BRASSEY

Mrs Brassey had already attended the opening of the Suez Canal, cruised the Arctic Circle and narrowly missed being run down by a large steamer in a howling gale in the English Channel.

She was one of the intrepid women of the late 19th century, scouting Mediterranean by-ways on cranky mules or waiting for Mt. Vesuvius to erupt all over again.

During a coffee party with Turkish princesses on the Bosphorus, she had heard the yearnings of Constantinople women for emancipation, or at least a trip to the theatre. One princess had brought along her white slave and black eunuch.

Now Mrs. Brassey was anchored off the Paphos coast in the family yacht, having already climbed the quivering rope ladder of a five masted man-o-war lying to called the "Minotaur"; there was to be an agreeable breakfast on board with the admiral of the fleet. It was November, 1878, four months after Britain had shipped troops over to Cyprus in an agreed takeover of the island.

There had been no seasonal rainfall, temperatures were uncomfortably high, and fever-ridden British troops in overcrowded bell-tents thought the island even hotter than India or the tropics.

It was to be a lightning, one-week visit to Cyprus for Mrs. Annie Brassey, her husband, Thomas, who was a British M.P. from Sussex, their three young daughters and guests. But they managed to tour the main towns, archeological sites and monasteries, Sir Garnet Wolseley's temporary H.Q. at Nicosia, and newly-opened army camps.

Although moving about when necessary by mule-train, they slept aboard the beloved family yacht, "The Sunbeam", whenever possible as she steamed along the Cyprus coast following their trail. The three-masted screw schooner, as she described it, was captained by Mr. Brassey himself, and for their current four-month Mediterranean tour she carried a crew of 20 along with a children's maid, nurse, cooks and a store-keeper.

The "Sunbeam" was 157 feet long with a displacement tonnage of 531 tons, Lady Brassey tells us, adding that life was not more expensive afloat than on shore. Some things were cheaper here, dearer there, and an average was maintained. On board a yacht, as anywhere else, expenses depended very much upon the disposition of the owner and his management abilities. Steaming, she went on, was much cheaper than sailing, as coal consumption was not nearly so costly as the wear and tear on sails and ropes, especially when flapping about in a calm. They never hired a pilot unless absolutely necessary. What did cost extra-budgeted expenses were alterations on board, however trifling, long land journeys, hotel bills and shopping on shore.

Mrs Brassey kept a journal of her several sea voyages, and her impressions of Cyprus are contained in her book "Sunshine and Storm in the East", published by Henry Holt in 1880. It was signed simply "Mrs. Brassey" and dedicated to "the brave, true-hearted sailors of England". She had already written another book called "Around the World in the Yacht, Sunbeam".

This time, the yacht had anchored just outside the ruined fort and harbour of Paphos, which had looked "very pretty" from the sea. Trees growing along shore were once part of the temple of Venus gardens while on the hills at the back was perched the little village of Ktima with its mosque and minaret. Above that stood the white tents and brown huts of the 71st regiment. Of 107 officers and men there, 27 were down with fever. "Others showed terrible traces of the disease, being hardly able to crawl about. There was no supply of fever medicine at the camp."

The previous morning on board the "Minotaur", Mrs. Brassey and her family had noticed one of the main decks curtained off into berths for invalid officers leaving Cyprus. Earlier, all the big guns on board had been fired for practice, she recounted, and the vibration stove in the bulkheads in the admiral's cabin. She had wondered the effect on the patients.

The group toured the immediate Paphos area riding bare-backed on horses owned by Arabs, she said; the children were mounted on donkeys. Lying about were a few broken marble columns, sarcophagi and inscribed slabs, while fields and roads were strewn with fragments of while marble capitals and acanthus-leaf ornaments.

Next morning the yacht and its passengers steamed close along the coast, passing Cape Blanco which the author thought much like the white cliffs of old England, and then to the modern town of Episcopi.

Here, General Cesnola had found his great treasures in three rooms under an ancient temple, she writes, quite full of gold and silver artifacts, vases and ornaments. The city's ancient inhabitants, according to one theory, had hidden their valuables under the temple when threatened by invasion. Either exterminated or carried off into slavery later, the population had left no clue as to the secret of their treasure.

Near Limassol was found the best wine of Cyprus and the most fertile district of the island where one could ride for miles through highly productive but almost uncultivated vines. But sheep or goats browse on the leaves at will, or trample in the dust the grapes gathered by the peasants, she said. Later, the owners crush and place the grapes into large jars to ferment, well-pitched inside and so vast as to "certainly hold Ali Baba and any of his forty thieves." But she thought the wine too sweet and strong, and with a marked flavour of tar.

Although the group had never seen anything so blue as the sky and sea at Limassol, they found the heat disagreeably intense. The mayor and the entire population had come down to greet them, thinking that they were another party of distinguished visitors. "When they found we only wanted to hire some mules, their interest abated." The mayor was very hospitable, nevertheless, presenting Mrs. Brassey with two specimens of ancient glass of which "great quantities are found in the tombs here." But excavating for antiquities was now forbidden, she writes, and government was to "take matters into its own hands."

Limassol's commissioner, Colonel Warren, she goes on, carried on an "amusing" barter with the visiting group, exchanging "new" newspapers for "old" pots and earthenware vessels from ancient tombs.

For dinner they were served beccaficos, or preserved birds "so well known in these parts. Delicious fat little morsels they would be, but spoiled by being dipped as soon as killed and feathers and all, into strong vinegar which spoilt the taste."

She thought Larnaca a "miserable looking place," with half a dozen wretched little jetties and broken-down quays in need of repair. It was, moreover, hot and steamy and unhealthy. The sea washes almost up to the doors of the houses and in many places it was necessary to make a detour by a back street to get into a house, she wrote.

The last of the Indian troops had embarked from the town the previous week, "leaving a good impression behind as the best behaved and most docile soldiers ever seen." Their surplus stores were sold at a fearful loss however, with horses going for less than a pound. Due to the fever, there was a lot of sickness and misery about, she added.

Reaching Nicosia that night by muleback, the party found the gates shut. After a long wait and much hammering and shouting, an old Turk appeared with lantern and keys to admit them.

There were many Venetian cannons lying about outside the walls, one of which the visitors later took away. At the invitation of Lt.Garnet Wolseley they stayed at Government House, actually a group of tents on the grounds of Kykko Monastery annex. Here Mrs. Brassey and her young daughters were housed, with her husband, in three huts opening into one another. Inside were sofas, easy chairs, rugs and writing tables, made as comfortable as possible for the visitors.

Their luggage arrived late next morning, "after Lord Gifford had kindly visited every khan in Nicosia to look for it. Finally it was found in a little inn just outside town, where the muleteers were still sleeping."

Some of the monastic cells were being used during the daytime by Sir Garnet, she tells us, especially when the tents became unbearably hot. "The British flag now waves over the monastery, having been blessed by the Patriarch before allowing it to be hoisted." The Archimandrite had already shown the group round the church and invited them to his own apartments where he presented them with beautiful sponges from Kyrenia. "His behavior was most polite and courteous."

During the summer, when temperatures had sometimes reached 120 Fahrenheit, the men were dropping off like sheep, Lady Brassey relates, sleeping together in hot tents on the ground, with nothing to distract their attention apart from who might be next to sicken. The Indians suffered as much as the British, she said. "The difficulties of interment were great amongst men of so many different religions and caste being considered. Some buried their dead with various peculiar ceremonies, others burned them."

"The Fever," as it was described, could have several causes. Some doctors thought that water very near the surface throughout the island, "although it doesn't actually appear," could be one reason. Another possibility was the habit of digging almost every well within ten feet of a Turkish or Greek cemetery. Yet others believed that the disintegration of sandstone and granite was the explanation.

In the meantime, a new Government House was being built on a place called Snake Hill, where two snakes had been found and killed. The view was to be a commanding one looking over river, plain, town and mountains. However, "some people seem to think the sooner we give it up (Cyprus) the better, as it is not likely to become more than a coaling station unless the climate changes."

Meanwhile, the Sultan was cross because the British flag was being hoisted on forts and public buildings. He thought his own should appear above it as he considered that Cyprus still belonged to him, Mrs. Brassey pointed out. ... "no one seems to know how long our sway is to last, or what are the exact conditions of our tenure of the place."

In 1925 Cyprus became a British crown colony, 47 years after the "Sunbeam" and her passengers sailed away forever. They had arrived home safely for New Year celebrations despite shipping sea in gale force winds off the Greek islands enroute.

DAILY LIFE UNDER THE OTTOMANS

Thousands of defeated Christians converted to Islam after the Ottoman conquest of the island over 400 years ago, according to court records of the time.

They had switched religion by choice, persuasion or force, historians say, and within three decades of the Venetian collapse at Famagusta about 31% of adult male Moslems were actually new converts. Any "infidel" of any age or sex who wished to become a Moslem had only to declare this intention in court along with name, occupation, residence and age. This was done in the presence of a Moslem "vekil" or agent, who vouched for the petitioner's voluntary adoption of the true faith.

Soon after, the new Moslem often appeared in his neighbourhood wearing a turban and, if female, accentuated her "new modesty" with veil and cloak in public. Some women adopted Islam to escape unhappy marriages and had no difficulty in finding new husbands, according to other sources.

There were certainly economic and social incentives behind the conversions, along with tax benefits; although it was forbidden to re-convert back to the former religion, some remained secret Christians for centuries after. The new Turkish administration reportedly kept accurate records of Moslems and non-Moslems (called "zimmis") for tax collection and other purposes.

The proportion of Orthodox to Catholic conversions is unknown, but it appears that a substantial number of Venetians and Franks from the former ruling class here remained in the island after the Ottoman conquest and that many went over to Islam. Previously, "in the process of the Ottoman conquest, thousands and thousands of Venetian soldiers were captured and carried away from Cyprus to be sold as slaves," one historian says.

Most Venetian holdings, including churches, buildings and land, were usurped by the new conqueror, then sometimes given to local Moslem communities or sold to support Islamic religious institutions. These properties included houses, shops, vineyards, orchards and sugar fields. If a local Moslem community petitioned that another mosque was needed, a fine abandoned church was usually available. If this was not adequate, there was also captured Latin property.

Many of the early founders of Efkaf, a pious Islamic charitable institution here, were from the Ottoman military class who remained after the conquest of the island in 1571. Before that, there were no residential Moslem communities here, historians say. All except a few local converts had been outsiders whose ties of home and family had initially been outside the island.

After the defeat of Cyprus, the Orthodox were permitted to maintain, buy and sell property, which caused their former Venetian rulers to sometimes opt for Orthodoxy instead of Islam. Others, including many of the Greek Cypriot intellectuals, had left for Venice or other parts of Italy, many to later return.

There are no accurate figures for the number of Latins who were eventually absorbed into the Turkish or Greek Cypriot communities, or information about any descendents who may still reside here under local names. One current historian, Costas Kyrris, maintains that about 25.000 people were forced to convert to Islam between 1570 and 1632 to save their lives and property, particularly Latins, including Venetians, French and other residents. Others record no massive conversions, just individual initiative or the proselytising influence of the new Mevlevi convent in Nicosia, for example.

The actual analyses of the big picture at the time, the real reasons for the Ottoman invasion, its impact and its aftermath, often depend upon which historical light you are standing in — Ottoman, Latin or Orthodox, and which are your sources.

Some historians complain that the defeated Latins, full of sour grapes at the time, had painted a highly inaccurate picture of their reign here and that life for the average Cypriot had actually been serfdom. (Slavery and the buying and selling of slaves from abroad was carried out under both regimes here.)

Others claim that the Ottomans boasted of their "voluntary" conversion rate in order to taunt the Latins. At the same time, Ottoman sources accuse the Venetians of leaving behind the economic and agricultural mess which so weakened the Cypriot economy, and which the new Ottoman administration here inherited.

One writer, Ronald C. Jennings, a professor of History at the University of Illinois, has recently published a study of life in Cyprus, "Christians and Muslims in Ottoman Cyprus and the Mediterranean World, 1571-1640".

In it, he includes such subjects as janissaries manning the castles and forts in Cyprus, the court system under the Ottomans, women in the island, slaves and slavery, smuggling and piracy, and the economy as seen through both Western and Ottoman eyes during the period almost 400 years ago. He adds that many Greek Cypriot had been agricultural slaves of the Latins, but were freed immediately after the Ottoman takeover.

The study was published in 1993 by the New York University Press, and the author dedicated it to "all the people of Cyprus, past and present, particularly those now in Turkish Cyprus".

For his comments and conclusions, he has relied on 20 pages of archival and modern sources, along with 76 original sources including Ottoman and Western writers and travellers from that period.

While he does cite Greek Cypriot or Greek sources, Jennings acknowledges his debt to the Turkish Cypriots "who befriended him here," and to the research facilities provided him at the Ethnography Museum in the former Mevlevi Tekke in Nicosia; the Kyrenia archives of Mustafa Hasim Altan; the Turkish National Library; and the judicial registers of the Efkaf Dairesi — all in the occupied north.

His interest in Cyprus and Turkey developed, he says, while

teaching for two years at the Maarif Kolej in Samsun, Turkey. He also salutes the people of Turkish Girne (Kyrenia) he tells us— "nearly every one an immigrant from elsewhere in the island," and the people of Turkish Lefkosa (Nicosia), "who live totally isolated and protected by their ancient city walls."

Meanwhile Jennings goes on to air other historians' theories, such as that of the Ottoman scholar, Katib Celibi, who blamed persistent Venetian tolerance of pirate attacks on Ottoman trading vessels rather than the Sultan "Selim the Sot's" penchant for local wine as the real reason for the Ottoman invasion of the island in 1571.

Another theory is that Cyprus was the last great conquest by the Ottoman empire, brilliantly executed, and which deprived Venice of a fine Eastern Mediterranean base.

The empire's loss at Lepanto shortly after was not so disastrous as described in the West, moreover. In fact, Ottoman historians had treated it rather lightly as a military defeat. Their galleys were back on the high seas in no time, and it was the unpreparedness of a careless Ottoman commander which had caused the loss at Lepanto anyway, it has been suggested.

Jennings, however, refers to Lepanto as the greatest Ottoman defeat since Timur beat the Sultan Bayezid I at the battle of Ankara in 1402. What did follow Lepanto, moreover, was a Holy Alliance against the Turkish empire by some worried European countries, a development which realised the Ottomans' greatest fear, according to historian Halil Inalcik.

Other remarks, theories or conclusions mentioned by Jennings:

Centuries of crusader rule in Cyprus had left a legacy of outstanding fortifications in Cyprus, mainly along the coasts. Because Lusignan rule was both exploitive and disliked by the Cypriots, there was wide-spread antipathy between Latin and Greek Orthodox Christians. These fortifications were therefore needed as much for internal as external security.

The position of the old aristocracy was quickly transformed when Ottoman troops overran Cyprus, and some of the Latin buildings were even handed over to the Orthodox or Armenian populations.

Although every Ottoman subject in Cyprus was equal before the law and could use the newly installed court system, some people were more equal than others. It was primarily a man's place and nearly all witnesses were men. While women were encouraged to resort to the courts, and frequently did so, their testimony counted for only half that of men's. Further, while their eyes were deemed the equal of men's, their minds were not.

Both Moslem and Christian women did make serious claims at court against family members, outsiders, janissaries or police. Their right to buy and sell property was also protected, as was their dowry for use in case of widowhood or divorce. The husband was obliged to pay all maintainence costs of wife and children, and there was actually very little polygamy amongst Moslems.

Marriages were usually arranged by fathers or other relatives, and Moslem divorces were relatively easy since marriage was a private contract requiring no official state or religious sanction. A divorced woman could marry anyone she wished, and there was no stigma attached to re-marriage by either party. A divorce was normally declared unilaterally by the husband, who paid maintenance costs during a "waiting" period to make certain that the wife was not pregnant. Marriage between Christian women and Moslem men was not uncommon, although the Orthodox Church discouraged it.

Almost a thousand janissaries came to Cyprus from Ottoman Turkey soon after the islands' defeat and were usually assigned to garrison the castles here. There were strong defences at Tuzla (Larnaca) says Jennings, Lefkosa (Nicosia), and Magosa (Famagusta), and it had been cheaper for the Ottomans to repair and restore existing fortifications than to build new ones.

The awesome janissary corps were originally an elite Ottoman infantry composed entirely of slaves whose loyalty was to the Sultan only. They had been conscripted for life as children from defeated Christian towns or villages throughout the empire, drilled constantly, converted to Islam and were garrisoned near the royal palace.

When the central government finally weakened, janissary discipline also broke down and the men sometimes skipped or otherwise avoided campaigns. Gradually, free men (Moslems) were admitted to their ranks.

By 1593, only 45% of janissaries were of slave-Christian origin, Jennings says. They were traditionally paid directly by the Porte, although the "spahis" or cavalrymen in Cyprus collected their own salaries through agricultural tax revenues. Early records in 1593 show a total of 937 janissaries in Cyprus, but this figure may be inflated by including men who could not or would not fight, or had secretly returned to the mainland, he adds.

Sometimes they became money lenders or tradesmen as a sideline, and some even passed on property to their heirs, as in cases recorded at Kaimakli and Pachna villages. Sometimes they were associated with violence — one janissary sought blood money from three Galata villagers on behalf of some orphans; another was killed by Christians after he had discovered them drunk.

In the meantime, unmarried girls from the Turkish mainland were brought to Cyprus as wives for the janissaries, along with thousands of other families included in a forced population transfer programme to Cyprus. Many were from nomadic Yuruk families from west Anatolia and were part of an Ottoman scheme "to restore the 14th century splendour" of Nicosia and Famagusta through new immigrants and craftsmen.

Another reason was to relieve overpopulation and unemployment in Turkey. But Cyprus was hotter and drier than home, and a large proportion either refused to leave Turkey at all or returned secretly at the first opportunity. Three eminent Ottoman historians —

Barkan, Inalcik and Avdag — agree that overpopulation in Anatolia had reached a dangerous stage, with lawlessness and brigandage sweeping the country as a result. A new life in Cyprus was therefore offered, and inducements included tax exemptions, free transport and free land.

According to Islamic law, Ottoman subjects in Cyprus were divided into two broad classes — Moslem and zimmis (Arabic dhimmi or protected people). The law knew no Turk, Arab or Kurd, only the true Moslem believer. But all non-Moslems who submitted to Ottoman authority and paid taxes were entitled to the protection of lives and property and could practice their own religion, Jennings writes.

In the Nicosia courts, the term "Greek Orthodox" or "Rum" was never used — always "zimmis". Although kadis were obliged to apply the same standard of justice, the word of a zimmi was not thought as honest as a Moslem's.

Maronites and Armenians — the latter remained mostly in their own Nicosia quarter — also had the same legal rights.

In general, Jennings says, Christians and Moslems lived in close proximity all over the island, as shown by land transfers back and forth. Both communities went to court for similar reasons — inheritance problems, civilian drunkenness, lascivious or rowdy behaviour, rape and loan defaults.

Some historians claim only a very fine line between Christians and Moslems here, and that the gulf between Christian and Moslem corsairs (the plague of the Ottoman administration) was not very wide. Piracy was rampant in the Mediterranean and smugglers often slid into remote bays here for trade. Some pirates were even on intimate terms with local Greeks and Turks whom they either pillaged or did business with.

PUTTING ON A CHEEKIN
TO SHARE WITH FRENS

If you were a first generation Greek Cypriot immigrant living in England, you hurried off to buy a "cheekin" in the "markettan" and then you "put the boiling" so that you and your "haspis" (husband) and children could eat it.

You might even ask other Greek Cypriot "frens" from the neighbourhood to share it - people like you who arrived from the homeland to cluster in the same area, blunting the strangeness and homesickness, or simply for mutual help. Most of your sentences would be in Greek, of course, and chances are that you would never learn the new language, English, very fluently. Just enough for basic communication.

In science-speak, to do this you would unconsciously employ a number of linguistic methods or combinations of them, to make yourself understood. This would include using "loan" words or blends and "code-switching". You would use snatches of each language, mostly your own, because it sounded better to you, more natural. Often you would mix up syntax, mispronounce foreign words because there were no equivalent sounds in your own language, or happily use Greek endings on English nouns and verbs.

On a long-awaited visit to the homeland, you would tell admiring but puzzled relatives in Greek that while you liked the new country, there was too much "fokess" in England. You meant "fog," of course, pluralising it. Your Greek - speaking audience wondered why there were so many seals in the U.K. You added and subtracted endings and sounds, not because you were dull or didn't care, but because you were already struggling fiercely in the new country with survival, long working hours, a new environment and sometimes profound adjustment problems.

Your life had changed forever.

London was a vast, intimidating city, larger than you had ever imagined, where you couldn't read the destinations on the big red buses, food was cooked differently and had other names, and the locals seemed distant and uncaring and didn't know any Greek. In the old, pre-migrant days, even visiting Nicosia from the village had been a culture shock. Now, the only secure and familiar institution was family and church, and the Greek Cypriot "frens" that you had made in the new country. These and, of course, the homeland and the Greek language, were the core of your identity, your comfort and solace.

As a "paren" in England, you would "kanei worry" because your growing, locally-born children might forget their roots or their Greekness. Usually bi-lingual, the second generation born abroad were struggling to integrate, thought their mother and other relatives too conservative, their father too patriarchal, and both too strict. "Nice girls" didn't go to discos, for example, or go out with boys. In the meantime, they urged their old country parents to speak English.

The same parents often had to look on helplessly as the younger generation "went from the frying pan to the saucepan" (the elders had already learned some of the local idioms!) when things looked bad and new habits threatened family stability.

It had taken almost 40 years for the Greek Cypriot community to establish a solid footing in Britain, and they are now one of the largest linguistic minorities in London, where most immigrants settled. At last count a decade ago, there were about 180,000 (figures vary) with second and third generations born in Britain not included in the Greek Cypriot census.

Researchers think that the first major group of Cypriot Greek immigrants arrived in Britain around 1911, as there was no mention of Cyprus-born residents in earlier censuses in England and Wales. Because of transport difficulties, many never saw their homeland again, or their relatives left behind.

Another wave was triggered following the Treaty of Lausanne

when in 1925 Cyprus became a British colony and islanders were automatically British subjects. It was a period when Cyprus was mainly dependent upon subsistence agriculture, education beyond the age of 12 except for younger sons was almost unknown, and only the wealthy could train their children for status jobs in teaching, medicine or the police force.

Local prospects were bleak and young people sought benefits they never found at home - employment, education and better financial futures. By the outbreak of the Second World war, Cypriot Greeks were firmly established in London, with regular earnings and full employment following difficult years of depression.

These findings were part of a recent study by a Greek Cypriot woman lecturer in Modern Languages at a British University, Irina Christodoulou-Pipis. Also a professional translator and interpreter, she launched an in-depth study into Greek Cypriot immigrants' lives in London, including their minority status, language, bilingualism and their interaction on each other.

Her work, which also drew on a number of related studies by other academics or researchers, many of them Greek Cypriot, was published as part of a "Diaspora Books" series called "Greek Outside Greece," Vol. III.

It was subtitled "Language Use by Greek Cypriots in Britain", and was based on research by Professors Robin Oakley and Floya Anthias, and by Dr. Maria Roussou. It had first appeared in 1991 and was based on her dissertation presented earlier for a Master's degree in Translation and Interpreting at the Department of Modern languages, University of Salford in the UK. Her postgraduate studies, along with the book's publication, were financed by the A. G. Leventis Foundation.

Thirty years ago, the two main destinations for Cypriots were England and Australia, but by 1950 England was preferred. Late in the same decade, Greek Cypriots were struggling for independence from Britain; ironically compatriots were migrating to the land of the enemy by the thousands.

The reasons were several -- demand for labour in Britain, a serious employment slump here, and rumours that British streets "were paved with gold". Three percent of emigrants gave other, political, reasons for leaving Cyprus, i.e Greeks opposed Britain, Turks opposed Greeks, and within each Cypriot group, factions such as left and right opposed each other. The third and last great wave of migration begun from the Second World War and finally ended in 1974 when Greek Cypriots abroad were suddenly joined by thousands of homeless relatives from Cyprus after the Turkish invasion of the island that year.

They often arrived with only the clothes they stood up in, says Christodoulou-Pipis. There were entire families, or mothers with children, teenagers alone, young children sent away for safety, and the elderly. The adults had lost property and livelihood and they turned to relatives abroad for shelter, clothing and food until jobs and homes could be found, she writes.

It was this last group - reluctant emigrants who had left under duress - who yearned the most strongly for repatriation; but it was on condition of a political settlement with return of lands and property certain, most said.

The author had become increasingly interested in the Greek Cypriot migrant community and the problems they faced after she spent six years studying in England, and then while working as a professional translator-lecturer there. A native Greek Cypriot bilingual who grew up speaking both Greek and Romanian, Christodoulou-Pipis was attracted to the particularities of the language used by immigrants; she decided to explore it in greater detail.

She dwells particularly on "the different types of linguistic interference"due to contact between two languages, as well as bilingualism and its maintenance or loss. In other words, what happens when Greek or Cypriot Greek speakers (the latter is a Greek dialect) confront the new, or second language, English.

She chose a small section of the Greek Cypriot minority in Britain, especially in London, for her study and found that the community does not possess a "uniform" linguistic background according to social class, age or degree of education. They do speak a "variety" of Cypriot Greek, however, which differs from standard Greek on the phonological, lexical and syntactic levels" (sounds, words and syntax).

The language of the first generation is Greek, or Cypriot Greek, even if they have lived for 20 or more years in England, she points out. Prior to their arrival, only a minority had any knowledge of English, while those with basic skills could not speak it fluently. Amongst themselves, the Greek Cypriot dialect was always spoken, a dialect which already contained many features from other languages which had crept in after centuries of home-land occupation by 14 different rulers.

"One can detect words or stems of words from French, Italian, Arabic, Turkish and English,"she writes. Nevertheless, Athenian demotic Greek was the island's standard language for use in formal education, in the press and media.

She also found that Cypriot children who came to England from the island after the age of five faced several language problems intially, but if younger than 11 had sufficient schooling in front of them to learn English and benefit from their schooling. Older children encountered "great difficulties."

Children born in Britain were in the majority of cases bilingual, although a portion spoke hardly any Greek, she went on. Some were later motivated to improve their Greek after discovering their "beautiful island" and their roots and origin. Others felt isolated because of the language problem and other obstacles they met during visits or extended stays there. This included restrictions on their freedom by relatively strict moral codes in the villages, or provincialism in general. In some cases "this led to alienation when parents insisted on instilling a culture that children were unwilling to share," the author points out.

Families who left the island after 1945 have closer links to their homeland than earlier emigrants, with Cypriot travel agencies offering special "ethnic fares" for travellers. Links are also maintained through letters, food parcels and remittances.

According to some studies, class divisions in the Cypriot community abroad were less distinct than in the island, mainly because the majority of early immigrants were skilled workers or peasants. Since 1960, however, small groups of better educated or professional people emerged and Cypriots themselves began to make distinctions on the basis of the amount of money or capital they possessed, or their business success.

"Those who live in Hendon considered those in Haringey as "horkates" or peasants, while the latter saw Hendon Cypriots as "pseudo aristocrats." Professional groups and successful businessmen are now lumped into one division, the small factory or shop owner in another, and the wage earner following. Political ideologies could also divide people into different groupings, even abroad, Christodoulou-Pipis writes- ideologies which had been bred within a family over time or through village friendships and organisational networks. Most groups vote for the Labour Party in Britain, as it is perceived as being more sympathetic to the Cyprus cause.

Unlike black migrants from the Commonwealth, the average Cypriot did not suffer racialisation as such, the author found. They were known as hard workers and there was little antagonism between Cypriot and Briton because the migrants had arrived in small groups. Moreover, they did not replace the native Briton in job positions but rather filled vacancies left by other immigrants, such as the Italians.

Cypriots were, however, sometimes exposed to xenophobia and ethnicity, particularly meeting some prejudice or stereotyping at schools in response to the EOKA uprising against Britain in the 1950's. But in general, they were considered part of the Greek world which in Britain enjoys prestige, she writes.

Through it all, however, family and the Greek Orthodox church have struggled unrelentingly to preserve migrant Greekness, identity and culture. Apart from attendance at local schools, children can also enroll in evening and weekend classes in the Greek language and culture - ie. mother-tongue teaching classes, or special, full-time schools offering a mixed Greek and English curriculum.

Possibly the most important factor in the survival of Greek Cypriot culture and identity is the powerful influence of the family, the writer says. The highest virtue is loyalty to it and often the Cypriot family of London is a replica of that in Cyprus,particularly that in rural areas.

Cypriot fathers were often compelled to modify their disciplinary powers over London-based families while adapting to new circumstances, she found, with a more liberal family code of behaviour, especially for girls, emerging after long years in England. But there was always insistence on maintaining ties to their own culture, customs, history, and sense of identity and belonging, even for children born in England. Otherwise, "all is lost." Sometimes, customs and traditions were maintained even more vigorously than in Cyprus.

Finally, what about language and bilingualism amongst Greek Cypriot migrants - generally described as the ability of the speaker to function in two or more languages? Much depends, of course, on their depth of interaction between both language groups, as well as motivation. But bilinguals are rarely equally fluent in both languages, with some speaking one language better than another, the writer explains. Judging by Christodoulou-Pipis's work, there are a number of traps involved for a bilingual person, and the Greek Cypriot migrant community, even second generation, is no exception.

While their elders tend to "Hellenise" their limited English vocabulary by slipping in mother-language sounds or tacking on more familiar Greek endings, the second generation will frequently use "loan words" from other languages such as "pizza" "czar" or "chilli" in the middle of Greek sentences. Still others come up with "integrated loans" such as "I am bookharismeni (booked) until Thursday, or "you cannot "controlaris" anybody.

There is a long list of other bilingual percularities or particularities, which include borrowing connectives from one language for use in another, re-arranging words in the primary language to correspond to the pattern of the second, and imposing idioms on the second language from the first, sometimes making no sense at all as a result.

Then there is something called "code-switching" which language experts describe as the use of two or more languages in the same utterance or conversation, says the author.

It goes something like this:

"Che ta dio; kapote kathoumai che milo tis ellinika alla leksis pou en te iksero lalo ta englezika. And then I start talking in English for a little while che istera pao piso sta ellinika."

Translation: "Both: Sometimes I sit and talk to her in Greek for a long time, but words I don't know I say them in English. And then I start talking in English for a little while and then I go back to Greek."

One of the big questions now in Greek Cypriot families abroad is, "what language or languages will the third generation be speaking?" It had better include Greek or the Cypriot Greek dialect. Otherwise ethnically they might go straight from the frying pan to the saucepan.

SEEING THE TEKKE

Are they still there? — the young Turkish Cypriot writers and poets who appeared in the government-backed "Cyprus Review" over 40 years ago and wrote such lines as "through the legs of a slow-moving camel one might see the Hala Sultan Tekke."

Or... "a bride dressed in green instead of white... the unfought battles of Bellapais and St. Hilarion... I like not your days, for they are full of agonies."

It was autumn, 1955, the magazine's early period, and Greek Cypriot writers, equally anxious for artistic exposure, were also contributors. It was also the early days of EOKA's underground war against colonial Britain.

The Greeks described life in their villages and unrequited love through their short stories, or wrote verse about solitude and yearning and leaving it all behind. Like their Turkish Cypriot counterparts, they too were "slaves of their environment," as one from that community had pointed out — "the palm trees crowding the shores of Larnaca, recollections from the pages of Shakespeare, the pines of Troodos." But as the anti-colonial rebellion gained momentum, new martyrs and sympathy, Greek Cypriot contributions sharply fell away, including those of a poetic nature.

For a time, Lawrence Durrell of later "Alexandria Quartet"and "Bitter Lemons" fame had edited the publication, hoping to slick up the Public Information Office's latest effort and at the same time provide literary space for Greek and Turkish talent. In a small island, scope as well as the reading public was limited. The Review also carried line-drawings and other art, side by side with the official "bumf", as it was known.

Hopeful colonial officials still thought that the rebellion might flicker and die away forever, like a Tolstoy heroine. Or why not passive resistance instead, like the Indians, authorities were to hint hopefully in those earliest days.

"We don't have a population of millions to lie down on railroad tracks," explained one churchman at the Archbishopric in Nicosia where on a nearby square brooded a memorial statue to another rebel ecclesiastic, hanged by the Ottomans in 1821.

But the "Review" soldiered on hopefully for a time. There was still no "them" and "us" between Greek and Turkish Cypriots, or an "other side". Just Greek and Turkish "quarters" with the Armenians in between. The word, "taksim" or partition in Turkish was as yet an unfamiliar word and nonconformist Greeks still went to "Chaglayan's" in the capital's Turkish quarter to smoke a nargile on Good Friday instead of going to church with the rest of the Christians.

Three languages crammed into a small island were still bandied back and forth and most people knew a smattering at least of each others'. More Turks could speak Greek than vice versa, "but then the Greeks could never really understand anything with a verb at the end," the Turks would say.

Eventually the "Review" was to falter, then cease altogether. The Archbishop was exiled, people were killed or hanged, and The Emergency was to continue another four years.

"And through Desdemona's closing eyes, night was falling," a Turkish Cypriot from Famagusta was to write. Mustapha Adiloglu was a graduate of the Turkish Lycee in Nicosia and had published two books of verse, including one called "Separate From Human Beings". He had already gained a wide reputation in literary circles in Turkey where he was also known for an epic poem about his own town.

According to Review writer, Salahi Ramadan, Adiloglu was one of many Turkish Cypriots who made up the Turkish literary movement in the island at the time. For them, he pointed out, Cyprus was "a constant source of inspiration and meditation," and offered "wonderful" material for their music, verse, drama and graphic arts.

"For years they have worked on this wonderful material like the craftsmen of the Stone Flower. For them, too, Cyprus was an island of sweet memories, dark recollections and dramatic adventures in love," says Ramadan. Another young Turkish poet, Taner Baybars, "adored" English literature and Greek mythology and moulded both into profound and wonderful verse, he said.

Baybars was then in England cooperating with an English translator on the works of the late Sait Faik, a famous Turkish writer, we are told. One of Baybars' poems was entitled "Oscar Wilde" and began "Couldn't you that night hear the heart of light being torn away...?"

Another promising writer was Ozker Yasin, according to Ramadan, whose poems frequently appeared in the literary monthly, "Varlik" (Existence, Being) in Turkey, where he was highly esteemed. The only outlet in Cyprus, apparently, had been a monthly periodical called "The Trellis" which was aimed at foreigners.

Meanwhile, there was growing admiration for the picturesque walled city of Nicosia and its Turkish quarter. One "Review" writer, M. Ferid, presents an unusual view with a tour "through Nicosia with a Turkish Guide". The article was called "Twelve Minarets" — they are stark and beautiful and uniform, he says, when seen from the pleasant heights of Kubat Pasha (Likavito).

"They draw us down to the centre of the walled city where the busy Municipal Market and Kuyumcular, the street of goldsmiths, leads to the twin towers of the Selimiye Mosque. It is Friday and a dense crowd is washing hands, feet and face three times at a fountain with dozens of taps before entering the mosque." The Sultan's Library is close by, he goes on, a small building that once housed more than 2.000 volumes of Turkish, Persian and Arabic works. Here, where an army of copyists once sat writing out the Holy Books in an ornate script, was also a glass case in which a few precious hairs from the beard of the Prophet were preserved.

Beyond the Haidar Pasha mosque was the Yeni Djami (mosque) where a domed canopy covered the tomb of Hassan Hilmi Effendi, the mufti of Cyprus in 1880.

Then there was the narrow street of the Turkish confectioners, and the nearby Buyuk Khan or Great Inn, built in 1571 (the year of the Ottoman invasion of Cyprus) by Muzaffer Pasha to accommodate visiting merchants. "The great doors were barred in those days; the merchants slept safely in the upstairs rooms while their servants occupied the lower quarters and their caravans the courtyard."

In nearby Asmalti Street was the "Khan (Inn) of the Itinerant Musicians", a onetime gathering place for Turkish artists who travelled the length and breadth of Asia Minor playing national music, according to Ferid. Beyond the Efkaf offices were the Women's Baths and the hamams (Turkish baths) still in use in the 1950's.

Some of the mosques were named after fruit or flowers, such as the Tourouchlou Djami (mosque), or Mosque of the Orange Tree, dedicated to a onetime Turkish governor here called Said Mehmed Aga.

Another, close to Ataturk Square, was the Laleli or Mosque of the Tulip, with a wrought iron floral design on its minaret. The Arab Ahmed mosque at the Paphos Gate end of Victoria Street, he comments, was named after a famous Turkish general who built the main water conduit that supplied the town from the upper Pedieos river.

One of the most picturesque was the Bairaktar, or mosque of the Standard Bearer whose tomb is there. It is on the Constanza Bastion where the walls of Nicosia were breached on September 9, 1570 by Ottoman troops. Its yard was made into a garden which still provided Nicosia with flowers two hundred years later.

The nearby Omeriyeh mosque within the walls takes its name from the Caliph Omer and is believed haunted by a benevolent spirit "invested with health-giving qualities." (Note: Like a number of mosques, it was once a Christian church before Ottoman rule.)

When it's time for folk-dancing, Turkish Cypriots have many to choose from, says Servet Sami in the February, 1956, issue of the Review.

They are the folk dances of Turkey, which Cyprus Turks have handed down from generation to generation, he says, and which would always be remembered and performed during celebrations despite the impact of other, more modern, forms of entertainment.

They include the well-known Harmandali, which can be performed singly or in groups, its haunting, bitter-sweet music full of emotion; the Sari Zeybek (zeybek means a swashbuckler from a village) whose words are first sung by the dancers standing in line; another is the Dadash, an important folk dance from the district of Erzurum in Eastern Turkey, which symbolises a youth who is "brave, generous, self sacrificing and sincere." It should be performed by a maximum of three men, and the dance loses its beauty if the numbers are altered.

The men begin in a semi-circle, and the slow and graceful movements are usually accompanied by drum and clarion. The leader is called the "barbashi."

Some particularly picturesque dances, Sami remarks, originated in the Black Sea's eastern coast, such as the dances of Trabzon-Rize, in which a group or "horon" take part. Trapezous was once inhabited by the Pontii - in ancient Greek "horos" meant the chorus.

The dances are gay and colourful, Sami writes, with intricate figures difficult to master. A viola at the centre of the circle provides the music.

He also mentions the dances of Hopa, Pazar and Hemshin,

usually danced to bagpipes. The Kars dances called for drum and clarion, trumpet, reed flute and tambourine. Some are danced by mixed groups of men and women in set formations, others, called "Bar", by men only in groups of eight or ten. Liveliest of all, the writer remarks, is the Turkish "Daghli" or the "Bengi" in which large numbers can participate. Many of the dances featured colourful, booted figures in turbans or kerchiefs, worn above loose shirts and embroidered vest, with a shawl flung over the shoulders and down the back.

During the barley harvest some Turkish communities dance the "Arpazli" on the threshing floor, he writes; sometimes an open-air banquet is given by the farmer producing the largest crop.

Yet another Turkish Cypriot writer tells us how the Turks remember their dead. Their tombs are visited frequently and are sometimes "imposing structures" if their survivors had been wealthy. "The tradition of visiting graves is common amongst all Moslems," Bedri says, "but particularly amongst the Turks." Religious holidays are the most sacred of days to visit lost relatives or friends.

"Men, women and children may visit the place of their dead relatives provided they have performed a ceremonial ablution i.e. the washing of face, hands and feet to the accompaniment of recitations from the Koran." They must also have carried ont "spiritual cleansing" through recitation of the "Yasin" chapter of the Koran. Devout Moslems then equip themselves with flowers, myrtle branches and containers of water which have been sanctified by a hodja through prayer.

On arrival at the cemetery, they stand at the eastern side of the tomb, the women with covered heads. They pour water over the grave and scatter flowers and myrtle while intoning prayers, their palms turned upward. When prayers end, the visitors wipe their faces with their hands to conclude the ceremony. ... "Moslems have a strong belief that the souls of the dead watch them throughout the ceremony, while water frees and purifies the soul."

According to Moslem belief all souls enter either paradise or hell, he says, and prayers "will go a long way in helping the soul on its journey to paradise. If at his last breath a person can pronounce the word 'Allah', he can go straight to paradise," relates Bedri: "This is why Turkish soldiers in a fight keep on uttering with a wild roar the sacred word, 'Allah,' just before and during an assault." The noise has the added effect of breaking the morale of the enemy. he says.

Although worship of the dead is strictly forbidden by Moslem tenets, ordinary people find satisfaction in believing that the dead can help them in times of need or distress. "This is more clearly exemplified by the number of candles that are being lit nightly by unknown people at the headstones of more than five holy graves in Nicosia."

Apparently they are those of Turkish soldiers who fell during the fight for the capture of Nicosia some three and a half centuries ago, he relates.

The graves are on the pavements of certain streets and are well-kept. A green ribbon, the colour of sanctity, has usually been wrapped round the headstone.

KOURION

Death came with little warning, says the archaeologist, certainly to hundreds and probably to thousands at Kourion and elsewhere in Cyprus on that fateful July morning 16 centuries ago.

There had been a massive earthquake, then another and another, its energy thought now to be 100 times more than that of the atom bomb dropped on Hiroshima.

The quake's epicentre was 30 miles to the southwest of Cyprus, under the Mediterranean, and overlooked by the ancient seaport city of Kourion from a bluff above.

The dying city quickly lay in ruins and for many of its inhabitants, entombed under massive toppling walls while most were still in their beds, it was the end of the world. Then, a great seismic wave from the sea, a "tsumani", hit the coast, drowning whatever had survived of Kourion life after the quakes. Over the centuries, sands blowing up from the shores buried the silent city until the scavengers, and finally the archaeologists, arrived.

When struck, the once-great city state was a new Christian settlement just emerging from its pagan past in the late Roman empire, the new faith still struggling for supremacy with other oriental religions.

The skeletal hand of one victim recently recovered still wore a ring inscribed with the initials "Chi Rho," the first two letters of Christ's name.

For archaeologists excavating at the site over the past two decades, the uncovering of the city and its dead seemed like a rescue operation 16 centuries too late. Even the pitiful skeletons unearthed, some with arms still entwined, were gradually given names in their numbered, carefully excavated rooms, even mourned as they were lifted out along with the smashed utensils from daily life that had surrounded them. There was pottery, glassware, oil lamps, Roman coins.

"The intimacy that exists between an archaeologist and the people he is excavating can be quite startling in its profundity," wrote David Soren, head of the Classics department at the University of Arizona and a renowned archaeologist.

He had excavated for three years at Kourion and the nearby sanctuary of Apollo of the Woodlands in the mid-1980's. Soren is known as a pioneer in the field of seismic archaeology -- that is, the excavation of cities buried by earthquake. He is currently digging in Italy.

After an initial shoestring start here, Soren's own excavating team grew to include co-director Diana Buitron (whose husband Drew Oliver is an authority on ancient glass) and scores of other archaeologists, scholars, specialists and supporters. At the time, the dig was sponsored by Dartmouth and the University of Missouri. Later, Arizona and other sources lent further, much-needed help. Eventually, the team was to unearth here the "earliest completely preserved Christian community ever discovered."

Soren's very readable story of the excavation, called "Kourion, the Search for a Lost Roman City", was written along with writer Jamie James and published in 1988 by Anchor Press, Doubleday, New York.

Soren also published a briefer account the same year in the "National Geographic" magazine, accompanied by several photographs taken by his archaeologist wife, Noelle.

The site of Kourion (called Curium in Latin) is about a mile from the modern-day village of Episcopi, and archaeologists believe that when fully uncovered eventually, it will rival Pompeii in its vividness, its poignancy and the scale of the tragedy which destroyed it.

Already a forum, shops, a spacious, patrician house, walls, a basilica and sanctuary, and other buildings have been unearthed.

But there is still a great deal underneath, according to Demos Christou, who has excavated at Kourion for 24 years and whose dream is to eventually see the city united once again.

Christou, who was Curator of ancient monuments with the Department of Antiquities and was also working at Kourion during Soren's dig, has recently retired as the department's Director of Antiquities. He subsequently launched another excavation at the early Christian basilica there, and points out that the site still hides further remains from the Hellenistic and Classical period.

He share's Soren's opinion that many archaeologists relate strongly to their excavation sites, and that amidst the cool, scientific approaches there are deeply felt emotions, especially when evidence emerges on how people actually lived at the time and what they thought.

Says Christou: "That feeling of discovery is very special, even more so when your own thoughts and theories eventually prove correct — theories that you have believed in over a long period. I still remember the first tomb that I excavated as a young archaeologist. I didn't feel comfortable at all, rather I felt guilty somehow because I was moving into that quietness surrounding the dead. Later, of course, I wished to find more and more of the offerings that were buried with them.

"These offerings are the treasures of the museums — the pottery and jewellery and other artifacts. All are important clues to people's lives at a particular time."

Says Soren: "The folks who lived in Kourion dreamed and napped and told lies and burned up with love and occasionally ate and drank too much, just like some people we know, just like us. The deeper into the rubble you dig, the more vividly you feel it. But as in any friendship, not all of the gaps are ever filled in... for the excavator there is always a quality of mystery, a final shadowy little corner that will never be revealed. That's what keeps us digging."

Soren offers other insights into the work and thoughts of a professional archaeologist in the field. He also describes the last moments of some of the quake victims at Kourion.

"They were in their bedroom," he wrote in the "National Geographic". "The mother, a young woman of 19, still clutched her 1½ year-old baby to her breast. The child, its teeth still coming in, grasped its mother's elbow. Over them lay a man of about 28, presumably the father, who had tried to shield the pair from a deadly rain of limestone building blocks weighing as much as 300 pounds.

... "bald skeletons now, they had been a family of three, clinging together for life as their home exploded and crumbled in an earthquake that devastated the city... 16 centuries ago.

"Nearby, a labourer of about 55 years had taken refuge in a doorway." His room had been decorated with frescoes and the wall collapsed against his skull.

After the massive quake, thought to have struck on July 21, in 365 AD, there followed a series of punishing shocks, he writes, accompanied by a seismic wave that also caused havoc as far away as Alexandria and the coast of Greece. Although a new urban centre emerged a few decades later, the great city of Kourion as it was known faded from historical record, he goes on. Founded in the late Bronze Age by Greek seafarers and finally containing a population of 20.000, it was gone forever in a few moments.

No one ever returned to collect the dead, Soren wrote.

Two miles to the west, the Temple of Apollo had also collapsed, the upper third of its wall sheared off. Scavangers later plundered what had remained standing, while earth and debris covered the rest.

Soren and other scientists think that before the major earthquake struck, earlier shocks had been felt only by animals. One 13-year-old victim, a girl named Camilia by archeologists who found her skeleton, had apparently rushed to the courtyard to calm a frightened mule. The first major quake then jarred everyone awake in a four-second episode, allowing time only "to reach for loved ones and huddle for protection" as buildings collapsed round them.

The young girl died trapped under her mule — archaeologists later found the skeletons of both — while the young mother and her family died in the second quake, the mother's neck snapped by a falling block as she huddled with husband and child, Soren writes. Their remains, along with other artifacts, are in the local site museum at Episcopi nearby. By the third quake, with the ground a "mass of quivering jell-o", most of the population were already dead. Thousands of others living in southwest Cyprus also perished, Soren adds.

A 4th century Roman historian, Ammianus Marcellinus, described the tragedy which he said had "devastated the Mediterranean" at the time. The tone is biblical.

"Just after dawn there were frequent flashes of lightning, and the rumbling of thunder. Then the firm and stable mass of the earth trembled and shook, and the sea withdrew, its waves flowing backward.

"The sea floor was exposed, revealing fishes and sea creatures stuck fast in the slime. Mountains and valleys that had been hidden in the unplumbed depths since the creation of the world saw the rays of the sun. Boats were left stranded in these newly created lands, and men wandered fearlessly in the little that remained of the waters, collecting fishes with their bare hands.

"But then the sea returned with an angry vengeance, roared and rushed through the seething shallows, dashing through every open space and levelling countless buildings in the cities and wherever else they are to be found.

... "The great mass of waters, returning when it was least expected, killed many thousands of men by drowning... other great ships, driven by the mad blasts, landed on the tops of buildings (as happened at Alexandria)...."

St. Jerome had also described an earthquake at the time

that "occurred throughout the world... the sea swamped the coastline and destroyed nations and cities of Sicily and many other islands."

Although shifting sands had blanketed Kourion for centuries, archaeologists have uncovered significant remains, including small live-in shops, thousands of fragments of wall frescoes, ample graffiti samples and drawings. On one wall, some 4th century AD artist had drawn a lady with a flower, another had written the Greek alphabet, yet another the words "O Jesus", and then "of Chr(ist)," Soren mentions.

Also unearthed were bronze cooking vessels, a "wonderful" bronze lamp in the shape of a duck pondering its lighted tail, a possible slaughter house, the bones of an enormous rabbit, ample barley, wheat and rye seeds, and coins dating from the period of Emperor Valens — some dated 365 AD when the earthquake levelled Kourion. According to Soren, the site is still well-stocked with the things that a good archaeologist prizes most — unanswered questions.

Kourion had remained in near-obscurity, he goes on, because until recently the profession had been traditionally prejudiced against Roman civilisation, particularly in its late period, believing it to have been copyist. Since the 18th century, the emphasis has always been on Greece and Greek art, and in the past on "classical" classical archaeology. The over-riding concern was the discovery or rather recovery of beautiful objects — "bigger was better and gold was the best of all."

But over the past 15 years, he thinks, there has been "a revolution of sorts in the way many of us are thinking in the field." Now, the "new archaeology" is a hybrid between science and the humanities. While still "healthily aware of the value of gold and beautiful objects," and the importance of museum displays, "our interest is more and more in what unearthed objects can tell us, a socio-economic as well as an aesthetic approach.

... "Now it is more a matter of motives — why does one dig — and of what one does with the stuff after it comes out of the ground?

"There are 6,528 Roman baths in the world, and we would all get along quite well if another one were never found. To excavate per se is boring and pointless, if all you are going to do is dig up more objects to be tagged and catalogued and put in display cases with little white cards."

There is nothing wrong with exhibits, he stresses, and museum studies will always be essential. But more interesting questions now are "What did people do with this thing? Exactly what went on here?" Previously, the archaeologist would cull out all the jewellery and ceramics from a tomb site, then throw out the rest, including human remains. "In Egypt, they once ground up crocodile mummies to mulch their gardens."

Today, archaeology makes use not only of specialist-scientists, but of computers. The latter has revolutionised the field, he says, and not only as a data base. Further, specialists have discovered along the way that the ancients had very few tooth cavities (lack of sugar) and that malaria has been with us since the Neolithic period.

Coins are now cleaned with a "highly ingenious" electrolytic process. The iridescent optical effect so common in excavated glassware, Soren explains, is caused by the leaching out of sodium and potassium ions (the components) into the soil during long exposure. Layers of silica are stripped away over a long period. But when used by the ancients, these objects were transparent, like modern glass.

According to Soren, "you are only as good as your last trench," and there are "people out there" waiting with glee to destroy your career.... "In archaeology, as in any field, nothing succeeds like success.

..."We archaeologists are all connected to one another by a giant, rather ungainly web, which consists of articles in scholarly journals, mimeographed newsletters and slide lectures at ceaseless rounds of conventions. There we keep shaking up one another's ideas. It can be deadly dull. It can also be exciting." And the rewards of the dig are large and deep as time goes on, he adds.

"At Kourion, they had all been dead for 16 hundred years when we unearthed them. It is just that distance that forged the deep connection between us. There is nothing more personal than death.

"Camelia (the 13-year-old girl) left this world all alone, except for the company of her mule, and she remained utterly alone until we butted in. She did not invite us, but she has graciously ... answered every question we have put to her; and over the course of the excavation, something very like friendship has flourished between us."

Archaeology, a microcosm of life, embraces the whole range of human activity. It can be infuriatingly incomplete in the field, full of random gaps, he points out. And what is "indisputably true one season becomes the outmoded fallacy of the next."

Perhaps that is what keeps them digging. That and the fact that a major excavation such as Kourion is never really over.

GOURMET DIPLOMAT

Not many of us know that Saint Zita is the 13th century patron saint of cooks, or that Sir Osbert Sitwell found roast saddle of iguana "very, very good," or that you should never chop up a good-hearted cabbage when you can serve it in quarters instead.

But Sir Harry Luke knew — that gourmet, diplomat and international food taster, who once shared a meatless, 14-course dinner with monks at Mt. Athos and "ate for his country round the world" for half a century as one of Britain's "gastronomic ambassadors."

His epicurian high points also included Cyprus where, early in his diplomatic career, he was private secretary to a popular British High Commissioner called Sir Hamilton Goold-Adams, in the early 1900's.

Sir Harry later helped to immortalise several gastronomic treats from the island which he included in an unusual and highly entertaining book called "The Tenth Muse", first published in 1954.

This tenth and final muse was an unacknowledged goddess whom he invented himself, and who was the inspiration for the food and wine of the gods. He called her Nectambrosia. The book is a collection of recipes and menus from the exquisite to the simply good, culled from years of international travel and much time spent at other people's dinner tables.

He recalls the splendour of pre-war banquets in great houses, and reminds us that birds' nest soup is really made of birds' nests and that bears' hams and good vodka as served in the Trans-Caucasian republics are an irresistable temptation to the unwary. He could never understand, he said, how the Georgian officers of those days retained their greyhound figures, given the enormous amounts of food they ate.

He also advises on the correct way to stuff a Cyprus sausage, and discussed the little "figpecking" birds called beccaficos which had been pickled in the island for centuries. They resembled the ortolan in size, and died a "cruel" death by liming.

Sir Harry is the same man who traced Ottoman rule in Cyprus through 300 years, a comparatively obscure period for scholars. His book "Cyprus Under the Turks, 1571 - 1878," was first published in 1921 by Clarendon Press, Oxford. Hearing at a Government House party in Nicosia in 1911 that there had been English consular representatives in the island as far back as the early 18th century, he had set about searching the lofts and cellars of government buildings for reports or any other material left behind.

Eventually, he uncovered some 10,000 documents in seven languages, stored and forgotten in an old wooden "sanduq" or chest normally used for keeping dowry linen. There were documents from the period of the famous Levant Company, established here in 1582 to further British trade in the Mediterranean (an amalgamation of two previous companies), and later consular archives covering almost two centuries until 1878, when Turkey handed over the administration and occupation of Cyprus to Britain.

But for him, food and its infinite variety was to hold an enduring fascination. For all of his adult life, he collected recipes, menus and wine lists from unforgettable dinners, official and otherwise, from every continent. His sources were his own cooks, the chatelaines and head chefs at British residences and government houses, famous cooks in European, South American and North American capitals, the chefs of Turkish Grand Viziers, and of Russia, China, Syria and even Polynesia.

His own introduction to the eating process, he writes, took place in the winter and spring of 1907-8, in the last months of the reign of Abdul Hamid II as absolute ruler of Turkey. With a friend from Oxford, they had been entertained by the Qaimaqam, or district commissioner, in the Empire's eastern province during a prolonged caravan tour where they stayed at the "noble Krak des Chevaliers."

The commissioner, who lived in the castle, had pulled the best pieces off the carcasses of sheep killed in their honour, rolling them into gigantic pills with rice, onion, pine kernels, cinnamon and garlic, and "then placing the resultant bolus firmly in their mouths." Later, returning the hospitality, the two rolled up suitably kneaded bits of bully-beef, which was all that they had to offer, and popped it into the amused Qaimaqam's mouth.

There are some recipes that he could never recommend, such as a favourite of a former Bey of Tunis that called for "the heads of parrots, tongues of nightingales, the brains of peacocks and of ostriches."

Sir Harry was later photographed sitting cross-legged on the ground while sharing "an appetising alfresco luncheon" of barbecued pig with Queen Salote, collecting clams in the Caribbean, and offering tea to the Prince of Wales in Sierra Leone. There is a large uncut cake set before them on a wicker table, and one wonders if Sir Harry had overseen its preparation personally.

He disliked unimaginative food; not for the gourmet the monotonous diet inflicted on some. While the Eskimos couldn't do much about blubber, or the wretched Alakaluf in the south with their main menu of raw sea urchins and mussels (for which their women plunged naked into the icy Patagonian fjords to obtain), he did think that his fellow Britons could vary their breakfast choices, given that it was the first meal of the day.

While hastening to say that he was not one of those who can find no good in British cooking — some of it was marvellous — there were other options than the "joyless, dyspeptic toast, coffee and cereal" served up in some homes, day after day. "It is sad to think that few are likely to see again the sideboard laden with that noble array... grilled fresh herring, the fried whiting swallowing his tail... the scrambled eggs... kidney and bacon... the cold bird."

While he does not suggest the breakfast of pork chops eaten by Lord Palmerston hours before his demise, he does feel that even bacon and egg could be a welcome change, or even a dover sole or modest kipper, or a mushroom or two. But then, neither would we wish to emulate that famous recipe for "ortolan into lark into thrush into quail into partridge into capon into duck into goose into turkey into peacock, each one stuffed inside the next," he says.

Naturally, he writes, it is the imperial and royal courts of pre-austerity Europe where one would expect to find the most complete achievement of variety. He had never seen a recipe that could compete with the range of ingredients and the subtlety of blending found in the famous state soup of the Habsburgs, which was served from the time of Empress Maria Theresa's father to that of her great-great-grandson Francis Joseph.

It took ten chefs, sous chefs and kitchen maids thirty two hours without pause to prepare the soup. The staff were all chosen for their endurance and conscientiousness.

It included veal, ham, mutton, venison and other game, roasted in butter and then boiled for stock, eight calves' feet and two cowheels converted into jelly, smoked and fresh pork, white cabbages, maize seeds, chestnuts, lentils, pearl barley and French carrots baked in sugar, ox liver, egg white and beef bones. When the finished product was drained through muslin bags, it was carried into the ballrooms in cauldrons and transferred to porcelain jugs. The soup was then poured into delicate gold and white cups from the Vienna porcelain factory. The soup served from 1,000 to 2,500 persons. (Note: One envoy from Ottoman Turkey visiting the Viennese court reported that some of the Habsburgs had strangely shaped heads and very large ears. He did not comment on the food.)

Sir Harry also describes Chinese banquets and North African feasts, and a luncheon in Quito, Ecuador which included a yearling pig with lots of crackling. The pig's head, he says, was adorned with horns cut out of large chillies. In Fidji, the population called those fiercely hot little red peppers so popular in Spanish America "goddamits," while a harmless mushroom, for some reason, was the "Devil's Umbrella."

There were some occasions when the author, during his long diplomatic career, was obliged to eat what he found most unappetising. "The paymasters of British government officials stationed in foreign parts have little or no realisation of the nastiness we are sometimes called upon to swallow so as not to offend," he remarks.

This could include the broth made of the roe of the sea slug, or roast flying fox (a large bat) or white grubs dug out of tree stumps. Another difficulty faced was the Oriental habit of stuffing the guests to the verge of suffocation and not taking no for an answer.

The best-cooked meals that he had ever eaten in the East, he said, were served by Said Beg, the hereditary head of the Devil Worshippers' at his castle in Mosul, and in the Asia Minor home of the high Islamic dignitary, the Chelebi of Konya (the hereditary head of the Mevlevi order of Dervishes). At the latter's, meat, vegetable and sweet dishes were interspersed with pleasant inconsequence, with the sweets being baklava, sweet rice pudding and finally melons.

Included in his "Don't" list of food preparation: it is a major gastronomic crime to permit an onion anywhere near caviar; clear soups require much labour and many ingredients and on most occasions it is better to stick to the thick ones, served hot; and please don't serve "wings only" of the chicken, which is a bad habit some hostesses have and which is the most tasteless part of the fowl.

Potatoes should be boiled before not after peeling, don't waste good food and wine on people who smoke between courses, and do add sugar when cooking peas, tomatoes and carrots. Further, don't chop up or skin French beans unless they are really old; confine yourself to stringing.

The Arabs, especially the Bedouin, prefer their coffee thin, bitter and powerfully flavoured with cardamom, while others prefer it thick and sweet. The word "coffee" comes from the Arabic "qahweh," he says, and when sugar is added to Turkish (or Greek) coffee, it is added to the coffee before boiling.

It is made in a long-handled pot which tapers toward the top so that the coffee may boil up quickly and produce the requisite froth, Sir Harry says. To make, place in the pot two teaspoons of powdered coffee and one Turkish coffee-cupful of cold water for each person. Bring to the boil three times. To evenly distribute the froth and sediment, only a little coffee should be poured into each cup at a time. There are three grades of sweetness, he adds.

Regarding St. Zita, the patron saint of cooks, she was born in a Tuscan village and sent to work in the house of a prosperous weaver at the age of 12. Deeply devout, she attended Mass daily and handed out to the poor much of the good food her employer had given her, keeping very little for herself, the story goes.

One year she over-reached herself and began secretly giving away her master's store of beans, there being famine in the land. Hoping to sell them at a profit, the master suddenly announced plans to carry out an inspection of supplies. Terrified of his quick-temper, St. Zita prayed for divine intervention, which was apparently quick in coming for the beans were mysteriously replenished. Angels also took charge of her baking chores whenever she was absent in church. St. Zita served the same family for 48 years.

In Cyprus, Sir Harry had a cook called Yianni, he writes, who could roast woodcock and the vanishing francolin to perfection, and who also cooked him the only camel's hump he had ever eaten.

Although he left behind no recipe for camel, Sir Harry did

include other local favorites including one for moussaka that he obtained from Lady Blackall, Kyrenia.

The ingredients: 1 lb. lean tender beefsteak, four large ripe tomatoes, 6 eggplants (aubergines), two tablespoons finely chopped onion, 1 tablespoon finely chopped parsley, salt, pepper, lard for frying, 2 tablespoons flour, 1 pint milk or milk and stock, 5 table-spoons grated cheese.

<u>Mince the meat</u>. Heat 2 tablespoons lard in a frying pan, add meat and onion, and fry until all the meat liquid is absorbed. Add tomatoes which have been skinned and cut up coarsely, and a little water or stock.

<u>Season</u> with salt and pepper and cover, simmering til the meat is quite tender and the tomato juice absorbed. Add the parsley.

<u>Make a sauce</u> with the butter, flour, milk and cheese. Wash, but do not peel the eggplants. Cut them lengthways in thin slices and fry in hot fat until a light golden colour, and drain on paper to remove all greasiness.

<u>Arrange layers</u> of fried eggplant and cooked meat alternately in a fire-proof dish, finishing with eggplant. Pour over the sauce, sprinkle with grated cheese and breadcrumbs, and brown in the oven.

He also tells the reader how to prepare Cyprus dolma (stuffed wine leaves), local sausages with coriander seeds and herbs to taste, and a spring delicacy made from a small, wild, low-growing thistle which is parent to the globe artichoke and cooked in Cyprus with scrambled eggs.

A good substitute for spinach or sorrel is the wild mallow (malva sylvestris) which is used in Cyprus villages, he writes, and was referred to in the first century B.C. by a Chinese poet who had said: "I'll pluck the mallows and make soup."

Cypriot cooks also pick the young leaves of the bladder campion, he adds, which they call "sparrow grass," or "strouthoudia."

<u>And finally, a Kyrenia recipe for Chocolate Mousse from Mrs Wilfred Bolton:</u>

6 oz. sweet chocolate

6 eggs

1/2 liqueur glass brandy

<u>Melt the chocolate</u> in a bain-marie. Beat the egg yolks and stir into the chocolate, adding the brandy.

<u>Whisk the whites</u> very stiffly, and fold into the chocolate. Put in a cool place to set, but do not leave more than 6 hours before eating. Serves 6.

And finally, for those turkeys that will not be with us on Christmas Day, a note on "How The Turkey Got His Names", according to Sir Harry. It is a confusing issue. The appellations given to this exotic bird from the New World in the languages of the Old, are geographically erratic and hopelessly perplexing, he says.

That in England he should be called turkey may be due to a 16th century confusion with guinea fowl and pea fowl, introduced into England from their respective homes via Turkey at the same time as the turkey arrived from South America and Spain. Other suggestions are that his gobble sounds like turk, turk, turk, or that his name is a corruption from one of the Amerindian languages.

The European world seems to connect the turkey with Indians, he continues, but is extremely hazy about what sort of Indians — those of the East Indies or those of the American continent? Actually, says Sir Harry, the turkey comes from Mexico and Central America.

"This is just one of the many examples of the permanent confusion into which Christopher Columbus plunged the world by thinking that he had reached the East Indies by a new route."

In Turkey, the bird is thought to originate in India or Egypt, according to the name given; the Arabs call it the Abyssinian fowl. Whatever, we should be grateful to the turkey, says Sir Harry, which has been making his notable contribution to "Christmas husbandlie fare" since the 16th century.

CAPTIONS

Page 149

1	2	3
4	5	6
7	8	9	10
11	12	13

1. Dionysos, Salamis. Famagusta, 2nd century AD.
2. Bird-faced goddess - 12th Century BC.
3. Female head, limestone. Arsos, 3rd century BC.
4. Artemis, limestone. Pyla, 5th century BC.
5. Aphrodite, Trikomo, 4th century BC.
6. Smiling head of woman. Cyprus-Archaic period. (700-745 BC)
7. Small cruciform figurine. Chalcolithic period (3900-2500 BC).
8. Plank-shaped fertility goddess. Early Bronze Age (2500-1900 BC).
9. Goddess, 8th century BC.
10. "Kore" style limestone head from Arsos (450 BC).
11. Emperor Septimius Severus. Roman period (50 BC - 395 AD).
12. Horned god, Enkomi. Famagusta, 12th century BC.
13. Aphrodite, marble, from Soloi. 1st century BC.

Photos from the Cyprus Museum, the Louvre, the Pierides Museum Larnaca.

Page 150

1	2	3
4	5	6
7	8	9
10		

1. Berengaria, a likeness.
2. Catherine Cornaro.
3. The Belle of Cyprus.
4. Sultan Abdul Hamid II.
5. Archbishop Makarios.
6. Sir Garnet Wolseley.
7. Mrs. Esme Scott - Stevenson.
8. Dr. Fazil Kuchuk.
9. A Cyprus village woman.
10. Enroute to Cyprus, 1878.

Photos from The Popular Bank Of Cyprus, Cultural Centre publications & The Leventis Municipal Museum of Nicosia; Lakis Demetriades; Holt, Rinehart & Winston, New York; Trigraph, London.

Page 151

1	2	3
4	5	6
7	■	8
9		

1. The Turkish Bedestan, Nicosia.
2,3,4. Villagers at work.
5. Victoria Road, Nicosia.
6,7,8. Village life.
9. Nicosia street scene.

Photos from Lakis Demetriades; Haigaz Mangoian
Voula Kokkinou; John Foscolo.
The Popular Bank Cultural Centre.

Page 152

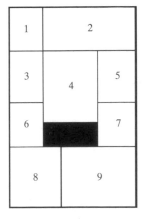

1	2	
3	4	5
6	■	7
8	9	

1. Stavrovouni Monastery.
2. Ancient Salamis.
3. Kolossi Castle.
4. Harbour Gate, Famagusta.
5. Nicosia mosque.
6. The last Lusignan Palace.
7. H.M.S. Himalaya.
8. The Beuyuk Khan.
9. Kykko Monastery.

Photos from Haigaz Mangoian; John Foscolo.
The Popular Bank Cultural Centre.

Page 153

1. St. Nicolas Cathedral, Famagusta.
2. Window, Lusignan Palace, Nicosia.
3. Kyrenia and its Harbour.
4. The Hala Sultan Tekke, Larnaca.
5. Larnaca and its Fort.
6. Paphos Harbour.

Photos from Haigaz Mangoian; John Foscolo.
The Popular Bank Cultural Centre.

Page 154

1. The Camel Driver.
2. Mountain villagers, Pedhoulas .

Photos from Haigaz Mangoian; John Foscolo.

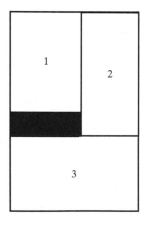

Page 155

1. Phini Village, Women potters.
2. A Cypriot Child.
3. St. Hilarion Castle, Kyrenia Mountains.

Photos from Haigaz Mangoian;
Lakis Demetriades; John Foscolo.
The Popular Bank Cultural Centre.

THANK YOU

I am indebted to a great many individuals and organisations for the assistance and time that they have given me in gathering material for this book. I have also been encouraged by readers' interest in the subject matter since the series first began appearing in the "Cyprus Weekly" three years ago.

Although generally well-acquainted with the Cyprus of the Homeric through the Byzantine periods, I found that many people, both Cypriot and foreign, are also curious about life here during the turbulent and lively times that followed.

I am very grateful to the "Cyprus Weekly" and its editors for permission to re-publish the series that I wrote for them.

Very special thanks are also due the following persons, organisations, academic and cultural bodies, research groups, institutes, museums and libraries, for the many forms of help and cooperation shown to me:

To my husband, Dr. Vassos Lyssarides, and to my nephew, Dr. George Christodoulou, archaeologist and Byzantine philologist; Dr. Vassos Karageorghis for his hospitality at New York's Metropolitan Museum; the Abbot of Kykko Monastery, Archimandrite Nikiforos; the Kykko Monastery Research Centre; Lady Hunt for her immediate permission to quote from "Footprints in Cyprus" edited by her late, beloved husband, David; Marina Vryonidou-Yiangou of the Cultural Centre of the Popular Bank of Cyprus; Loukia Loizou Hadjigavriel, curator of the Leventis Municipal Museum; Nicosia; Dr. Sophocles Hadjisavvas, director of the Department of Antiquities, and other archaeologists in the department; Dr. Demetrios Michaelides, director, University of Cyprus, Archaelogical Research Unit; Mrs. Eleni Chrysostomides; Dr. Nancy Serwint of the Cyprus-American Archaeological Research Institute and its staff; Dr. Costas Hadjistephanou of the Makarios Foundation; Stuart and Lena Swiny, formerly of CAARI; Androulla Mouyarou of the Cyprus Parliament Library; Dr. Costas Kyrris; Maria Roussou of Cyprus and London; Ruth Keshishian and Aileen Stavrinides of the Moufflon Bookshop; and of course Voula Kokkinou of En Tipis.

A word, too, in memory of those writers and diarists of the past, of some very fine photographers, and of course that superb writer-translator, Claude Cobham, author of "Excerpta Cypria".

Barbara Cornwall Lyssarides

ACKNOWLEDGEMENTS

Every effort has been made to trace copyright holders in all copyright material in this book. In the event of any oversight, the writer would like to apologise sincerely, and will be happy to correct mistakes or omissions in future editions. The following sources and permissions are gratefully acknowledged:

Agnes Smith, *Through Cyprus*, London 1897; M. C. Kareklas *Hassan Poulis*, Police H.Q. Archives, Nicosia; Claude Cobham, *Excerpta Cypria*, *Materials for a History of Cyprus*, Cambridge University Press 1908; C. Kokkinoftas, I.Theocharides, *Handbook of Kykkos Monastery*; Kykkos Research Centre, Nicosia, 1995; *Vasilios Barsky*, Institute of Cypriot Studies, Albany, New York, 1995; Anne Cavendish, *Cyprus 1878, The Journal of Sir Garnet Wolseley*, The Cyprus Popular Bank, Cultural Centre 1991; Esme Scott-Stevenson, *Our Home in Cyprus*, Chapman Hall, 1880; Diana Wood Conroy, *From an Excavation Diary*, Heat 3, Australia, 1997; Alexander Kinglake, *Eothen*, Everyman Edition, London, 1908; Dr Frosso Egoumenidou, *Traditional Forms of Nutrition in Cyprus from the 18th to the early 20th centuries*, University of Cyprus, Archaeological Research Unit, 1997; Abbe Giovanni Mariti, *Travels in the island of Cyprus*, translated by Claude Cobham, Nicosia; John Gillingham, *Richard Coeur de Lion*, Hambleton Press, London, 1994; Mairin Mitchell, *Berengaria, Enigmatic Queen of England*, A Wright, England 1986; Henry Rider Haggard, *A Winter Pilgrimage in Palestine, Italy and Cyprus*, Longmans, 1901; John Thomson, *Through Cyprus with the Camera, in the Autumn of 1878*, London 1878; Lady Murphy *ABC of Flower Gardening in Cyprus*, The Times of Cyprus, Nicosia, 1956; Alexander Kinglake, *Traces of Travel brought Home from the East*, Oxford University Press, Oxford 1991; Einar Gjerstad, *Ages and Days in Cyprus*, Sweden; Michael Toumazou, *Athienou Archaeological Project*, Davidson College USA; David Lavender, *The Story of the Cyprus Mines Corporation*, Huntington Library, USA, 1962; *The Cyprus Review*, The Public Information Office, Nicosia 1950; Clea Constantinou Hadjistephanou, *Athletics in Cyprus and the Greek Tradition;* Linda & Kostas Myrsiades, *Karagiozis, Culture and Comedy in Greek Puppet Theatre*, University Press of Kentucky USA, 1992; Cyprus Today, Ministry of Education and Culture, 1994, Costas Yiangoullis *The Art of the Karaghiozi Shadow Theatre in Cyprus,* Nicosia 1991; Yiannis Kissonerghis, *Memories of a Puppeteer;* Sir Harry Luke, *Cyprus Under the Turks*, Clarendon Press, London 1969; H V *Morton, In the Steps of St. Paul*, Methuen London 1935; Andrew Oliver Jr. *Beyond the Shores of Tripoli*, Archaeological Institute of America,1979; Andrew Oliver Jr, Diana Buitron, *Lorenzo Warriner Pease, American Missionary in Cyprus, 1834-1839,* Cyprus Antiquities Department Report for 1988; Sir Ronald Storrs, *Orientations*, Nicholson & Watson, London 1937; Rupert Gunnis, *Historic Cyprus,* Methuen London 1936; Maynard Owen Williams, National Geographic July 1928; Christopher Walker, *Visions of Ararat*, Tauris Press 1997; Susan Paul Patti, *Faith in History*, *Armenians Rebuilding Community*, Smithsonian, 1997; George Martelli, *Whose Sea?* Chatto & Windus, London 1938; Sophocles Hadjisavva, *Ayia Napa Excavations at Makronisos and the Archaeology of the Region*, Cyprus Antiquities Department Nicosia, 1997;Cesnola, *Cyprus*, its *Cities, Tombs and Temples*, Star Graphics, Nicosia; Sir George Arthur, *The Life of Lord Kitchener*, Macmillan and Co, London 1920; Mrs Brassey, *Sunshine and Storm in the East*, Henry Holt London, 1888; Ronald Jennings *Christians and Muslims in the Mediterranean World, 1571-1640,* New York University Press, 1993; Irina Christodoulou-Pipis, *Greek Outside Greece,* Diaspora Books, Vol. III; David Soren, Jamie James, *Kourion, The Search for a Lost Roman City*, National Geographic, 1988; Sir Harry Luke, *The Tenth Muse,* London,1954.